Woodcarver's
Pattern & Design
—— Book ——

Woodcarver's Pattern & Design —Book—

E. J. Tangerman

Sterling Publishing Co., Inc.   New York

Library of Congress Cataloging-in-Publication Data

Tangerman, E. J. (Elmer John), 1907–
    Woodcarver's pattern and design book.
    Includes index.
    1. Wood-carving. I. Title.
TT199.7.T378 1986   736'.4   86-904
ISBN 0-8069-6298-4
ISBN 0-8069-6300-X (pbk.)

Copyright © 1986 by Sterling Publishing Co., Inc.
Two Park Avenue, New York, N.Y. 10016
Distributed in Australia by Capricorn Book Co. Pty. Ltd.
Unit 5C1 Lincoln St., Lane Cove, N.S.W. 2066
Distributed in the United Kingdom by Blandford Press
Link House, West Street, Poole, Dorset BH15 1LL, England
Distributed in Canada by Oak Tree Press Ltd.
% Canadian Manda Group, P.O. Box 920, Station U
Toronto, Ontario, Canada M8Z 5P9
Manufactured in the United States of America
All rights reserved

Table of Contents

I
Before You Begin

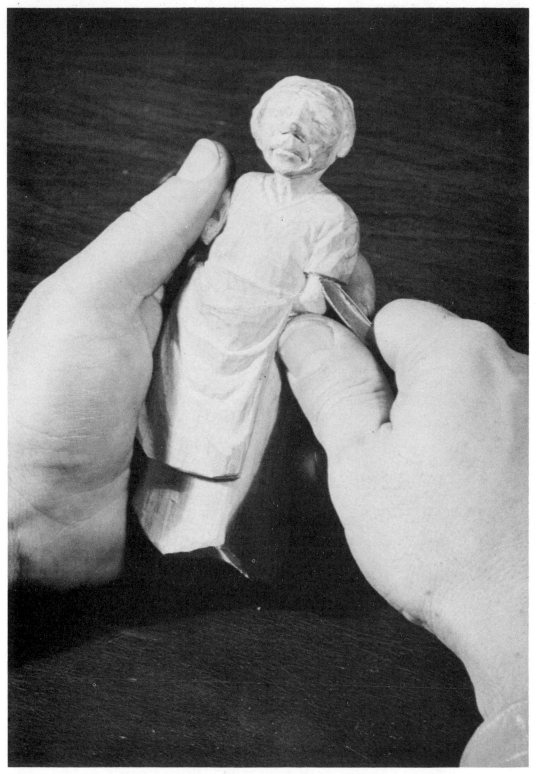

Fig. 1. Whittling with the knife alone is the most common carving technique.

A MAN once ordered a birthday cake decorated with the initial "B." When he returned for the cake, he expressed disappointment at the plainness of the block letter on top—he'd expected something fancier. The baker apologized and asked for an additional hour. When the buyer returned, the cake bore a script letter B surrounded by swirls and frosted flowers. The buyer was still disappointed, so the baker agreed to try one more time. The third design was an Old English B surrounded by cherries and chocolate drops, with a rainbow of colored frosting. The buyer was ecstatic and paid the bill without demur. The baker, proud once again, started to take the cake away to box it. "Never mind wrapping it," said the customer, "I'll eat it here!"

I'm reminded of that old yarn when I listen to whittlers and woodcarvers in search of a design. No matter how many patterns and books I have with me in class, at least one student has in mind something totally different, or just doesn't go for the available designs, so it's back to the old drawing board. The same thing is true, I suspect, of many of my readers. I have published perhaps 5,000 designs in fifteen books thus far, and hundreds more appear in other books and magazines, yet a recent survey of representative carvers showed patterns as Need Number One! Beyond all that, many carvers are semi-professionals, making what will sell or what buyers or collectors think they want. Like the baker, they need a new and different way of reproducing the letter B.

This is a further effort to satisfy these requests for more patterns, and to show in a number of examples the step-by-step procedure in carving them. I have also tried to show how various designs and patterns can be adapted to the wood, the tools, the need, or the desire. Most of the drawings are half the size of my originals, to provide a starting point.

The tools I used on many step-by-step projects are pictured or listed and I have included a special chapter on the V-tool, which many carvers do not use effectively, if at all. As always, I have tried to group associated ideas and designs, and to present them in order of difficulty. I have not, however, separated in-the-round and relief carving, or knife and chisel carving, both because they overlap and because an increasing number of carvers tend to be broad-gauge in their selection of patterns, woods and tools. This is a companion volume to my *Complete Guide to Wood Carving* (Sterling, New York), which contains basic data for the beginner, so here there is a wider range of ideas, with my choice of wood, tools and techniques for you to accept or reject as you will. I have also emphasized ways in which preliminary carving time can be reduced by using saws, drills, routers and large tools to get rid of waste wood quickly.

There is information on woodcarving around the world, on the use of locally available or "bad" wood, on the use of gesso, on some outstanding carvers and their work, and more examples of traditional native carving from remote and unpublicized parts of the world. Happy carving!

NOTE: This is my conversion of a very long surname into a carvable signature.

1

Where Do Patterns Come From?

IT SHOULD BE POSSIBLE to prepare a pattern and design book that will provide every reader with the information he needs to make a successful carving. Practically, however, readers vary tremendously in background, training, experience, and a number of other factors. Some can read and interpret a "blueprint" or pattern; some cannot. Some people read and comprehend easily; others do not. Some are familiar with the specialized terminology of woodcarving; others are only beginning to use chisels, or use the knife alone. Thus, an explanation suitable for one sort of person is inadequate or over-adequate for another.

Let's try to untangle the matter of patterns a bit: There are thousands of patterns available from books and magazines—if you have access to them. In my books alone, I estimate that there are more than 5,000 patterns and design ideas; there are well over 500 in this collection. If any of these meet your need and if you can find one of the modern Xerox or other photocopying machines capable of reducing or enlarging, you can readily produce a pattern of the desired size. If you don't have access to such a machine, you can make a standard same-size copy and reduce or enlarge it by one of the methods I shall describe later in this chapter.

Also available are presawed blanks for various simple designs, pattern kits of full-scale drawings for a more limited number, and more recently some books and magazines with full-size drawings, usually for

objects to be whittled. In my books, I try to make drawings half the size of the object carved. This is, however, arbitrary, because in many cases I adapted my design to the wood I had at hand, or to fit a specific place or purpose. There is no real reason why you should make *your* carving *my* size. The same goes for the carvings of others that I have photographed and sketched. Also, in the case of relief panels, a clear frontal photograph of the carving is itself a pattern and can usually be copied by Xeroxing without damaging the binding. Also, in such complex relief carvings as my polyglot panels, there are incorporated a host of units, any one of which may be copied for a single pattern.

You may want to develop your own patterns from the designs in this book. Incidentally, it is relatively easy to make patterns for panel carvings and simple reliefs, but somewhat more complicated for in-the-round work, because a good in-the-round pattern includes at least two views of the subject, sometimes more. Thus, you may find it difficult to produce a useable pattern for an in-the-round piece. But paradoxically it is easier to carve an object in the round than it is to carve it in relief, because of the necessity of compressing the third dimension. In these days of wood from a supplier, the usual piece is a plank or a rectangular block purchased to fit the pattern rather than the other way 'round. However, I have in this book shown a number of projects in which I adapted an idea or made a design, or fulfilled a com-

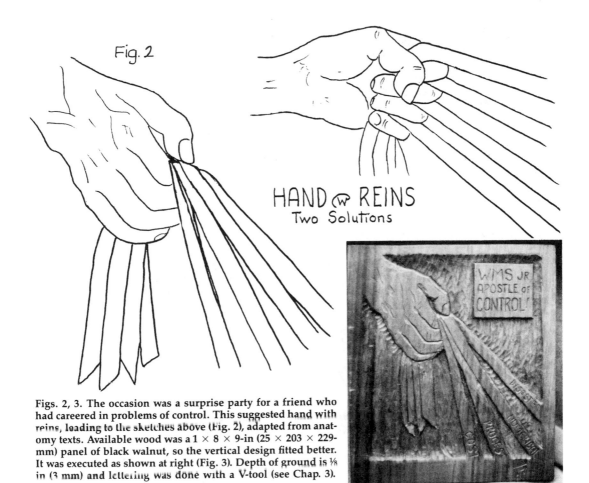

Fig. 2

HAND (w) REINS
Two Solutions

WMS JR
APOSTLE of
CONTROL

Figs. 2, 3. The occasion was a surprise party for a friend who had careered in problems of control. This suggested hand with reins, leading to the sketches above (Fig. 2), adapted from anatomy texts. Available wood was a 1 × 8 × 9-in (25 × 203 × 229-mm) panel of black walnut, so the vertical design fitted better. It was executed as shown at right (Fig. 3). Depth of ground is ⅛ in (3 mm) and lettering was done with a V-tool (see Chap. 3).

mission by adapting a pattern to fit the premium wood available (see above).

How to Pick a Pattern

There are some cautions about pattern selection, of course. Don't pick a pattern that requires tools that you don't have, or a skill too far beyond yours. (It's always good to stretch a little, however!) Avoid detail unless your wood will take it and you're willing to spend the added time; don't try to put scales on a basswood dragon. And make certain that you study the pattern or idea you propose to develop so you understand it thoroughly before you begin, or you may waste a lot of time and some expensive wood.

If you have a specific idea, try to find a design for it in this or other of my books. Also try a big or craft-oriented library; usual libraries will not have a great number of woodcarving books. Local woodcarving clubs and local woodcarvers sometimes have impressive book collections. If these fail you, try to think of some general reference book, a bird guide, tree guide, or other field manual, or a book or magazine devoted to the particular field, such as dogs, cats, horses, specific sports or technology. Often, they will contain photographs that you can photocopy directly. Even some fiction book jackets may have paintings that you can adapt. The children's room—if the library has one—may have files of tear sheets classified under headings that will include the one you're looking for. Another source of good-sized patterns is children's coloring books. If any of these prove suitable, photocopy. If you can't get the size this way, read on . . .

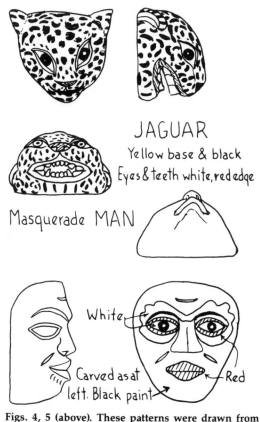

JAGUAR
Yellow base & black
Eyes & teeth white, red edge

Masquerade MAN

White

Carved as at
left. Black paint

Red

Figs. 4, 5 (above). These patterns were drawn from miniature masks carved in Mexico. The masks, about twice this size, were laid on paper and outlined, then detailed by eye.

Making Your Own Design

If none of the above sources is of any help, you may want to consult a good encyclopaedia or dictionary for a generic picture in the area in which you are interested. (I've found *Webster's Unabridged Second Edition* particularly useful in this respect.) Such a picture is usually a fairly dead sketch, like a mounted specimen in a museum, but it will give you starters. Often, the poses in field guides and other books tend to be standardized as well, so you may want to try to change them. Or you may want to incorporate them in a scene. Further, the illustration or illustrations may be so small that you can only really get a starting silhouette, but that of itself is a step in the right direction. It is even better if you can get equivalent pictures from several sources so you can com-

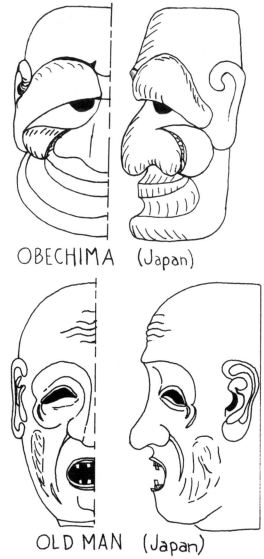

OBECHIMA (Japan)

OLD MAN (Japan)

Figs. 6, 7 (above). These mask patterns were made from photographs, so only a front view was available. The side view is, therefore, half guess. Designs are unusual in having ears.

pare them. (You may discover, as I did in the case of the "bug tree" designs, that two artists don't always interpret the same subject the same way—"artistic license" is sometimes used in strange ways.)

To go on from there takes a bit of nerve and some artistic ability. Figure out the pose or arrangement you want and try to draw it. (Sometimes, if you do a bad enough job, some other member of the family will pitch in and help—they do for me.) Don't worry about details at this point; try to get the major silhouette or arrangement. Try to be certain that the outlines are right; I find that if it is anything reasonable, I can ask someone else to critique the pattern at this point.

Now you can begin the tricky part—you can add detail. But don't add too much; the abiding sin of most woodcarvings is that the carver tries to get in too much detail. I say this with feeling because some of my panels, in particular, are over-detailed. There are times when detail is necessary, but they are far fewer than most amateurs realize, and detail often tends to confuse rather than explain. I've often wished I had a nickel for each nail some carver has delineated in the siding on a house, or each feather on a bird—when such details are not visible from a relatively short distance on the real thing. Also, remember that a carving is monochromatic unless you paint it, so don't expect it to look realistic unless you plan to spend a great deal of time painting it after you're done carving.

Parenthetically, I should point out that, contrary to popular opinion, it is considerably harder to make a good relief carving than it is to make a three-dimensional or in-the-round one. Even experienced relief carvers tend to lower the background unduly in the effort to carve in effect a half-round subject. Or else they undercut to such a degree that it would be easier to carve the subject in-the-round and appliqué it to a background.

The difficulty in carving in relief, par-

ticularly scenes involving perspective, is that most of us haven't studied perspective. On top of that, we may not understand that, in relief carving, the third dimension must be greatly and proportionally reduced, but in such a way that the finished object looks realistic. You may have found scenes in which the base of a house seems to stand out from the ground or the roots of a tree seem to have grown out in the open. In-the-round carvings can be rotated to study proportions as you carve; relief carvings cannot. And you'll find that your pattern may look fine on paper, but it changes when you start to adjust that third dimension on the wood.

There are certain things to watch out for in selecting a pattern, or particularly in making one up. Telephone wires, ship rigging, clouds, spray, transparent draperies, soft edges and fine lines (like bowstrings) are very difficult and sometimes impossible to carve. Expression on a face is difficult to achieve if you can't carve a plain face. A portrait is quite difficult unless you

BEAVER HOCKEY PLAYER

Figs. 8, 9 (right). These patterns were adapted from references. I needed designs for Christmas-tree decorations at a sports club with "Beaver" in its name. These caricatures were drawn after study of pictures of beavers and of hockey players in action. They were about 4 in (102 mm) tall, in mahogany.

BEAVER GOAL TENDER - Mahogany

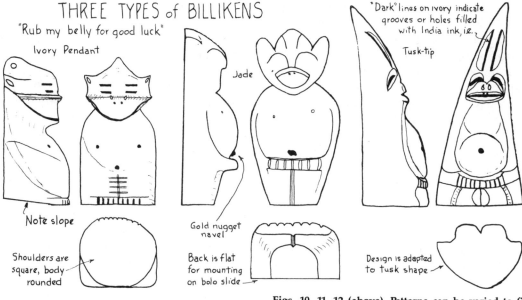

THREE TYPES of BILLIKENS

"Rub my belly for good luck"

Ivory Pendant

Note slope

Shoulders are square, body rounded

Jade

Gold nugget navel

Back is flat for mounting on bolo slide

Dark lines on ivory indicate grooves or holes filled with India ink, i.e.

Tusk-tip

Design is adapted to tusk shape

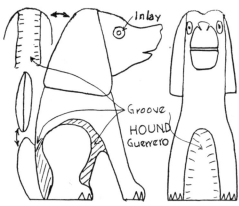

Inlay

Groove

HOUND Guerrero

Figs. 10, 11, 12 (above). Patterns can be varied to fit available material shape (see Fig. 2). Here are three variants of the Billiken pattern made by Eskimos in pieces of walrus ivory and jade. Good luck supposedly comes from rubbing the navel, which may be inlaid. Similar adaptations are common in the Orient and Africa.

Fig. 13 (left). Basic blockiness is not a problem for this carved hound—he's *designed* to be blocky, and rapidly carved. Only the eye inserts take time, and they're optional additions. Note the use of grooves to outline legs.

have considerable training and a God-given skill, particularly if the subject is a child. (See later chapters.) Multiple elevations—like a road spiralling up a mountain, or a stream running down one, or a series of buildings along a street at an angle to the viewer—can be real trouble.

My best advice: Do as children do, at least try to crawl before you walk; even Michelangelo wasn't famous as a child. Don't try to make a pattern that is shaded like a sketch; it may become so confusing that it is troublesome to copy on the wood, as well as to check against when you're carving. Also check the pattern for thin sections that will be cross-grain; they'll be difficult to carve in almost any wood. The

same caution applies to long-legged and long-necked animals or birds, or the stems of flowers, or even a picket fence or a row of telephone poles.

In a relief carving, it is sometimes possible to suggest such elements by reversing them—actually cutting grooves to represent them rather than having them above the surface as they would normally be. You'll find this trick used in several instances shown in this book like, for example, the tennis player's racket in the Victorian garden figures (see Chapter 21). It is also possible, if you have the patience and intend to coat the finished carving with paint or foil, to appliqué some small elements across grain, making them of wood or some other more suitable material for the size and complexity, and gluing them on the surface. I have done this, for example, with the arrow on the shield of my coat of arms; Gardner Wood has used Masonite (pressedboard) on ark doors for Jewish temples for major parts as well as for smaller units (see Chapter 16). It is also possible to build up a particular area so it projects above a surface by gluing on plates or blocks of matching wood, particularly on darker woods like walnut—thus saving hours of work cutting away a background and smoothing it again, to say nothing of the saving of the premium normally paid for thicker wood.

How to Change Pattern Size

The usual pattern is often too small for your purposes, so you'll probably want to enlarge it to fit. The best and easiest ways are photographic. As mentioned earlier, if you can get to a Xerox or other photocopying machine that enlarges and reduces, that's cheapest and easiest, although you may have to take several shots to get to the size you want, because such machines work to arbitrary sizes only.

More flexible is a photostatting machine (one brand is Velox), which some advertising agencies and graphic-arts companies have and which makes a photographic copy on good-quality paper without a negative, as does a Xerox. This works like a zoom camera lens, so you can enlarge or reduce an exact amount. Cost is somewhat higher than for Xeroxing and quality is probably better than you need.

The other photographic method requires a projector—an old-fashioned photograph projector if you have one, or a modern slide projector if you can start with a transparency. You simply project the image on a flat board carrying a piece of drawing paper, enlarge it to the required size by moving the projector, and sketch it in with a pencil. The lines can be refined later. I have used this method very effectively for combining elements of several scenic transparencies.

Art stores have pantographs, an arrangement of hinged arms by which you can enlarge or reduce flat copy like a photo or drawing. This is not highly accurate and the enlargement or reduction is arbitrary in ratio, but it will usually serve well enough for normal enlargements or reductions. Major changes of dimension might result in distortion.

Some artists also use a right-angle lens that can be mounted on a drawing board in such a way that you see the enlarged or reduced image of an object on paper so you can draw it; this takes a pair of good eyes and is a bit tricky.

Beyond all those, there are three standard and familiar methods of mechanically changing dimensions. One is to use an elastic band, or chain of bands, as shown in one sketch. This is a very rough and somewhat clumsy method, but it will serve in an emergency. The other two are the point-to-point and the method of squares. My favorite is the point-to-point, which re-

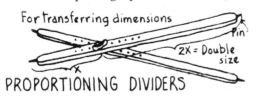

PROPORTIONING DIVIDERS

Fig. 14

Both these devices can be made from strips or purchased & are adjustable for various ratios.

Fig. 15

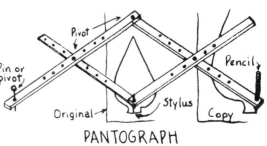

PANTOGRAPH

quires a little ability to sketch and resembles the drawing by numbers that one sees in Sunday comics. (See the illustrations.)

One other suggestion that may help: If you are planning to make a miniature of a life-size or heroic statue, as I have on several occasions, use a camera. Take pictures of the original from the four points of the compass *without changing focus* and from a height about the middle of the original if that is possible. Then have enlargements made—to the size of your planned piece if you can afford them in these inflationary days—and draw your patterns from them. It's best to use a good camera and lens to reduce distortion at the outer limits of the subject, and you may find even so that our old friend perspective will get in its licks. For example, when I took such photos of

the Russian "Beating Swords into Plowshares" figure at the United Nations, I had to stand well below the base level. When I got my enlargements, I found that the smith's hammer, raised high over his head, was differently located in the various views because of perspective, and I had to adjust between them to get a proper location. A similar thing will occur if you try to copy a full figure from a photograph or magazine illustration. The camera and the artist both put in perspective, so if you copy directly you'll find that your figure may be standing on its tiptoes. So . . . if you're developing such a pattern, make certain before you transfer it to the wood that the feet are parallel with the ground on the bottom and that horizontal and vertical surfaces are truly horizontal and vertical.

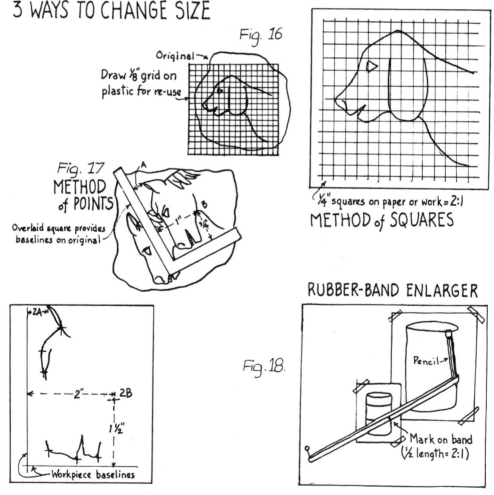

3 WAYS TO CHANGE SIZE

Fig. 16

Original →

Draw ⅛" grid on plastic for re-use

¼" squares on paper or work = 2:1

METHOD of SQUARES

Fig. 17
METHOD of POINTS

Overlaid square provides baselines on original

2"

1½"

Workpiece baselines

Fig. 18.

RUBBER-BAND ENLARGER

Pencil →

Mark on band (½ length = 2:1)

The Pekingese Dog and His Pattern

I mentioned early in this chapter that in modern days it is usually necessary to think in terms of planks or blocks, because that's what commercial sources supply. (This often is the source of the blocky and clumsy-looking carvings you see—the carver merely rounded the corners and did not get rid of the flat planed surfaces.) The old-timers usually started with a twig, branch or trunk and adapted the design to it, or even developed a design from something they saw in the conformation of the wood, its figure, or whatever. This is still evident in carvings like those of the Makonde in Africa, or of the Balinese. While we are accustomed to rectangular bases on carvings, the Makonde may be round or oval as the tree was, with the design following a fork in the limbs. The Balinese carving may have a triangular base and be disproportionately tall, because that's how the wood happened to split out of the chunk he had. I have had this problem again and again with larger carvings when I started with tree trunks instead of ultra-expensive "boughten" lumber that would have to be glued up, and even with smaller pieces when I had an idea that didn't naturally fit the available wood. The case of the little Pekingese dog may illustrate what I mean.

This all started because another carver and I "liberated" some blocks from a mutual friend who had brought a van-load of wood home for his fireplace. The pieces happened to be scrap butts of timber from the Steinway piano factory. Many were mahogany or maple, and a few were walnut. They tended to be 4 in (102 mm) or more thick and up to 15 in (381 mm) wide, but only about 6 or 7 in (152 to 178 mm) long, and were scrapped because they had good solid wood on one end.

One day I picked up one of the liberated blocks. It was mahogany, about 7 × 4¾ × 11 in (178 × 114 × 279 mm) mahogany, with the idea of making a doorstop or floor-level carving. Floor-level suggested a dog or a

cat. Dogs are easier to carve than cats. This piece was longer than it was high, and if I was to match grain direction to leg direction, I immediately thought of a dachshund. But a dachshund has four very visible legs and a long nose, as well as a tail that tends to stick out straight in back, so there were grain problems. I shifted to a long-haired Pekingese, which is also long but has a plume for a tail, long floppy ears, a pugnose and enough hair to hide his legs.

No sooner said than done. I found a picture of a Pekingese in *Webster*, and roughed out a sketch the length of the block. I decided to stylize the dog and have him carry an oversized plume of a tail, and have his body hair go right down to fade into the base, which could be substantial. I could simulate the long-hair effect by a series of long gouge scallops running with the grain.

Mahogany gives a good color for the dog and for a doorstop, but can splinter and split when you try to scallop across grain. Also, the tail overhead meant that the small-cross-section tail base could go with the grain rather than across it. The face could be detailed with a knife and the bulging eyes and dewlaps featured. What's more, the silhouette could be sawed readily on a neighbor's bandsaw. So the block was laid out with the checked end down and the carving made as pictured.

Fig. 19. The pug as I made him was 4 × 7¾ × 11 in (102 × 197 × 279 mm), with grain vertical to strengthen tail. Ears and pelt flare only slightly because of limited block width. Eyes bulge and are stained darker to emphasize this. Face modelling and forepaws are the only intricate parts. For pattern, see next page.

Figs. 20, 21. A piece of scrap mahogany from a piano timber made this Pekingese pug dog—a case of fitting the pattern to the wood. Intricacy in suggesting hair is avoided by fluting pelt and tail with a flat gouge, and only the forepaws show, avoiding the difficulties of pierce-carving between body and base. Front pattern (21a) is enlarged to show detail.

Fig. 21a

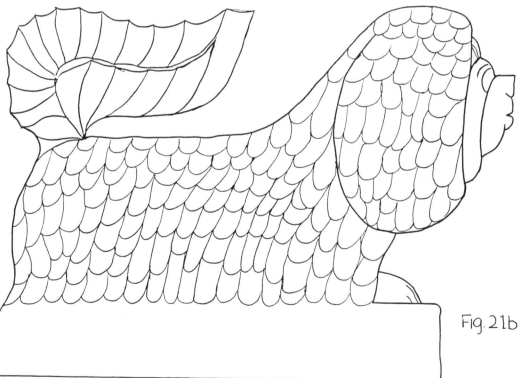

Fig. 21b

Figs. 22, 23 (above). Sometimes the easiest way to arrive at a suitable pattern for carving is to model it first in clay or other modelling material. Here is an example by Hugh Minton of Aiken, SC. It is a grotesque or chimera from the Cathedral of Notre Dame in Paris, and Hugh had only a telephoto picture to work from. The eventual figure was in pine, at right. Note the stub base for holding the work in a vise during carving. The tongue would have been longer, but was cut short by an overzealous instructor.

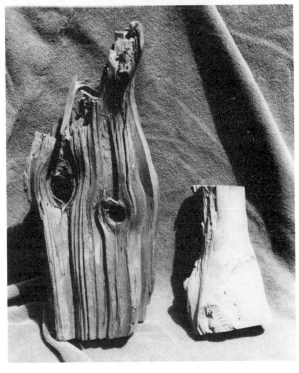

Fig. 24 (right). Wood is normally a fragile material, but these two pieces belie this belief. Left, Virginia cedar found in an Ohio marble pit and 8,500 years old. Right, Alaska fir, found beneath a glacier at Juneau, Alaska, and 10,000 years old. The oldest known wood is 12,000 years, so these two are second and third. I made 500 miniature shingles from a piece of the cedar for a model of an ancient barn.

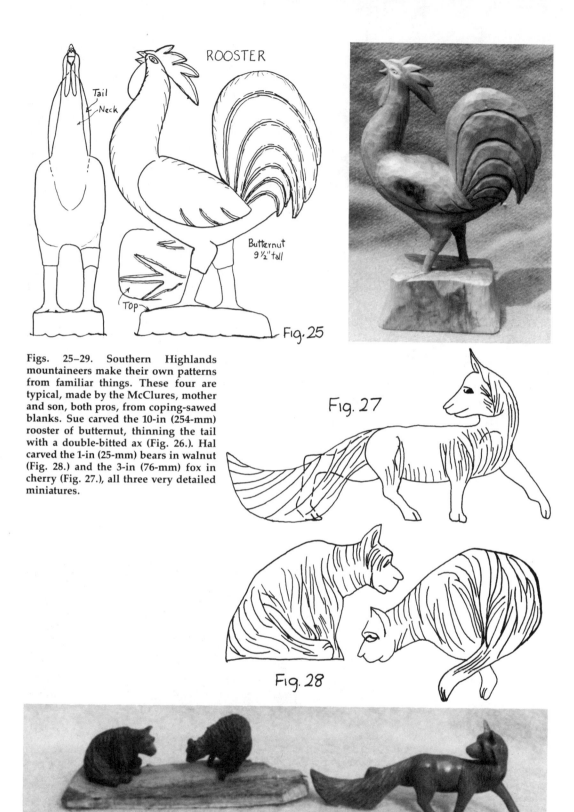

ROOSTER

Tail

Neck

Butternut
9½" tall

Top

Fig. 25

Figs. 25–29. Southern Highlands mountaineers make their own patterns from familiar things. These four are typical, made by the McClures, mother and son, both pros, from coping-sawed blanks. Sue carved the 10-in (254-mm) rooster of butternut, thinning the tail with a double-bitted ax (Fig. 26.). Hal carved the 1-in (25-mm) bears in walnut (Fig. 28.) and the 3-in (76-mm) fox in cherry (Fig. 27.), all three very detailed miniatures.

Fig. 27

Fig. 28

2

The Tools You Need

SOME YEARS AGO, I had a boss who had an engineering degree but who was primarily a theoretical physicist. As he neared retirement, he bought a metal-cutting lathe, drillpress and milling machine—all used—for a home shop. I helped him set them up and make the necessary basic tooling. Meanwhile, he loaded up on accessories—drills, toolbits, boring tools and so on. When he got through with all that, he began to make steel and brass candlesticks, until his wife threatened to throw out an old pair each time he came up with a new one. He simply couldn't think of anything else to make on all the equipment he had bought!

I am reminded of him regularly when I talk with a neophyte woodcarver who brags about the number of tools he has, a bandsaw, two or three kinds of vises, sander, rotary tools, chain saw and Lord knows what else—to make copies of the age-old projects, as if the tools possess some magic or inspirational value. Other carvers ask me what tools or what brands to get, or show me what some sharp peddler has sold them. Often, it is a set of tools adequate for a pro who is making life-size statuary, while they're planning to make small panels. Or they have the most expensive of imported tools. I've seen even one school shop that has an elaborate cabinet filled with a thousand dollars worth of tools—wrong shapes and sizes almost without exception because the man who bought them had no idea what was needed and the dealer who sold them simply got rid of some dead stock. And I've known

Fig. 30. Professional sculptor Georg Keilhofer is carving life-sized Nativity figures of basswood. Note tools arranged on bench at right with cutting edges towards him, so he can make a quick selection. Mr. Keilhofer served his apprenticeship in Germany. Figures such as these are made frequently there, so carvers use large tools and heavy mallets to remove wood rapidly. He has brought these techniques to the United States and teaches in Frankenmuth, Michigan.

Figs. 31 (left), 32 (below, left). Balinese carvers have long thin chisels and use mallets on hard woods. Only tools used on soft woods without mallets have handles. Uniformly, carvers sit on mats on the floor, holding the work with a foot or a leg as needed. Their work is extremely delicate and detailed, so mechanical holding might do more harm than good. These figures are an elongated priest and a vase.

potential carvers who were scared off by tool costs.

What I'm getting at is that tools will not make you a good carver. They won't even speed the learning process, particularly if they're the wrong tools for what you're trying to do. If you're simply trying various hobbies, or various types of woodcarving, to see what you'd like, make a minimum investment in tools and equipment. Then you can supplement it as you see the need and as your interest develops. Only the specialist pro or the amateur dilettante needs a whole packet of tools; I find that for my typical project, I use eight or ten at most. For my most frequent projects— small panels—I use inexpensive short

tools that sell for about one third the price of standard ones. These are tools designed by H.M. Sutter for his students to use in carving floral panels in pine, but I've used them on walnut, teak and ebony with a neoprene-surfaced light mallet with only one casualty—a V-tool I drove in too deep. And for very large work, I've used carpenter's gouges and chisels for roughing because they again are cheaper and sturdier than conventional woodcarving tools of equivalent size. To help you decide on the tools you may need, I have listed the tools I used on many of the projects in this book.

Obviously, if you are making small hand-sized objects like the very common cowboy caricatures, old shoes, hound dogs, or the like, your best tool is a good knife. You don't even need several knives; if you think you do, get a knife handle that

Fig. 33 (below). Common knife-blade shapes. I prefer the curved-edge blades at left, although many whittlers use straight cutting edge, at right. Above all, blades should be short.

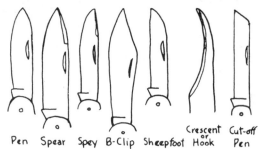

Pen   Spear   Spey   B-Clip   Sheepfoot   Crescent or Hook   Cut-off Pen

Fig. 34. Carvers in Kenya work much like the Balinese, but usually in larger groups—as many as 1,000 in a series of thatched sheds! This man, working on a mask, relies on the dirt floor to hold it. Roughing is done commonly with the adze, finishing with knife or chisel. He may carve up a tree per month and may have an assistant or two to do rough cutting, according to Vernon Swearingen, who took this picture at the Akomba Cooperative near Nairobi. Bali and Kenya are presently the largest producers of carvings for sale.

will take interchangeable blades. There are some very good knives available, but be sure your interest and your ability make the investment in additional and special knives worthwhile.

If you are going in for relief carving or carving of objects larger than hand-size, you'll need chisels. I'd suggest a half-dozen for starters, either the little ones I talked about above or full-size ones, depending upon the size of the object you expect to carve and the hardness of the wood. Be careful when you're offered a "set" or "kit" of tools; often the set will include tools you'll never need. I, for example, never use a skew firmer, and al-

most every set includes one. I also find a full set of gouges stepping up in sweep (radius of the curve) by sixteenths of an inch or by millimetres is more than I need. And the long-bent and short-bent tools I need relatively rarely and for fairly specialized work. So, I'd say to start with that you might want ½-in (13-mm) and ¼-in (6-mm) firmers, ⅛-in (3-mm) flat gouge, ¼-in (6-mm) medium and deep gouges, and a small V-tool. I prefer the neoprene-covered potato masher or traditional mallet, light in weight for small work, heavier if you're planning a cigar-store Indian (which is really a chain-saw job anyway). You'll need something to hold the work. A vise will do nicely if the work is a block; or if it's a small panel, you can make a bench plate yourself. When the panel gets much bigger than $1 \times 12 \times 15$ in ($25 \times 305 \times 381$ mm), it will probably be big enough that it will stay in position under relatively light cuts.

What you need in auxiliary equipment is

Figs. 35, 36. Some typical carving-tool shapes and nomenclature. Macaroni, fluteroni, and back-bent tools are specialties used largely by pros. Fig. 36 (right). Three heavy-duty tool shapes. In Fig. 35 is a long-bent 1-in (25-mm) gouge; a straight tapered (modified spade) V-tool, and a short-bent firmer. All would be used on large carvings only.

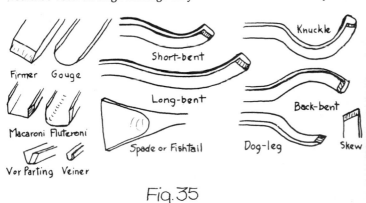

Firmer Gouge

Short-bent

Knuckle

Macaroni Fluteroni

Long-bent

Back-bent

Spade or Fishtail

Dog-leg

Skew

Vor Parting Veiner

Fig. 35

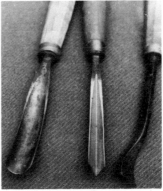

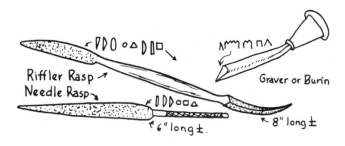

Riffler Rasp
Needle Rasp
Graver or Burin
6" long ±.
8" long ±.

Fig. 37 (left). Useful accessories for cleaning up hard-to-reach portions of carvings include small rasps, available in the shapes sketched, and the engraver's burins, useful primarily on very hard woods in my experience.

dependent on how well you like to buy tools. I use a couple of coping saws, one with 14-tooth blades, the other with 22-tooth, a ¼-in (6-mm) electric drill with sander, and a router for big hard-wood panels. I have no bandsaw, and use a rotary power tool only on bone or ivory.

I have about a hundred chisels, but when I teach I take a canvas roll with about

ten full-size tools, and two rolls of little ones. My students most frequently borrow my 2-in (51-mm) flat spade gouge, my ⅛-in (3-mm) V-tool and my two or three ¹⁄₁₆-in (1.5-mm) veiners, V-tools and fluters—because such tools are not in the sets they've bought. Their usual projects are panels or 10-in (254.0-mm) animals or people in walnut or cherry.

Fig. 38 (below). There are tricks in every trade. Here are some of those involving woodcarving tools. Hand positions vary depending upon chisel and cut when no mallet is used, as shown in the three top examples. The phrase "setting-in" means simply to drive a firmer or gouge vertically into the wood to outline a shape. This is done *before* cuts are made from the sides towards the subject, as in "bosting" or

"grounding," two terms meaning removal of background around the subject of a panel in relief carving. A stop cut is essentially the same as setting-in, but done primarily to prevent a chisel from splitting out wood or "running" beyond a desired point. The gouge swing to ease cutting will come to you naturally.

Heavy & straight cuts
Heel of back hand pushes handle end
Near hand guides, prevents overcuts & slips

Light & curving cuts
Back hand presses forward & steers
Near hand restrains, rests on work

Side cuts & V-tool cuts
Back hand presses
Near hand pulls, rests on work

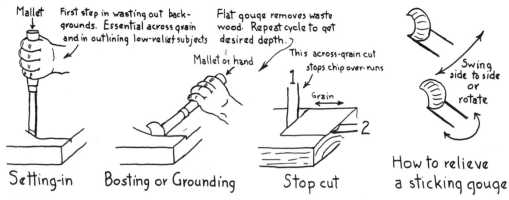

Mallet
First step in wasting out backgrounds. Essential across grain and in outlining low-relief subjects

Flat gouge removes waste wood. Repeat cycle to get desired depth.

Mallet or hand

This across-grain cut stops chip over-runs

Grain

Swing side to side or rotate

Setting-in   Bosting or Grounding   Stop cut   How to relieve a sticking gouge

3

The V-Tool for Victory

MY FAVORITE CHISEL has been the V-tool (also called parting tool), especially since I learned to sharpen it and use it effectively. It is rapid for outlining, for suggesting hair, for cross-hatching and shading, for a whole host of services. In relief carving, it can be tilted slightly to create a V-groove with one vertical and one sloping side, thus making one portion of the carving appear higher than another. And it is a lifesaver in incising lettering, such as on the cartouches in this chapter.

These words of praise are amplified by my recent experience with the pictured panels, part of an elaborate vanity table designed by a local cabinetmaker. My part was to carve two panels and three splats or cabinet-top decorations. The wood selected was straight-grained ash, which is fairly hard and has a tendency to split and splinter, thus leaving nasty little burrs after carving. However, with a ⅛-in (3-mm) V-tool, I was able to cut the necessary grooves in my Spanish-Colonial designs with relatively little grain trouble. If the Vee became very close to parallel with the grain, it was sometimes necessary to cut the two sides in opposite directions, but the carving was done with V-tool, ½-in (13-mm) firmer, and a fixed-blade knife for the corners and tight curves.

I also used a backsaw to cut the deeper sloping grooves in the two bosses, because their depth exceeded the size of my V-tool and this avoided split-outs. By sawing along the groove lines at an angle, then chipping out from both sides with a firmer, I could attain the desired groove of rapidly increasing size from the middle. However, the middle circle was outlined with the V-tool as well. I also roughed out two pineapple-shaped capitals with saw, chisel and

Fig. 39. Seth Velsey relied heavily on V-tools in carving this yellow-poplar panel titled "Salt." It is 3½ × 6 ft (1070 × 1830 mm) and was one of several he carved for the post office in Pomeroy, Ohio, in 1937. Simple outlines are created by tilting the V-tool to cut one side vertical while fairing the other out to make one surface appear higher than the other.

Figs. 40 (left), 41 (middle). Simple elements for a vanity table I carved in straight-grained ash. The drawer front is an assembly of three ½-in (13-mm) pieces, and the "pineapple" finial above it is one of two based on 2-in (51-mm) squares. These were cut from the splats below, which are 2 and 2½ ft (610 and 783 mm) long and 2 in (51 mm) thick. Most of the carving was done with a V-tool and mallet, with the V-grooves widened and rounded by firmer. Pieces were sanded and stained (really antiqued to bring out the carving) before assembly.

Fig. 42 (below). Spanish-Colonial motifs like these are regaining their popularity, even in the East—the panels above are a case in point. The motifs are simple and regular and can be cut easily and accurately with a V-tool. It is advisable to make knife stop cuts at the ends of rays to prevent splitting and to keep the V-tool very sharp so it does not tear the wood when a curve is cut.

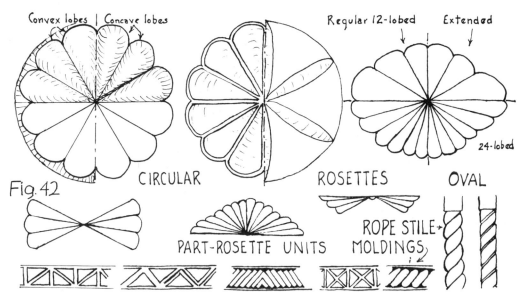

Fig. 42

Convex lobes | Concave lobes   Regular 12-lobed   Extended

CIRCULAR   ROSETTES   OVAL

24-lobed

PART-ROSETTE UNITS   ROPE STILE MOLDINGS

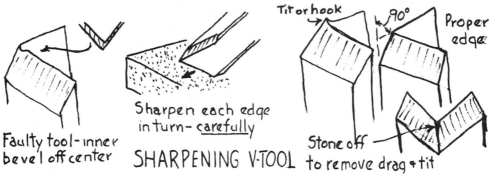

Fig. 43. V-tool sharpening hints.

knife, then put in the cross-section markings with the V-tool.

Another application of the V-tool in relief carving in particular is to remove splinters and incomplete spots along the outline of an object. After I complete setting-in, for example, I often run a V-tool along the right angle between outline and background to smooth it up. It can also undercut slightly, or emphasize the carving outline.

To cut properly and minimize tearing at the edges, a V-tool must be properly sharpened; it is not enough merely to have the two faces sharp, and the modern habit of sharpening on a buffing wheel is likely to harm more than it helps, because the cutting edges will be bull-nosed (rounded) and the bottom of the Vee will be damaged as well. Also, it is essential to have a V-edged slip that will fit inside the Vee of the tool and remove any slight burr there, or the tool will drag.

The principal problem in sharpening a V-tool is the bottom of the Vee, which is always thicker than either side, hence tends to drag. Also, be sure that the V-tool you buy is properly forged and rough-sharpened; I have seen some that are scored on one side or with sides of different thickness so they cannot be sharpened properly, even by hand. Basically, the two cutting edges should be at right angles to the tool length, neither sloping forward nor backward. Further, the sides should be sharpened evenly, or one side will "lead" the other slightly and pull the tool off the

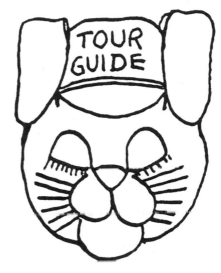

Fig. 44. Pendant in holly depicts the White Rabbit as a tour guide in "Alice in Blunderland," a satire. The piece, about 1½ in (38 mm) high, was a natural for V-tool carving.

Fig. 45 (below). Lettering on a rebus-type family breadboard was incised with a V-tool. The breadboard is oak 8 in (203 mm) wide, and depicts Mike, Jim(my), Jill (as "gill"), and Pat (as a butter pat) Salerno. In this case, the V-tool was tilted to create vertical walls around the designs, while the background was faired.

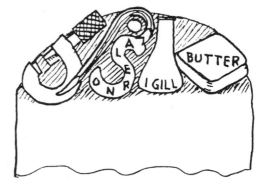

desired line. Often, when properly sharpened, the tool will have a slight "tit" projecting at the bottom, the result of that extra thickness there. This can be removed by stoning or honing a slight flat spot on the bottom of the Vee, supplementing this, if necessary by honing *inside* slightly with the slip. It may also help in cutting if you hone a very slight angle on the inside of each cutting edge.

I have V-tools ranging from ¹⁄₁₆ in (1.5 mm) on a side to more than 1 in (25 mm). The small ones I sharpen with a slip so I can control the angle on the edges. This is difficult to do on a larger stone, which usually is faster-cutting as well. A strop for the V-tool can be made by cutting a suitable notch in a piece of leather. However, V-tools are made with several different included angles: 30, 45 or 60 degrees (mine are all 30°, the commonest form), so you may have to make several grooves to accommodate your tools.

The Very Useful Cartouche

THE CARTOUCHE is an architectural form that is drawn from a tattered scroll. It has been used since ancient Egypt (there to surround a Pharaoh's name), particularly to provide a base for limited lettering, such as the street number or name on a building, a short quotation on a tomb or altar, and the like. By extension, the word also covers any oval decorative shape. But my purpose in including it here is to suggest a very useful device for certain special needs. It will give added dimension to a nameplate or a commemorative plaque, and is readily adaptable to suit a shape.

There are dozens of small variations in the design of a cartouche. I used one for the commemorative plaques in oak on a portable altar, a more rectangular one for teak plaques to be set on posts at the base of trees planted on Arbor Day at a school and a church, other shapes just to give lettering or numbers a little more importance and decorative quality.

The usual cartouche is relatively small. Mine have been in the general range of 4 in (102 mm) to 6 in (152 mm) × 7 in (178 mm) or 8 in (203 mm) and usually from wood about 1 in (25 mm) to 2 in (51 mm) thick, thinner for application on other wood surfaces, thicker for standing alone in the weather. The essentials of a cartouche design are the tattered curls at the edges, but it also helps if the central surface on which

V-TOOL DESIGN—Swiss

Figs. 46, 47 (left). V-tool carving decorates this simple lindenwood bowl and spoon from Switzerland. Similar designs are carved in the USSR and Poland, but are usually filled with a color or cut through a painted surface to show the bare-wood color beneath. Fijian carvers do the same thing on masks.

Fig. 48 (below). The runic alphabet of the ancient Vikings lends itself to V-tool carving. It is older than the Roman which we use and is said to have mystic qualities; it was used to "read" sticks cast on a surface. Fig. 49 (next page). The Norse symbol of eternal life is another natural for V-tool incision. I used it on the back of a Kubbstol. Blind Helen Keller loved this finger-traceable and "endless" form.

a ᚠ, b ᛒ, c h, d ᛝ, e ᛋ or M, f ᚥ, g X,
h ᚾ, i l, j ᛊ, k ᚲ, l ᚱ, m ᛘ, n ↑, ng ◊, o ᛟ,
p ᛉ, r ᚱ, s ᛋ, t ↑, u ᚾ, w ᛈ, y ᚻ, z ᛉ.
(This a simplified form, with no q, v, or x)   Fig.48

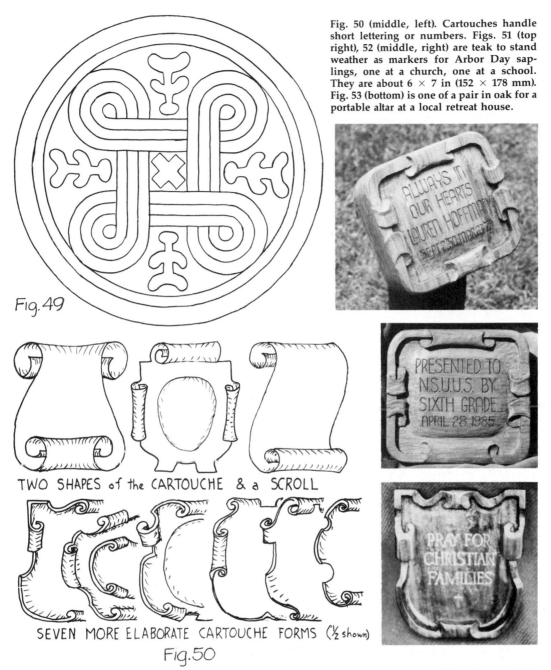

Fig. 50 (middle, left). Cartouches handle short lettering or numbers. Figs. 51 (top right), 52 (middle, right) are teak to stand weather as markers for Arbor Day saplings, one at a church, one at a school. They are about 6 × 7 in (152 × 178 mm). Fig. 53 (bottom) is one of a pair in oak for a portable altar at a local retreat house.

Fig. 49

TWO SHAPES of the CARTOUCHE & a SCROLL

SEVEN MORE ELABORATE CARTOUCHE FORMS (½ shown)

Fig. 50

the lettering is to appear is either convex or concave, rather than a flat plane. The curls can be carved fairly deep, say ½ in (13 mm) or more, to provide realism, and it helps to undercut the curl and to tint at the base to give the illusion of shadow and depth.

The only tools usually necessary are a gouge of the curvature desired for the edges of the curls, a smaller firmer and flat gouge for setting in the background, a knife for details, and a V-tool for incising lettering. The lettering, if incised, is helped also by coating with darker color inside. Be careful, however, to avoid spreading any color into the grain around the letters—a sealant is usually advisable. If the lettering is raised, the number of letters or numbers should be limited.

4

That Troublesome Lettering

LETTERING continues to be a problem for many carvers. I have written about it frequently (including the preceding chapter), and provided many examples as well as alphabets in previous books, but . . . So I will provide several further examples here, although I suspect the problem is as much the design and layout as it is the carving in most instances, and goes all the way back to the laborious learning of letter-printing in grade school. All my life, I have done printed letters as a kind of doodling, and the use of special letters and alphabets was part of my work as an editor. So it is easy for me. I have difficulty understanding the fear so many carvers have.

The Roman alphabet does tend to be blocky and difficult, and such lower-case letters as "e," "a," "o," "c," and "s" require practice to do well. An easy remedy is to stick with capital letters as far as possible, and to avoid the elaborate cursive and uncial shapes, as well as the serifed forms. Further, it is preferable to incise the lettering rather than to carve it in relief. In most cases, I use incised lettering, which can be carved cleanly with a V-tool in the harder woods. Further, it is easy to accentuate incised lettering by making it darker or lighter than the surrounding wood. I do this by spraying the lettered area with a matte varnish to seal the grain, then painting in and immediately wiping off a darker stain, even on walnut. In this way, the surface of the wood will not be discolored, but some stain will remain in the lettering and create contrast. It is also possible to use black stain or paint for accentuation, but I have found that usually too strong and not very aesthetic. The same holds true for white pigment brushed into lettering; inevitably, it seems to get into adjacent grain and make the lettering look messy.

If the lettering is limited and sufficiently large, it is always possible to cut the letters from thin wood, plywood, or other material and to appliqué them. With that in mind, I have included here the designs of the letters that are made in West Sumatra and used extensively. These are much more decorative than our hardware-store letters of plastic with "jewels," wood composition, or whatever, and suggest themselves for initials or short words and numbers. They are made in three or four sizes in a West Sumatran carving village, roughly 3, 4 and 5 in (76, 102 and 127 mm) tall. They are of a soft wood and painted in colors.

One problem that many woodcarvers seem to have, by the way, is the matter of signature and title. I have seen signatures, poorly carved, scrawled across the lower half of panel carvings, in some cases actually spoiling an otherwise passable scene, and titles poorly carved into the bases of statuettes that were quite obvious and not in need of titling at all. After all, if you've copied a Toby jug, or Rodin's "Thinker," a title is scarcely necessary. The best of painting and sculpture, you will note, is untitled—the title being listed in a subdued and discreet separate plaque or card. And the artist's name does not dominate the lower right-hand corner and distract the viewer.

Further, many woodcarvings of long ago have no identification whatsoever; they were carved by very competent craftsmen who saw no reason to use their work as a billboard. I feel that every carver should sign work that has an element of originality, or of which he is particularly proud, but the title, if it must be there, should be an attached engraved brass plate, or something else subdued and within reason.

If your name is Horace Jonathan Winterbottom, it is advisable to develop a chirograph, a symbol that will identify your work for ages to come. Use a monogram, your initials, or something like the simplified V-tool logo or chirograph that I use, a vast simplification of the first five letters of my last name, "Tange." It is far better to be just a little modest in signing, and to let the viewer do a bit of deciding what the title of your work is—before deciding how competently you have depicted it. If you have done your carving properly, a viewer will *hunt* for title and name. If you haven't, an oversize signature only builds a more negative attitude towards the carving.

To dismount from the soap box, let me point out that the simplest sort of lettering is that on the cartouches (Chapter 3). This is straightforward block lettering, easy and fast with a V-tool. It has been enhanced as I described, with a darker stain in the lettering. Another simple letter form that our ancestors enjoyed is Runic lettering (page 28), which even today carries the connotation of magic. It did have some connection through the throwing of a handful of short sticks—the way the sticks landed when thrown on a surface could be interpreted into letters and forecasts. The alphabet, however, is hard to find, so I have shown it there.

I used it on a Kubbestol (block stool) I carved to identify the gods and goddesses depicted and for an inscription girdling the seat, "May you sit on the seats of the mighty." It was fun to use an alphabet that the viewer was very unlikely to be able to read, even if he was of Swedish or Norwegian descent. More normal alphabets are readily available; I've included them at least three times.

The *design* of lettering is extremely im-

Fig. 55. San Quentin prisoner carved this panel perhaps thirty years ago. The likeness of the general is better than most, but the scalloped background of the scroll appears busy. Handling of the general's name is unfortunate; "Arthur" should have been upper and lower case like "General Mac." The lettering was done with a fluter, then filled with darker color that blurred a bit. All in all, the carver should have avoided the lettering job; he'd have come out ahead.

Fig. 54. Counter for a boat in oak with deeply incised lettering. By coincidence, the owner's name has a nautical ring. Note the handling of the date—an effort to create dynamic balance on a difficult shape—not too successful.

portant, and somewhat difficult. The type-writer allows equal spaces for an "i" and a "w," but the skilled letterer gives the "i" or the "l" half the width of an "n" or other normal letter, and allots 1½ widths to "m" or "w." Further, he alters letterspacing because of the extended top of a "t," the circularity of an "o" and the projection of a crossbar on an "f." All I have discussed is in standard lettering handbooks, readily available. They'll repay your study before you try to do extensive lettering.

Two Major Examples

My two major examples here again compare the difficult and the easy. In each case, the lettering is a major component of the design. But in the case of the little boy with the pig, it is simple incised upper and lower case, and in the letter panel it is quite an elaborate form of Old English raised letters. They are worlds apart in the problems of execution.

The panel of boy and pig deserves a bit more explanation. The daughter of a Colorado friend wrote asking me to make a birthday present for her father. There was danger there, because he is a skilled carver with a tricky sense of humor. The fact that his name is Ken Thompson led me into recalling that old English nursery rhyme: "Tom, Tom the Piper's son/Stole a pig and away he run/The pig was eat and Tom was beat/And Tom went crying down the street." After all, "Tom" and "Son" combine into his name. So I put the lettering into a scroll at the side of the figure, the only innovation being that, because it was a scroll, I lettered the reverse portions backwards. Also, I added in the background the Scottish phrase, "D'ye ken (for "Do you know"), which gave me the "Ken." The carving was made in walnut about 10 × 15 in (254 × 381 mm) with the lettering simply incised and antiqued. I am happy to report that the recipient figured it out at once.

The second major example is a panel commissioned as a motto for a skating club. It was to be placed over the doorway to the clubroom, so had to be readably large. I had available the mahogany leaf from a hand-made table at least 150 years old. (You will note that the left- and right-hand lobes are not exactly the same shape.) It was approximately 12 × 36 in (305 × 914 mm) and had quite a nice patina under the grime. So I decided to reverse the usual procedure, and show the lettering dark (preserving the patina) against the lighter natural mahogany background. The edges of the leaf were beveled off, so could be preserved to make a natural frame.

I chose an Old English form of lettering from the tomb of Richard II (*circa* 1400 AD) in Westminster—it is somewhat simpler and more readable, as well as more carvable, than the elaborate typical Old English. However, there the design became a problem. No matter how I approached it, the quotation formed two equal lines, and there was no space for credit to Goethe, the author. ("Power perfected becomes grace".)

As you can see, it was necessary to put in the credit in vertical lettering at the right. Actually, this lettering is only about ⅛ in (3 mm) above the background, but the contrast between patina and natural wood is more than sufficient to make it readable. However, although I selected the letters for readability and ease of carving, I had to make a careful layout to size on paper and carbon-copy it on the wood. Any change of mind, either in the layout or the carving, would have destroyed the patina.

This kind of raised lettering requires meticulous care and attention. It is not something that can be dashed off as an afterthought. This is true as well of any plaque you may design that contains a quotation or lettering of any length. You will find that if you lay the lettering out twice independently, the lines will vary in length, so you must be certain that your ultimate layout is correct before you apply it to the wood. This must be followed by careful setting-in and removal of background to avoid chipping letter surfaces. In this case,

Fig. 56–58. When Ken Thompson's daughter commissioned a birthday present for him, I thought of the old nursery rhyme, "Tom, Tom, the Piper's son . . ." It blanked out any other idea, so I carved it, putting "D'ye KEN" (Do you know . . .) from the Scots above the head of the rhyme. Thus "Ken" and "Tom son" are hidden in the lettering, and Ken got it right off. (He later admitted he'd filched a piglet as a youngster.) To add a fillip, I reversed the lettering with the scroll. Lettering was all done with a V-tool. Wood is walnut and size 10 × 12 in (254 × 305 mm). (The sketch is 40% of actual size.) With the antiqued finished piece, I match a photo of the panel before antiquing, as a reminder that finishing is vital.

Fig.58

Fig. 60

Figs. 59 (above), 60 (middle). Exact layout of complex lettering like this Old English variant is essential, including form and spacing, as shown in the half- **length sketch. The 33-in (838-mm) panel is a 150-year-old table leaf of mahogany, so patina was preserved on letter faces, with the background lighter.**

I scalloped the background with a flat ½-in (13-mm) gouge to create contrast with the plane surface of the lettering, and finished the plaque with a coat of matte varnish, followed by Kiwi® natural shoe polish.

Obviously, every lettering problem will have its individual characteristics, and these should be considered in the design stages. It is not advisable to make a rough layout and trust to luck; it's too hard to replace wood that should not have been removed in the first place. If the lettering *is* the subject, as in the panel just described, you are in a sense fortunate, because all of

your skill can be applied to it. But if it is simply an adjunct to a carving, as in the case of the Tom, Tom panel, it must be done so that it does not destroy or compete with the subject of the carving. Which conveniently returns me to what I wrote earlier about signatures and titles: Play them down rather than up. The viewer wants first to see and understand the carving— your name comes later. And if you must have a title, there may be something lacking in the design of the carving itself. A good carving tells its own story, without words—to that extent Confucius was right.

II
Designs by
the Hundreds

5

Fun with the Ball-in-a-Cage

ONE OF THE FAMILIAR tricks of whittling, here and abroad, has been the ball-in-a-cage. American whittlers carve a ball, a bird, a fish, a girl, even the ubiquitous ugly cowboy within the four corner bars of a simple cage. The Chinese have for centuries made the nested spheres in ivory—one ball within another and another within that, carved integrally, and those visible through the holes in the outer one also surface-carved. I have heard of such spheres having a total of 24 balls; I have one reputedly with fourteen. (Obviously, special tools are needed for such work.) Then there is the Welsh love spoon, and the Chinese bamboo back scratcher, each with two nested balls in the handle. In the case of the Welsh spoon the two imprisoned balls supposedly represent the happily married couple, and adjacent chain links depict the carver's suggestion for the number of offspring. Carving it is a knife job, pure but not simple.

All this was in my mind when I looked at a 4-in (102-mm)-dia section of ash limb 4 in (102 mm) long. It had white growth wood surrounding a golden-brown center and for some reason suggested a lion head. No sooner said than done—I started a lion head, but with one variation that turned out to be major: the ball in his mouth. The picture sequence shows what happened thereafter, but gives no indication of the amount of time spent removing tiny chips in the roof of the mouth, over the tongue (which is non-existent, fortunately), and behind the teeth. The idea is, of course, to

Fig. 61 (above). A simple version of the Welsh love spoon, with the two balls in a cage representing wedded bliss, and the three chain links a coy suggestion of number of children. The block at the end of the chain carries a monogram. Pine was the wood.

Figs. 62, 63. Two examples of the ball-in-a-cage. At left are the nested spheres—at least four balls, one within the other, and carved through the holes with special tools. At right is a lion in a cage.

make the ball as large as possible, at least large enough that it cannot be taken out. This one ended up so large that, even if the fangs were implanted and not integral, the ball would not come out. And it turned out to be almost round, which was as much luck as good carving.

Obviously, the first step is to carve the lion head, making certain that the mouth is open about as wide as possible. This puts wrinkles behind the mouth and makes the eyes squint, so it would be helpful to find a good, clear, photo of a lion at full roar, particularly a side view. I've seen such, but couldn't find one when I needed it; all

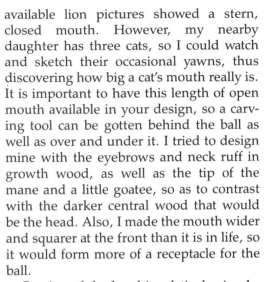

available lion pictures showed a stern, closed mouth. However, my nearby daughter has three cats, so I could watch and sketch their occasional yawns, thus discovering how big a cat's mouth really is. It is important to have this length of open mouth available in your design, so a carving tool can be gotten behind the ball as well as over and under it. I tried to design mine with the eyebrows and neck ruff in growth wood, as well as the tip of the mane and a little goatee, so as to contrast with the darker central wood that would be the head. Also, I made the mouth wider and squarer at the front than it is in life, so it would form more of a receptacle for the ball.

Carving of the head is relatively simple. If you have carved lion heads before, you can adjust the design slightly to accommodate the relative colors of the wood. I left a ridge at each side of the jaws to be shaped later into the side teeth, and formed the lips and located front fangs. Then began the carving of the ball. In contrast to the usual procedure with a ball-in-a-cage, in which a square shape is carved for the ball, then rounded as it is separated from the corner bars, I had to begin the rounding at once, sighting frequently to make certain that the ball was round rather than oval or

Fig. 64 (above). Lion head with ball in mouth, head before ruff being about 4 × 4½ × 4 in (102 × 115 × 102 mm). The wood is ash, with a 1 × 5 × 7-in (25 × 127 × 178-mm) oval of holly behind it to expand the ruff. In the ash limb, growth wood could be used to give white touches to mane, nose tip, and goatee. The integral ball is just under 2¼ in (57 mm) in diameter.

The Lion Head Step by Step. Figs. 66–69

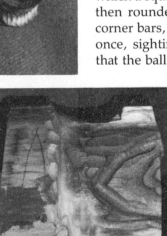

Step I (Fig. 66). The original piece of ash was ½ in (12 mm) longer, as shown, to provide clamping surfaces. Here the growth wood has been retained for nose tip and goatee, as well as the outlining of original mouth opening.

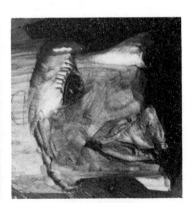

Step II (Fig. 67). After the head was shaped, except for the mane ruff, shaping of the ball was begun. Note the ridge left for back teeth within the side of the lip. Teeth, which are, of course, across grain and very fragile are still attached to the ball blank.

otherwise misshapen. Also, I realized that I had to widen the mouth at the back still more; it could not open with a V at the back—it required a U for tool clearance, as shown in the photos. It was particularly difficult to clear the back of the ball, but once it was free, it could be shaved and rounded by holding it against the mouth wall with a finger in back, while flat gouges and a knife are used for shaving in front. (This operation must be done very carefully, for the ball has a tendency to slip and rotate, and the back finger may be the victim.)

Once the ball was roughly rounded, I could get at it with an offset rasp to smooth

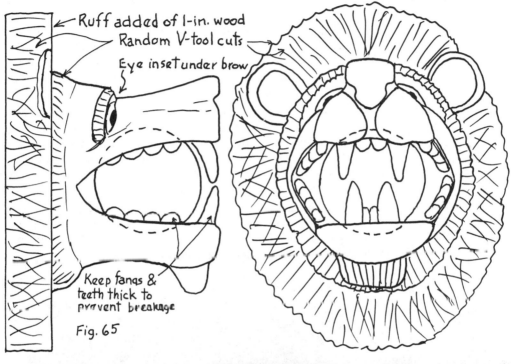

Ruff added of 1-in. wood
Random V-tool cuts
Eye inset under brow
Keep fangs & teeth thick to prevent breakage
Fig. 65

  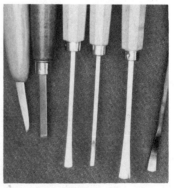

Step III (Fig. 68). The ball blank has been rounded and teeth shaped but are still attached. The back end of the mouth has been changed from V to U shape to provide added tool clearance. Also, gum ridge was thinned inside to the minimum, again to clear tools.

Step IV (Fig. 69). The ball has now been separated from teeth and is being rounded with gouges and firmers in the slow process of separation. The back has been cut through from the sides, and this cut is being extended up and down to meet cuts worked from between the fangs in front.

Fig. 70. The Tools: These tools served for both projects. They include ⅜-in (10-mm) short-bent and long-bent flat gouges, ¼-in (6-mm) short- and long-bent firmers, all full-sized tools. A ¼-in (6-mm) small firmer and a whittler's knife were considerable help as well. For this, special tools are essential.

it. I increased the mane diameter with an oval of 1-in (25-mm) holly, cutting about ½ in (13 mm) off the back of the ash so the growth wood blended into the holly. Touching up with stain finished the piece.

Not content with the lion, I designed a hippopotamus, also with a ball in his mouth, this time in a piece of silky oak from Florida, which I had not previously carved. This is a grey wood with some visible grain and looks something like rhino hide in color. However, the piece was only 1½ × 2½ × 6½ in (38 × 64 × 165 mm), so I unintentionally violated my own preachings about not undertaking a design which is too big or too little for available tools. This one was too little.

The rhino design was blocky, with the head as wide as the body and squared off in front, again to provide space for the ball. The carving of the animal body and head is easy, but the ball was a real joker. Sides and front were easy, despite the large front teeth, and the ball could be cleared readily in all the visible areas. (The silky oak is rather easy to carve.) But I had to use every small bent tool that I had in order to get in back, on top, and under the ball. Even so, it took hours to get it loose and ready for the tedious work of rounding. But it was all worthwhile, because the piece excites the interest of everyone who sees it, although most insist that the ball was put in later, despite the visible evidence that it cannot be done. The ball in the rhino's mouth is just under 1¼ in (32 mm) in diameter, while that in the lion's mouth is just under 2¼ in (57 mm), as compared with jaw widths (outside) of 1½ in (38 mm) and 3 in (76 mm). Finish on this piece was simply wax, because no retouching was necessary. On the lion head, I used matte varnish as a sealant, then oil stain to get the darker color where it was needed.

If you try these two, keep the fangs thick to avoid breakage, and leave spaces between fang and teeth to get tools in. Also, put the ball as far forward as possible, allowing only space for eventual separation from the fangs.

Figs. 71, 72 (below). This 1½ × 2½ × 6½-in (38 × 64 × 165-mm) hippopotamus with ball in mouth proved challenging, particularly because most of my tools were too big. The wood is silky oak, a fragment from a Florida tree that froze. The ball is almost 1¼ in (32 mm) in diameter, so clearances are close, requiring bent tools and careful cutting. The wood is relatively soft, with a pleasing grey color and some figure. Modelling is simple.

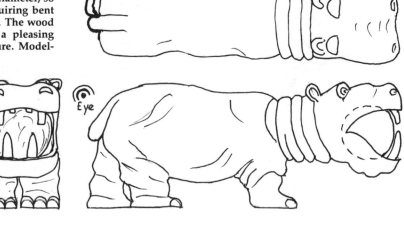

Fig. 72

6

Holly Is Versatile and Useful

HOLLY has been familiar to me all my life as a decorative bush or small tree, the source of Christmas wreaths, but I didn't realize it was also a rather unique decorative wood, even though I wrote about it fifty years ago. Then, a decade or so ago, I rescued a 2-in (51-mm)-dia trunk of dead holly that a neighbor was discarding, and my education began. It is America's whitest wood, and one of the densest—it will support very small detail and allow the carving of such elements as fingers the size of a pencil lead, and across grain at that. Further, it can be finished to look almost like ivory. It shows little grain, but may on occasion be gray in color, apparently from absorbing stain from water passing through black soil. It has little or no tendency to split. The nearest approach to it is English sycamore, used as a substitute for holly inlaying, etc. (also called sycamore maple, and *Acer pseudo platanus* in Latin). This latter wood has a decided crossfire figure in a fiddle pattern, so is often dyed silver-gray and called harewood commercially. In its natural state, it is almost as white as holly.

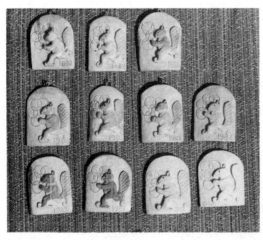

Fig. 73 (above). Olympic-aspirant skaters showed their skill at a local winter sports club. Pendants like these, ¼ × 1½ × 2¼ in (66 × 38 × 57 mm), were given the girls, and similar ones mounted on walnut wedges went to the boys. The face shows a beaver (club emblem) in relief, on skates, juggling the five Olympic rings incided on the rounded background. The date is incised at lower right. Holly sometimes has a darker layer near the surface, which was used on several of these pieces to create a cameo effect.

Fig. 74. Holly only ⅛ in (3 mm) thick formed these ballet figures for a mobile. The tallest are about 4 in (102 mm), but holly will support the carving of extended pencil-lead-size fingers, for example.

Figs. 75, 76. 1-in (25-mm) pendant with monogram on one side (right) and a scene taken from a club logo on the other (left). Similar ones became key-chain ornaments.

Figs. 77, 78. Valentine's Day pendant for a teenager, whittled in holly (left). It is piece-carved and modelled on both sides. About 1½ in (38 mm) tall, it has a silver screw-eye and jump ring.

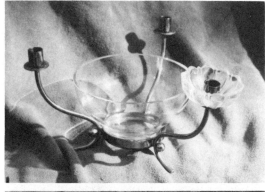

Brasstown carvers of the Campbell Folk School in North Carolina carve Nativity scenes and very exceptional Christmas-tree ornaments of holly. I have made all sorts of pendants, some with figures, some with scenes, some with miniature lettering. I have also made a great many other things, including buttons, flowers, scene assemblies, awards. Several recent ones, ranging widely in type, are described here. You may not have holly, but the designs are useable for other woods, although you may have to increase size a little.

The original 2-in (51 mm) trunk has been succeeded by some 4-in (102 mm)-diameter

Fig. 79 (left, above). This triple-candle table center-piece had bobêches (drip-wax catchers) to match the glass central bowl. When two were broken, they could not be replaced. Fig. 80 (left). Holly flowers were carved to replace the bobêches. Now if the hostess prefers, she can insert mushroom-shaped holly figures instead of candles. The cross-hatching is done with a V-tool.

Fig. 81 (left). Flowers were carved from blanks like that at right with only four tools, 1-in (25-mm) medium-sweep gouge, ⅜-in (10-mm) half-round gouge, small firmer, and V-tool.

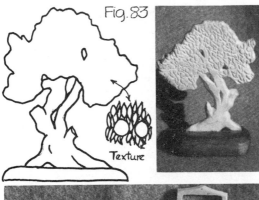

Fig. 83

Texture

Fig. 82 (above). Planned Nativity had these figures, plus Wise Men and shepherds. All were ⅛-in (3-mm) holly, with Joseph about 4 in (102 mm) tall. Shepherds were grouped on a base of walnut.

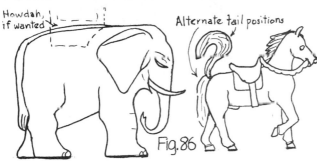

Howdah, if wanted

Alternate tail positions

Fig. 86

Fig. 87

Figs. 83–88 (above left, left, and below right). Various elements have been added annually by the owner. They include olive (top left), carob, and palm trees, mounts for the Three Wise Men, and a cow, all on separate walnut bases. All added figures are carved on both sides so they can be posed as desired.

Fig. 89 (below). The creche as it appears now. The palm tree (shown at right also) is 8 in (203 mm) tall. Closeups of original figures are in my *Carving the Unusual* (Sterling).

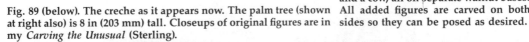

pieces, and even a 1×6×8 in (25× 152×203 mm) piece, because holly grows wild in the Southeast. However, if you attempt to air-dry a green piece, it can both warp and check badly.

My preceding remark about tiny fingers is prompted by the fact that I made a mobile of ballet figures, none more than 4 in (102 mm) tall and some with fingers extended. The wood can be carved readily with either knife or chisels, and has been used extensively by cabinetmakers for inlaying in oak or ebony. The first four examples are basically whittling projects, all in thin sections of wood. Slightly larger are the twin sea horses, 3 in (76 mm) long, which accompany a starfish in maple and a fantail goldfish in mahogany as floating toys for a child's bath. Any of the three can be chewed without danger—the starfish and goldfish are in fact finished by soaking in vegetable oil.

The next example is one of those things that happen. A friend had a brass table-top decoration that combined three candle holders around a glass bowl matched by fairly elaborate glass bobèches (catchers of wax drip) on the holders. But two of the bobèches had been broken and were not replaceable. Could I carve something? My solution was three holly flowers about 2 in (51 mm) in diameter with cross-hatched centers. However, they had an added fillip: The flower centers were mushroom-shaped and could be replaced by candles.

The next example includes some inherent marketing advice. It is a Nativity scene originally intended to be somewhat experimental. The figures for it are not in-the-round—they are in ⅛-in (3-mm) holly mounted on bases, singly or in groups, and against a walnut background. It originally included the Holy Family (carved on one side only), with a kneeling donkey on a walnut base, plus two doves, a Star of Bethlehem and a three-Angel choir on the background. There were also three separately based Wise Men, plus three shepherds with assorted sheep on a single base. When I had it almost completed, a friend saw it—and bought it.

But that was only the beginning. Since then, I have been asked to add a kneeling cow, an elephant, a camel, a pony (these three for the Wise Men), a palm tree, a carob tree (also known as St. John's Bread and the source of artificial chocolate), and an olive tree to expand the scene!

Fig. 90. A pair of sea horses 3 in (76 mm) tall in holly, plus a mahogany fantail goldfish and a maple starfish, form a group of bath playthings, or can be mobiles. Maple and mahogany pieces are soaked in vegetable oil.

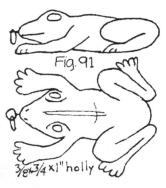

Fig. 91. Holly makes interesting three-dimensional pieces, of course. This 1-in (25-mm) frog with ebony-insert eyes was carved as a pendant with a silver screw-eye and jump ring. Other examples are shown elsewhere in this book, like dragon door handles.

7

Bad Wood Made Good

WOOD IS relatively plentiful in the United States, so carvers tend to start out with clean kiln-dried planks of known softness—with a predictable less-than-interesting result. Odd-shaped branches, knotty or spalted pieces, checked sections and odd shapes are discarded—and their

Fig. 92 (above). A student gave me this piece of palmetto, with the comment that it is useless as a carving wood. But it made this crude pig!

Fig. 93 (right). Ted Haag of Tualatin, Oregon, sent me this cup and spoon. They are whittled from myrtle wood that he salvaged from a downed tree on an Oregon beach.

Fig. 94 (below right). A sourwood stump from North Carolina became the head of Big Bird from TV's "Sesame Street" simply by the addition of a left eye and a bit of shaping of the bill. The right eye was already there—a flaw in the wood, as was the mouth—a split when the sapling was cut. I debarked the bill and widened the mouth, then stuck the assembly on a dowel in a piece of scrap olive wood.

Fig. 95 (below). I saw this swan one Sunday in the front window of a furniture store in Scottsdale, Arizona, and photographed it through the glass. This was mesquite, and the swan is about 30 in (762 mm) long.

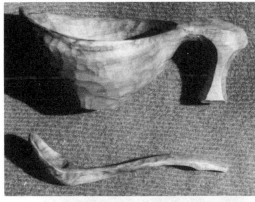

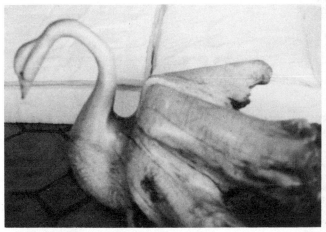

potential is lost. Carvers in other countries, where wood is scarce or relatively expensive, make good carvings from what we throw away as scrap. (Examples of this from Mexico are pictured in the chapter on gesso.) Because I have made many carvings from odd pieces of wood, friends have taken to sending me more. I enjoy trying something new. These are examples of what can be done with them. You may have to look at a piece for a while, and it may defeat you in the end, but it's fun to try to make something different and new from what is otherwise scrap.

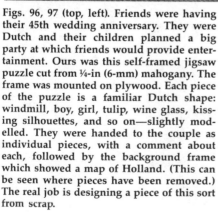

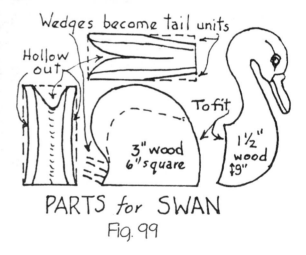

PARTS for SWAN
Fig. 99

Figs. 96, 97 (top, left). Friends were having their 45th wedding anniversary. They were Dutch and their children planned a big party at which friends would provide entertainment. Ours was this self-framed jigsaw puzzle cut from ¼-in (6-mm) mahogany. The frame was mounted on plywood. Each piece of the puzzle is a familiar Dutch shape: windmill, boy, girl, tulip, wine glass, kissing silhouettes, and so on—slightly modelled. They were handed to the couple as individual pieces, with a comment about each, followed by the background frame which showed a map of Holland. (This can be seen where pieces have been removed.) The real job is designing a piece of this sort from scrap.

Figs. 98, 99 (top, right). From Ted Haag came the two pieces of big-leaf maple above, so badly spalted that Ted "stabilized" them by soaking in a mixture of paraffin and acetone. The curved block suggested a swan's body to me, so I hollowed out between the wings and cut off wedges at the sides to thin the piece to the front. (It was originally 3½ × 5 × 7 in (89 × 127 × 178 mm). The wedges became the two tail sections. Head and neck are a scrap piece of butternut ("white walnut") that also had an interesting figure, with an ebony eye inserted and a double tassel like those on my Korean wedding ducks (next page). The wings were shaped inside and out. Assembly proved difficult; I had to nail the tail pieces and neck to the body, because you can't glue paraffin! The square block became a decorative panel with a Greek motif, shown elsewhere in this book.

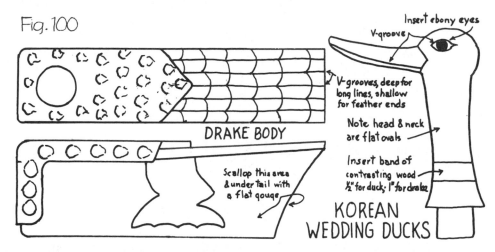

Fig. 100

DRAKE BODY

V-groove

Insert ebony eyes

V-grooves, deep for long lines, shallow for feather ends

Note head & neck are flat ovals

Insert band of contrasting wood ½" for duck; 1" for drake

Scallop this area & under tail with a flat gouge

KOREAN WEDDING DUCKS

Fig. 102 (below left). Hurricane Gloria uprooted a 4-in (102-mm) ash with a wisteria vine around it. The wisteria now is a serpent with a tulip-wood head, brass eyes, and forked aluminum tongue nuzzling an apple, while an owl and a mouse in branch sockets watch.

Fig. 103 (below middle). Three lion heads, one utilizing a projection, are carved through the bark on this slab of camphorwood, good practice for me in a different species.

Figs. 100, 101 (above, left). In 1983, a New York store introduced "Korean wedding ducks," absurdly shaped, supposedly good-luck tokens as wedding gifts—at a very substantial price, of course. A neighbor who liked the shape but not the gaudy painting called them to my attention, so I made a drake and his mate (left, with a later loon) with rosewood bodies, maple heads with beefwood rings, topknot of pink ivory wood and eye inserts of ebony. No paint! She insisted upon buying them to hide until her 50th wedding anniversary in 1985, and they have now gone to her daughter for her 25th in 1986. Other friends who saw them demanded copies—I made 13 and used up all my 2 × 2–3 × 4-in (51 × 51–76 × 102-mm) scraps of rare wood, as well as other bits.

Fig. 104 (below). Bill Heynen carved these ferrets in a spalted stump. Many roots and distorted branches lend themselves to carving.

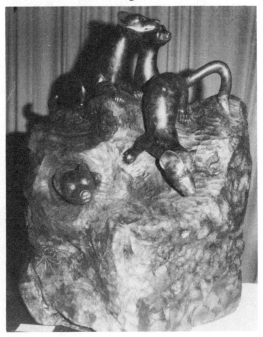

8

Caricatures Create Comedy

PRESENT-DAY beginning whittlers rarely carve the chain, the ball-in-a-cage or the fan; instead they go in for broken-down cowboys, boots, hounds, sea captains, old nags—mostly caricatures. Some even violate one of the old rules about whittling: They carve heads, bodies, arms and legs separately, then assemble the lot to get a desired pose. (As a woodcarver, I assemble carvings all the time; it is whittling tradition to make the carving monolithic.) Caricatures can and do serve a purpose; they bring a smile to the burdens of present-day living, and they poke gentle fun—if they're properly done. As emphasis for this, I picture first three caricatures by Harold Enlow of Dogpatch, Arkansas, acknowledged king of the cowboy caricaturists and admittedly the producer of the ugliest mugs extant. His carvings are masterpieces, as were those of Andy Anderson, who inspired two of the three pictured here.

However, a major problem in caricature is that a high percentage of the so-called caricatures are merely crude. They are poor copies of what has been done, and are often produced by rounding up a sawed-out blank. There is no input on the part of the carver, and the finish may com-

Fig. 105 (left). This caricature of an old-time cowboy is my friend Harold Enlow's "stock in trade." As Harold says, "I think he's plenty ugly enough for people to recognize who carved him." This is true; it's skilled caricature by a master; every line bites—but with a smile.

pound the felony. The usual wood for caricatures is white pine or basswood, because they carve easily. However, neither reacts well to oil stains, tending to darken in cross-grain areas and showing every flaw in the carving. It is preferable to use a harder wood that has some grain or figure, or to seal the surface and provide an antiqued finish, as described elsewhere in this book.

Obviously, I have made my share of sea captains, cowboys, hounds, broken-down horses and the like, some good, some bad. I have even taught beginning classes how to make them, particularly Skipper Sam'l, whom I first described in print more than fifty years ago. But here we go on another one—this one a cowboy caricature, an effort as well to produce a caricature of former President Lyndon Johnson.

This carving is in avocado wood and is a foot (305 mm) tall. I didn't intend him as a demonstration of competence, but as a sort of caricature of cowboy caricatures. He serves as an example of how to go about carving a cowpuncher if you hanker for one. He even has his hands jammed into his pockets, so you won't run into trouble caricaturing them. It is hard to caricature hands without making them look crude or ungainly. Not so the face: crossed eyes, huge nose, crooked teeth, underslung jaw and other emphasized deformities are usually encouraged.) A wide nose and oversize, even stand-out, ears are common on this kind of figure and the mouth may often be distorted as well, with "rubber" lips. Bowlegs and big feet are also standard. Boot toes tend to turn up, pants are too long—and usually have cuffs. The hat will be exaggerated, of course, and may or may not be creased in one of the "regional" standards. I found out some years ago that black Stetsons are not necessarily worn by the bad guys; they are worn commonly in Wyoming, as I recall.

Remember that caricature is the humorous exaggeration of the characteristics of an individual, his features, his form, his way of walking or gesturing or whatever. Thus, it will be much more fun for you later to caricature people whom you know,

Fig. 106 (above). Favorite subjects of the late Andy Anderson, famed carver-caricaturist, were the convict and the nurse. These two are interpretations of Andy by Harold Enlow. The convict's number is the date the figure was completed.

Fig. 107 (right). Former President Lyndon Johnson in my caricature. The blank was California avocado wood 4 × 4 × 12 in (102 × 102 × 305 mm). Note the jutting chin, large nose, and big ears. Hands in pockets avoid the necessity of carving them.

if you pick out the things about them that are distinctive. This ability comes, I am told, with practice; I guess I've never practiced enough. But I've seen many so-called portraits of notables, such as Abraham Lincoln, John Kennedy, Winston Churchill and Charlie Chaplin that were in reality caricatures because the carver over-emphasized certain well-known characteristics like Lincoln's wart and thin jaw, Kennedy's thick hair and plump face, Churchill's fat face, small eyes and big cigar, Chaplin's moustache, big shoes, bowlegged shuffle and cane. There is a thin line between portraiture and caricature, and it is very often overstepped.

HERE'S HOW TO CARVE A COWBOY . . .

COWBOY CARICATURE
Avocado
Fig. 108

STEP I

Fig. 109 (below). My blank was 4 × 4 × 12 in (102 × 102 × 305 mm). It can be smaller, of equivalent 3:1 proportions. Sketch on front and side silhouettes. Saw the back and far side first to preserve layout lines. Then saw off the front as a single piece and replace the scrap (tack or tab it in place) to provide the final sawing guide, particularly around the head.

STEP II

Fig. 110 (left). Rough the body to shape. Remember to leave wood for the bulge of the hands in the pants pockets and for the ears. Leave plenty of wood at the nose as well; if you try to keep the features in proportion, you may end up fighting for a likeness instead of a caricature. Draw in and carve vest and Windsor tie.

STEP III

Fig. 111 (right). The back of the figure is relatively simple. Be sure to carve the legs bowed and the toes of the oversized boots turned up. A narrow waist emphasizes the width of his seating area. You may find it easier to drill between the legs than to saw them apart; in either case, stay well below the crotch because his pants should look oversized and baggy. Put in hip-pocket slits, vest strap, arm holes and creases.

STEP IV

Fig. 112 (left). With general outlines shaped, detail and shape the vest, arms, and face. It seems to be traditional to leave the vest open, to use a string, bandanna, or Windsor tie, and to have cuffs on the pants. The hat is usually turned up at the sides, but the creasing or denting of its top is a function of geography. I used a front and two side dents rather than a top crease. There should be a suggestion of a paunch, and the clothes should look slept in, so carve wrinkles and bags.

STEP V

Fig. 113 (right). The front is finished similarly, with buttons and buttonholes suggested, a wide belt below the bulging shirt, the cravat in the soft and spreading shirt collar. The ears are intentionally large, of course, with the hat jammed down on them, and the nose is overly wide. The face is grinning and the eyes have drilled pupils so they stare a bit. That's my Lyndon!

9

Why Not a Pumpkin? Or Two?

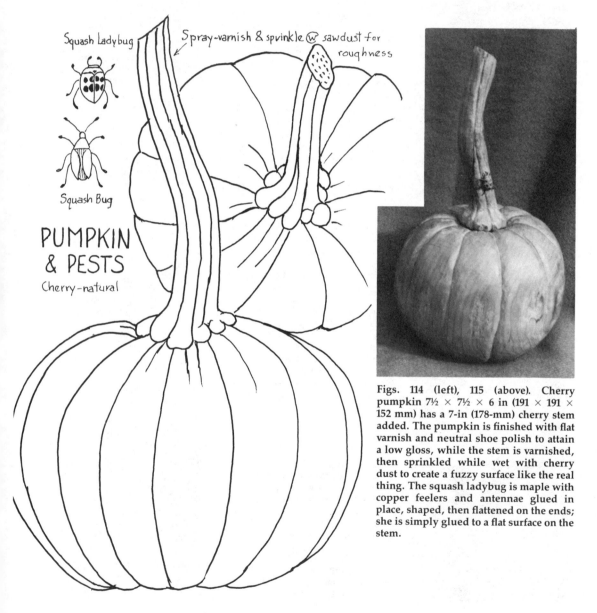

Squash Ladybug

Spray-varnish & sprinkle ⓦ sawdust for roughness

PUMPKIN
& PESTS

Cherry-natural

Squash Bug

Figs. 114 (left), 115 (above). Cherry pumpkin 7½ × 7½ × 6 in (191 × 191 × 152 mm) has a 7-in (178-mm) cherry stem added. The pumpkin is finished with flat varnish and neutral shoe polish to attain a low gloss, while the stem is varnished, then sprinkled while wet with cherry dust to create a fuzzy surface like the real thing. The squash ladybug is maple with copper feelers and antennae glued in place, shaped, then flattened on the ends; she is simply glued to a flat surface on the stem.

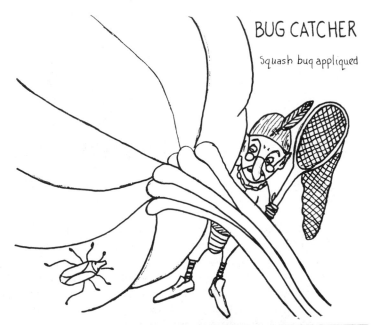

BUG CATCHER
Squash bug appliqued

Figs. 116 (right), 117 (below, right). This panel in curly maple, about 10 × 11 in (254 × 279 mm), resulted from an extra bug. The squash bug mounted on the pumpkin was left over, so the panel was designed to go with it. The bug is in Macassar ebony. The elf is adapted from a design by Arthur Rackham.

THE COMMISSION was from a young lady who wanted a "different" Christmas present for her fiancé who raised pumpkins, of all things. Whether it was in-the-round or in relief was immaterial, and the design was up to me. I thought the most unusual idea would be a wooden pumpkin, so I selected a block of home-grown cherry and set to work. The pumpkin that resulted is 7½ × 6 in (191 × 152 mm), with a stem about 7 in (178 mm) long added. The color was quite good, and the cherry had a couple of bad grain spots that suggested what happens to a pumpkin in contact with the ground.

But the piece lacked distinction somehow, so I decided to add, for fun, a bug or two. Phone calls to the local office of the U.S. Dept. of Agriculture and others got me finally to a lady biologist at the Nassau County (New York) Farm Agency. She named four pumpkin pests. I found sketches of three in *Webster's New International Dictionary, Second Edition*. So I carved a squash ladybug and a squash bug, each life-size, the ladybug of maple and the squash bug of Macassar ebony. Each had copper-wire feelers and legs, these shaped pieces being glued in drilled holes and flattened on the ends with a hammer. They looked very life-like to me, but the ladybug on the stem was enough.

The leftover squash bug led to an additional carving, this time a panel, with an elf (copied from a design by Arthur Rackham, modified to hold a butterfly net) hiding behind a pumpkin and preparing to net the squash bug mounted on the front. The panel itself was of curly maple, about 10 × 11 in (254 × 279 mm), so provided some interesting grain on the surface of the pumpkin. The panel went to the young lady for *her* Christmas present, so I got double use from the idea.

10

Gargoyles and Griffins Can Get You

WITH SOME FREQUENCY, readers ask for patterns for "gargoyles"—usually because they want something a bit more challenging than another caricature of a cowboy or a tramp. As often as not, they don't mean a gargoyle—which is strictly a device for getting rid of roof rainwater—an outspout. What they have in mind is sometimes a griffin and sometimes a chimera (or chimaera), the latter being a term used loosely in architecture for any grotesque, fantastic or imaginary beast used in decoration. (It has also become the word describing any fantastic idea or fiction of the imagination, and "grotesque" is an alternate for "chimera" in architecture.)

The chimera in Greek mythology was a fire-breathing female monster resembling a lion in its foreparts, a goat in the middle, and a dragon behind. The best-known example was the one slain by Bellerophon after she devastated Caria and Lycia in the *Iliad*, *vi*, 179. In art, it is now depicted basically as a lion with a goat's head and neck rising from the middle of the back found in Arezzo, Italy. The French version, *chimère*, is applied to the grotesque beasts that decorate the parapets of Notre Dame Cathedral in Paris.

The gargoyle of ancient Greece was often a relief lion's head (as in Pompeii) which did not carry rainwater out far from

Fig. 118. Not a gargoyle but a grotesque or chimera, this is a copy in pine by Hugh Minton of the original on the Cathedral of Notre Dame in Paris. It serves no architectural function except decoration. See Figs. 23 and 24, Chap. 1.

Fig. 119. Griffins were legendary guardians of treasure, so should be fierce in aspect. This one is in teak, with maple and ebony eyes. The basic design is Roman, but the stylized eagle head is medieval in origin.

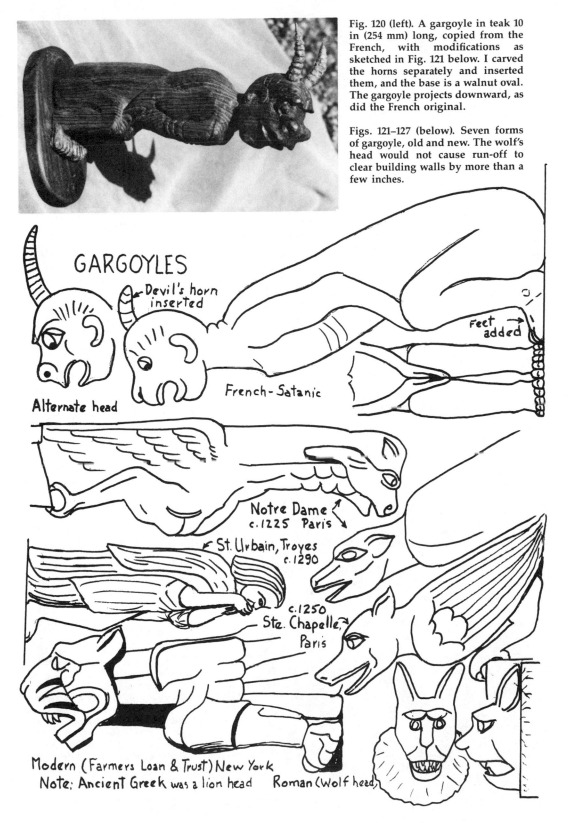

Fig. 120 (left). A gargoyle in teak 10 in (254 mm) long, copied from the French, with modifications as sketched in Fig. 121 below. I carved the horns separately and inserted them, and the base is a walnut oval. The gargoyle projects downward, as did the French original.

Figs. 121–127 (below). Seven forms of gargoyle, old and new. The wolf's head would not cause run-off to clear building walls by more than a few inches.

GARGOYLES

Devil's horn inserted

Feet added

Alternate head

French-Satanic

Notre Dame c.1225 Paris

St. Urbain, Troyes c.1290

c.1250 Ste. Chapelle, Paris

Modern (Farmers Loan & Trust) New York
Note: Ancient Greek was a lion head   Roman (Wolf head)

STEP-BY-STEP CARVING OF A GRIFFIN

STEP I

Fig. 128. My blank was teak, 3 × 7 × 12 in (76 × 178 × 305 mm), and I adapted a Roman relief design for 3D to fill it by putting more stride in the hind leg and curling the tail in to meet the leg to reduce fragility. The original had a conventional eagle head, as shown in the sketch and this sawn blank. The outline was cut with a coping saw, and the legs are now being separated, largely by flat gouge and mallet.

STEP II

Fig. 129. The tail has been cut almost to size and is being shaped to angle over the left hind leg. The forelegs are separated and in process of being shaped. The wings have also been separated by hollowing down to the body line and veeing outwards at the top. Some of this work can be speeded by sawing, because the head is narrower than the body. Thus, if the head is thinned with saw and chisel, there is clearance for some sawing between wings—but be careful! The wing is also being hollowed outside with a flat gouge.

STEP III

Fig. 130. Because the head as designed looked insufficiently fierce, I altered it to a stylized and staring one. The eyes are ¼-in (6-mm) maple dowels in drilled holes, which are in turn drilled for ⅛-in (3-mm) ebony insets. The left front claw has also been shaped and ridged, and the upraised right claw is in process of being similarly treated. The feather pattern on the wing—a stylized treatment—has also been carved in low relief.

STEP IV

Fig. 131. The head has been completed—note the outlining of eye and mouth—feathering is complete, as are foreclaws. This is largely V-tool work, with assistance from a small flat gouge. Some modelling has been done on flank and chest, and hind legs are being shaped. The tail still requires some smoothing of curvature; the end lies over the hind leg. Gouge marks will be left on the body to avoid the sanded and polished look.

STEP V, SEE PAGE 58

Figs. 132-138

GRIFFIN - in a publisher's mark (colophon)

WYVERN - dragon or griffin variant?

GRIFFIN - on final arms of the Austro-Hungarian Empire (1915-18)

These are "supporters" for heraldic arms - the latter two each being one of a pair.

GRIFFIN - French Renaissance   Sicilian   Italian, w serpent tail

GRIFFIN

Roman - adapted for 3D (Greek was similar)

Fig. 139. The tail has been shaped more precisely and toes and claws defined on hind legs. The body is being smoothed to show small gouge marks rather than long lines or ridges and to remove flat surfaces visible in Step IV on upper legs. When completed, the lines of the feathers and head will be accentuated by "antiquing" a bit with dark stain immediately wiped off surfaces but left in grooves. Feathering on neck has been extended in a crescent on the breast, and a tongue is outlined in the mouth.

building walls. The Romans used the stylized lion's head (see sketches) that had the same fault. The Gothic gargoyle, however, was usually a grotesque bird or beast squatting on its haunches on the face of a cornice moulding, so it projected outward horizontally, or even downward. The design was usually elongated so that it carried rainwater out several feet from the building wall. For decorative companions it had grotesques which stood at various points—just standing.

The griffin (also griffon or gryphon) in ancient myths was a four-legged rapacious beast with an eagle's head, legs and wings attached to a lion's body and tail. In some cases, however, the tail became a serpent, or the hind part of the body was like that of a serpent or dragon. Quite commonly, also, the head resembled that of a horse or a lion, having a mane and ears, but the face was that of an eagle. The griffin was supposed to guard gold mines and hidden treasures, to hate horses, and to be consecrated to the sun. Thus, ancient painters often showed the chariot of the sun drawn by griffins, and sometimes those of Jupiter and Nemesis as well. The "griffin" mentioned in the Bible is probably the osprey. The legendary griffin was said to inhabit Asiatic Scythia, and to attack and rend anyone who approached whatever he was guarding.

Mandeville, in his travels, said a griffin was eight times the size of a horse. It has been used architecturally in Greece, Rome,

Syria, France, Italy, and on some earlier American buildings as a decorative element, for example, on pergolas and various buildings of palatial estates at the beginning of the 20th century. It is also frequently found in heraldry, particularly in France and England—it was the badge of the Upper Franconia tourney society in 1000 AD, and later the badge of the Arundel in England and the dragon in Switzerland.

Also in heraldry there is the wyvern (wivern, wyver, wivere, wiver), a monster with the forepart a winged dragon and the hind part a serpent or lizard. (The word is a doublet for "viper.") In some heraldic usages, it is hard to distinguish between wyvern and griffin, but the griffin has more tradition. Alexander the Great carried the griffin east to India, and from there it has spread into Indonesia, with local variations, such as a head with elephant face and trunk, the emblem of the Sultans of Tenggarong in Borneo, or the version with bull horns in Syria.

Occasionally, one encounters the basilisk or cockatrice, a fanciful and horrid monster said to have been born of a hen's egg, so it has a winged dragon body with a hen's head. It serves as a supporter in the arms of Basel. Its hissing was said to drive away all other serpents and its breath, or even look, was fatal. Among present day animals, the basilisk is a species of lizard and the griffin a kind of vulture—*sic transit gloria*!

11

Delve into the Mythical

SOMEHOW, dragons and their modern counterparts, alligators and crocodiles, have a sort of horrible fascination. They have appeared extensively in art all over the world and there's at least one present-day wood collector who specializes in trading carved dragons for wood samples he doesn't yet have. I have carved a number of dragons, in relief and in the round, and find they continue to appeal. Here are a few more examples. I've also included sketches and a photograph of the traditional Chinese symbols for the years of their calendar, as well as sketches of several mythical animals that, like my dragon door handles, earn their keep.

The crocodile was worshipped in ancient Egypt and has had its adherents ever since in those countries where the croc repre-sents a recurring danger. I have found crocodile carvings in as disparate places as Sri Lanka, India, Nepal, and Papua New Guinea. Of these, by far the finest is the door handle from the Sepik River shown here; it was partly, at least, the inspiration for the holly dragon door handles I carved recently, the other part of the inspiration coming from Nepal. I include sketches of these two handles as well—you may have a door that fits one or the other.

For contrast, there are also several sketches of door knockers in England, which also depict somewhat mythical or fanciful figures—after all, St. George did have a dragon to fight. Also mythical, and from the other side of the world are the lion door guards and cheepu from Nepal. You may find one or more of these worthy.

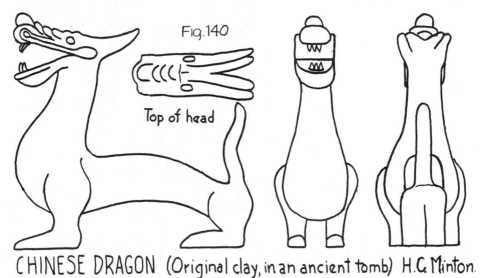

Fig. 140

Top of head

CHINESE DRAGON (Original clay, in an ancient tomb) H.C. Minton.

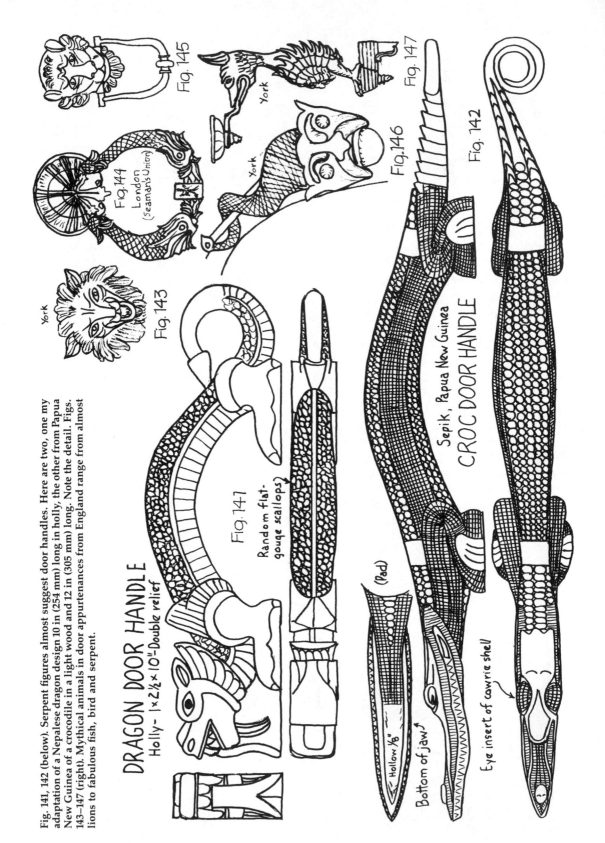

Fig. 145

Fig. 147

Fig. 144
London
(Seaman's Union)

Fig. 146
York

York

Fig. 142

York

Fig. 143

DRAGON DOOR HANDLE
Holly~ 1 × 2½ × 10"—Double relief

Fig. 141
Random flat-gouge scallops

Sepik, Papua New Guinea
CROC DOOR HANDLE

(Pad)

Hollow ⅛"

Bottom of jaw

Eye insert of cowrie shell

Fig. 141, 142 (below). Serpent figures almost suggest door handles. Here are two, one my adaptation of a Nepalese dragon design 10 in (254 mm) long in holly, the other from Papua New Guinea of a crocodile in a light wood and 12 in (305 mm) long. Note the detail. Figs. 143–147 (right). Mythical animals in door appurtenances from England range from almost lions to fabulous fish, bird and serpent.

EMPEROR'S PET—China, Han Dynasty
Fig. 150

Teak 1×1⅝×⅜

Figs. 149 (above), 150 above, right). China is unearthing some interesting caricatures in clay from ancient tombs. This dog and the dragon of Fig. 140 are examples. This design can now be bought from museums in bronze or silver—at a price.

Fig. 151 (below). This crocodile door handle is from the Sepik River in Papua New Guinea, therefore supposedly crude. It *is* primitive, but quite sophisticated and detailed, with good stylization. The carver must have known about doors in the Western world, because in his a cloth hanging on the entrance ladder shows the owner is absent.

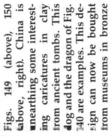

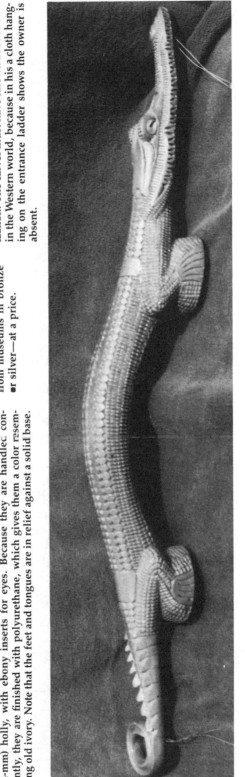

Fig. 148 (above). These handles for French doors are 1 × 1½ × 10-in (25 × 38 × 254-mm) holly, with ebony inserts for eyes. Because they are handled constantly, they are finished with polyurethane, which gives them a color resembling old ivory. Note that the feet and tongues are in relief against a solid base.

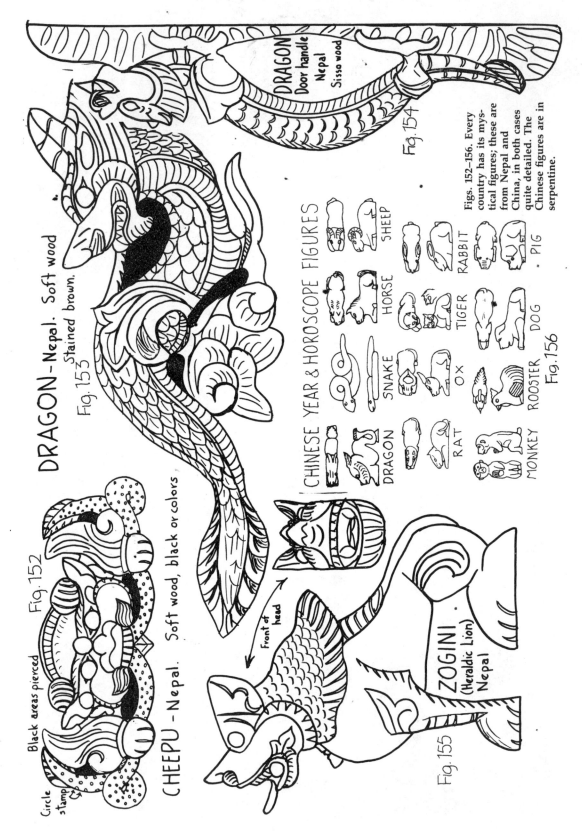

DRAGON — Nepal. Soft wood
Stained brown.

Fig. 153

DRAGON
Door handle
Nepal
Sisso wood

Fig. 154

Figs. 152–156. Every country has its mystical figures; these are from Nepal and China, in both cases quite detailed. The Chinese figures are in serpentine.

CHINESE YEAR & HOROSCOPE FIGURES

SHEEP

RABBIT

PIG

HORSE

TIGER

DOG

SNAKE

OX

ROOSTER

Fig. 156

DRAGON

RAT

MONKEY

Black areas pierced

Fig. 152

Circle stamp

CHEEPU — Nepal.   Soft wood, black or colors

Front of head

ZOGINI
(Heraldic Lion)
Nepal

Fig. 155

Fig. 158.

Fig. 159.

Fig. 161.

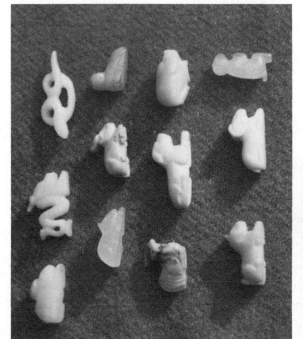

Fig. 157 (above). The Chinese still designate their years by the names of animals, rotating among twelve, although each has a modifying adjective. These are in a soft stone, and only slightly larger than pictured here. Figs. 158–161: Nepal is isolated and remote, so its art is quite different, as these examples show. Again there is a dragon as a door handle and a dog-lion as a temple guardian, plus the cheepu, who is a guardian ogre over doors.

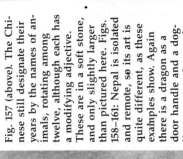

Fig. 160.

MYTHICAL CREATURES   63

12

Eric Carved Fine Horses

WHILE DIGGING through my extensive and poorly organized files for this volume, I came across the accompanying photographs and correspondence dating back a dozen years, with the late Eric Zimmerman, who wrote the very successful book, "Carving Horses in Wood" (Sterling, 1983). Three of them appear in his book, but his notes about them do not, and they are worthy of inclusion here, because they bring up points of importance. We had known each other, I as a technical editor and Eric as a technical advertiser, for many years, but it was only after we both had retired that our letters concerning horses began.

Eric was a whittler—he used only knives—and kept very busy carving horses, so busy that he never got around to completing the carousel he describes in his book, even though I did succeed in locating a source for the music box he needed. (I collected big music boxes for a time.) Also, after we had reworked his manuscript twice over, he abandoned it temporarily. But he did try carving horses in a large variety of woods, and had his share of finishing problems. Neither of us was a devotee of sandpaper, rasps, or hand grinders, nor of "shiny" finishes. He went far beyond me in exploring the possibilities of reproducing his carvings—one such casting is pictured here. And he had several Christmas cards showing his horses in color. So, thank Eric for his extensive research into the anatomy of horses, for the design of a practical carousel model, for his straightforward advice about carving, and for his experiment in reproducing worthy carvings by some mechanical means.

Figs. 162 (left), 163 (right). A sawn blank of manzanita and the finished carving. Eric wrote: "I spoiled the finished look by oiling the surface; the color darkened from the beautiful deep red to a chocolate. Mostly, I just wax the surface—never file or sandpaper. All [the horses] I've made are knife-finished. To me, it's sacrilege to sand a hand-carved piece." Amen!

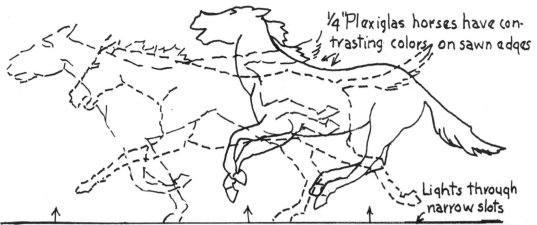

¼"Plexiglas horses have contrasting colors on sawn edges

Lights through narrow slots

Fig. 164 (above). An idea of Eric's only partly completed was this device for simulating a jumping or galloping horse. Horse blanks were sawed from ¼-in (6-mm) Plexiglas and mounted in sequence over a narrow slot from which lights of various colors would flash in turn. Sawn edges of the horses would be colored in a comparable series of colors, so they would stand out in sequence. Wrote Eric: "I seem to enjoy the fun of developing more than the operating." This is supported by his failure to finish his carousel.

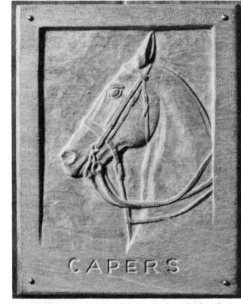

Fig. 165 (right). Eric rarely carved in relief, probably because of the difficulty of doing a good job with a knife. This panel is in red mahogany on a birch plywood ground.

Fig. 166 (below, left). A yearling colt and his goat mascot were whittled from a single piece of curly buckeye and proved to be very difficult because of the recalcitrant wood.

Fig. 167 (below, right). This bronze casting on a marble base originated as a walnut whittling.

13

Whittle Your Own Netsuke

NETSUKE are decorative toggles of wood, ivory or metal that were threaded on the thongs of small bags carried under the obi, or sash, on a Japanese kimono. They had two connected holes in the back so the thong could be slipped through, then put on the bag as a drawstring. A Japanese gentleman merely slipped the thong under his sash so that the netsuke hung out over the top. Obviously, the netsuke became obsolete when Japanese men shifted to Western dress—they wear kimonos now only at home.

But the netsuke became an object of art and was cherished in families and later collected for museums and individuals. Americans in particular have become interested, so that the netsuke is now eagerly sought after and is being made in increasing quantities as a tourist item.

Older ones, like those sketched, are now quite valuable, and there are three or four elaborate books of colored pictures for the collector's library. Significantly, all the books are in English, and more available outside of Japan than in. Also, the Chinese are making netsuke for export as well, although the original Chinese equivalent was somewhat larger.

Anyhow, the netsuke can be extremely well-carved by an expert, and certain signed ones are now eagerly sought after. The subjects can be anything, and the old netsuke carvers seemed to delight in developing a new design, just as the Chinese carvers of ladies' snuff bottles did. Those that I have sketched were collected some years ago before they became so popular. They make an interesting variation on American whittling projects, and you can try one or more of these, or develop your own. These are all miniature carvings, in no case larger than 1½ in (38 mm) in their longest dimension. They should be in a hard wood, like holly or walnut or ebony, so detail can be worked in, and they should not have snagging projections. The ideal is to attain a rounded shape that will not catch or bruise the wearer, of course.

Fig. 168 (below, left). The pop-eyed scholar and the seven lucky gods on a chicken-shaped ship are typical complex older netsukes in ivory. The ship rests on an ebony base—loosely. The little judge or scholar has eyeballs on tiny pistons so they pop out when he is tilted downwards. Fig. 169 (below, right). Merchant, badger, and toad are also ivory, but stained dark brown. The badger is a bit over 1 in (25 mm) tall. Badger and merchant are drilled in back, merchant and toad through the belly.

Fig. 170. Six more-modern netsuke of the Chinese sort, including two miniatures of Peking horses, and a large rabbit, plus a seated lady and a working man. All are in boxwood.

Among the group I have sketched, the most complex is the seven lucky gods aboard a chicken-shaped sailboat. It is necessary, in carving these gods, to distinguish between them, as I have described earlier, because each has certain skills and attributes. In this particular case, the thong holes are in the flat bottom of the ship. Note that the mast and sail are quite low, and that a general roundness is retained. The most unique netsuke is the judge or scholar—I'm not sure which. He is an attractive little figure, but his most startling trait is popping eyes. If the figure is leaned forward the eyes move forward more than ⅛ in (3 mm)! The eye sockets are bored deep into the head, and the eyeballs are black ends on tiny ivory dowels, fitted loosely so they will slide outward like pistons; normally they sit discreetly back.

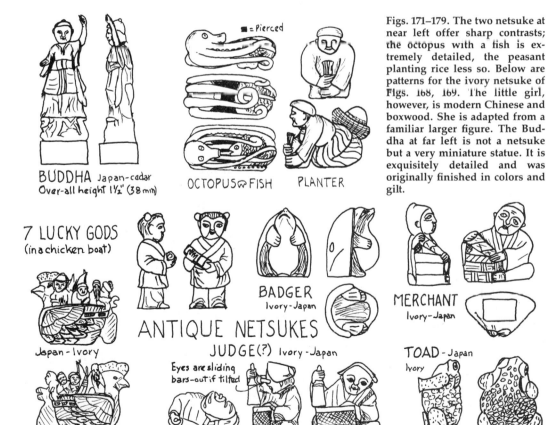

Figs. 171–179. The two netsuke at near left offer sharp contrasts; the octopus with a fish is extremely detailed, the peasant planting rice less so. Below are patterns for the ivory netsuke of Figs. 168, 169. The little girl, however, is modern Chinese and boxwood. She is adapted from a familiar larger figure. The Buddha at far left is not a netsuke but a very miniature statue. It is exquisitely detailed and was originally finished in colors and gilt.

BUDDHA Japan-cedar
Over-all height 1½" (38 mm)

■ = Pierced

OCTOPUS & FISH

PLANTER

7 LUCKY GODS
(in a chicken boat)

Japan-Ivory

ANTIQUE NETSUKES

BADGER
Ivory-Japan

JUDGE(?) Ivory-Japan

Eyes are sliding
bars-out if tilted

MERCHANT
Ivory-Japan

TOAD - Japan
Ivory

14

Doleful and His Dino

WOODCARVINGS do not have to be formal; they can be just the opposite. And caricatures do not have to be of cowboys, sea captains, hound dogs, or broken-down horses or mules; they're better if you think up your own subject. This one was largely the result of my having a piece of Alaska cedar 4×4½×15 in (102×115×381 mm) long that I wanted to carve to see how it would go. For some reason, a doleful elf suggested himself to me, and the only additional step needed was to give him a reason for being doleful. I thought a good one would be a pet that was not yet housebroken, but I wasn't sure that an elf would have a puppy. So I gave him a baby dinosaur.

Having no pattern made it necessary for me to improvise as I carved, thus the head of the figure was designed and shaped before I ever figured out the body. And the head and cap were so long that I had to seat the elf to keep from running out of wood. Also, the dinosaur had to be held quite closely. As is usual in such carving, a quite large knot located itself on the elf's left shoulder. So the sketch for the body had to take all that into account. I originally intended to have the long feet hanging near together, down the face of the rock on which the elf was seated, but it seemed to work out better to modify the design to cross the feet and make them longer.

When the carving was completed, the dinosaur didn't stand out as much as he should, so I sprayed the surface with matte varnish and "antiqued" it by putting on a

dark stain and rubbing it off rapidly, to leave it in the crevices only. Much of this is evident in the photographs.

Finally, the elf won the ultimate test in my book. I took him along to show a friend—and brought home a check instead. I am reminded of William Steig, the famous cartoonist, who back in the Thirties made some wooden caricatures in pear, walnut, and tangerine. (One lady he carved had a "polka-dot dress"—studded with brass tacks.) He made them originally as a hobby, but when they sold he decided they were just "more business."

Fig. 180. Doleful is a blocky figure.

Fig. 182 (above, left). The head was roughed out before the body was finally planned, so there was only wood enough left for a seated figure—or a dwarf. Here rough shaping of the body has been started. The chin and shin profiles were saw-cut. Fig. 183 (above, right). Once the front was proportioned, the back of the figure could be worked out as well. Here the arms and shoulders are roughed (leaving wood for the dino's tail), as well as the buttocks and rock. Compare this with Fig. 184 (below, left). After final shaping of the body and head, the ears are smoothed up and the hair suggested by V-tool lines. Is the knot on the left shoulder depicting something the dino did? Fig. 185 (below, right). The feet were made long and thin. Also, the crossed feet suggest embarrassment.

Fig. 181 (above). Antiqued to show carving lines and accentuate shadows (compare with Fig. 185), this doleful elf is in Alaskan cedar—but only the proportions are important. He is a caricature, with a pet baby dinosaur.

15

A Leprechaun for You

Fig. 186 (left). The first leprechaun was short and in California apricot. Fig. 187 (middle). The second little man was actually 2 in (51 mm) taller, because of relative wood dimensions and variations in sketching the design on the wood. Hands in pockets reduce carving problems and add to piquancy, as does the ruffled shirt front, knock knees, and heavy brogans. Fig. 188 (right). Oversized tricorn hat, bulging "chest," and white-growth wood on the ash figure are quite visible here, as well as the tailcoat fluting. This figure looks thinner because of its added height. Note the differences in foot pose and holly pipe position.

IN IRISH FOLKLORE, the leprechaun is a fairy, usually pictured as a sly old man about child-size, who if cornered will reveal the location of hidden treasure. He is an attractive sprite, much beloved by children with Irish blood. I have one granddaughter with a touch of the Irish, so . . .

As a carving project, the leprechaun is best made from a section of tree trunk, particularly one that is bent as at a fork.

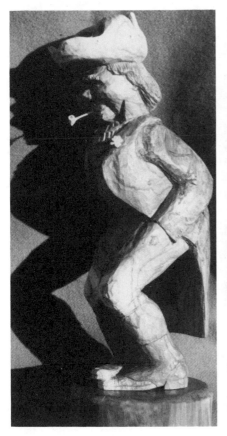
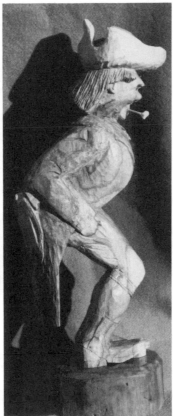

Fig. 189 (left). The shadow here gives a profile of the traditional Irish face, which is relatively short, with a long upper lip, pug nose, and beetling brow. Note also the stand-up shirt collar. Fig. 190 (middle). From the opposite side, the dangling handkerchief utilizing available white-growth wood is visible, as well as the growth wood on hat and kneecaps. Note the engaging smile. Fig. 191 (right). From the back, the handkerchief and arm positions can be seen, as well as hair treatment. The "target circle" marking the base of the limb sawed off is barely visible. This became the lion head of Chap. 5.

The bend gives the figure its built-in stoop. The two shown here include one from an ash fork and one from a section of bent apricot trunk, both exhibiting the difference in color between growth and core wood. The bent blank markedly reduces grain problems. Taken from the same pattern, they are somewhat different in shape because of the wood, one ending up 15 in (381 mm) tall, the other 13 in (330 mm).

The figure can be carved from a conventional block, of course, but that wastes some wood and isn't as much fun. My design was made with the ash fork in mind. I

Fig. 192 (above). The face close-up shows the overhanging eyebrows, forelock on the sloping brow, pudgy cheeks, long upper lip, and short chin of the round face. The eyes are made to stare by drilling holes for the pupils. Note also the hair coming well forward and stand-up collar.

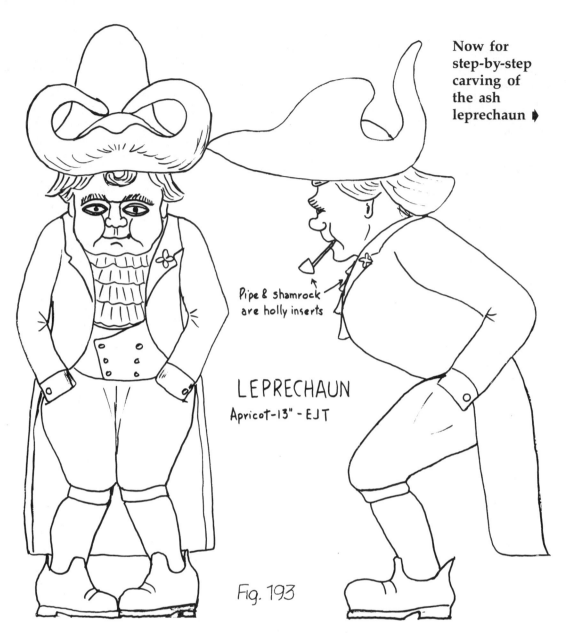

Pipe & shamrock
are holly inserts

LEPRECHAUN
Apricot-13" - EJT

Fig. 193

had the piece with the fork, well air-dried, and as a matter of fact later made a lion head with ball in mouth out of the limb cut off. This did mean that there was an unusual bull's-eye grain pattern on the leprechaun's lower back, but it added to the figure and caused no serious problems in carving.

In a section of trunk, it is difficult to do a nice and correct side and front view, to be cut in turn on a band saw. It is easier to put in the rough dimensions and sketch in the

figure to fit with a soft-tipped pen, then get some of the wood out of the way with chisels before you refine the drawing. This is inexact if you're a past mechanic or patternmaker, but it's good mental exercise—and is the reason my two leprechauns are alike, only different. There may well be some variation from the base pattern if you guess as you go, but the result may surprise you—and favorably, for a change! Try it. You will note that one of my leprechauns has toes crossed; the other

Fig. 194. Smaller branch of fork cut off. Bent figure drawn to fit with ink marker.

Fig. 195. Wood blanked out at waist, chin, top of hat, under coattails.

Fig. 196. Hat, head, and upper body rough-shaped. Stock left for nose and ears.

Fig. 197. Head and hat detailed; the face must be right or other carving is useless.

Fig. 198. Flared coat front, lapels, and shoulders formed. Handkerchief roughed.

Fig. 199. Ruffled shirt carved and vest roughed. Coat flare and facial details done.

Fig. 200 (right). Lower-leg notch sawn and chiselled out. Vest completed. Hand bulges shaped in pants.

Fig. 201 (far right). Hollowing under the tailcoat is a chore, but necessary to give proper appearance. Handkerchief is carved. Only lower-leg roughing remains to be done. Shoes should be round-toed, high and heavy. Then the entire body is rounded, wrinkles and tailcoat pleating done. Pipe, shamrock, and base are added, and antiquing and touch-up of growth wood complete the figure.

has feet side by side. (This sort of thing seems to happen to me no matter how conscientiously I try to make an exact copy. I hope it happens to you, because I find it fun!)

Side views of the ash figure show how the curve of the tree trunk is utilized, and one back picture shows where the forking branch was cut off. Also, if you're lucky in your choice of trunk, you'll be able to tie in the growth wood for decoration; one of my leprechauns has white hair, white knees, toes, elbows and white elements on his hat. I did have to darken a spot or two where the white growth wood was inappropriate, so it is not an unmixed blessing.

I made both leprechauns without bases, but added bases later to give them greater stability, particularly the one with the crossed toes; he teetered on his triangular base. The bases were pieces of walnut, in one instance the rounded section of a trunk, in the other a rectangular block.

Also, I carved the pipe and shamrock boutonnière for each separately and glued them in place; they're holly so they stand out. The double-breasted vest in one case has "buttons" made of brass escutcheon pins in drilled holes, and one has a handkerchief (there was growth wood there) hanging conspicuously out of a side coat pocket. There is one area of carving in this design—the lengthy tailcoat—that is a bit of a nuisance. Carving the legs up into the tail of the coat takes some careful maneuvering, but perhaps no more so than carving the double curve of the oversize hat. This hat, by the way, should not be as thin as it would be in life; it should be thin at the edges only and thicker inside to add to its strength. This is true as well of the projecting coat lapels; thin the edges but leave them thick immediately behind. This is also true of the coattail, and something to remember for other carvings.

16

Gesso and Other Timesavers

SOME YEARS BACK in Mexico, I commissioned an Indian carver to make me a 3D Madonna and Child about 10 in (254 mm) tall. He elected to carve in mesquite, and when I saw the piece nearing completion, I was dismayed to see several knots and checks in the wood, one check running through the Madonna's face. Fortunately, I

said nothing, because when I picked up the finished piece, there were no visible traces of the faults. The carver had filled the flaws with gesso tinted to match the color of the wood. Although I had the carving for at least ten years, the gessoed areas did not fail nor become visible.

More recently, I visited a very compe-

Fig. 202. Jenero Almanza Rios of San Miguel de Allende, Mexico, with arms for a Christus. Each is three blocks of wood, glued together. The wood provides a strong core for the gesso, best when applied in a thin coat. Senor Almanza uses chisels on the arms, but does the hands with a knife.

Fig. 203. Here two blocks of colcho wood have been glued together and are partially rough-shaped. The face of the Christus is a plaster casting glued in place. The wood will be carved to complete the head and any visible joint filled with gesso before sanding and finishing with oil paints.

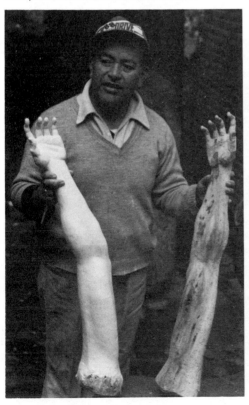

tent sculptor of religious figures in a totally different area of Mexico, and found that he, too, used a great deal of gesso. He, too, had to depend upon wood locally available, most of it a tree called colorin, petál, or colcho. He sticks three chunks together with gesso, glue, and hope, and proceeds to carve the assembly into an arm or leg for a statue. He speeds the carving of a Christus by gluing a cast plaster or gesso face to a head block of wood.

Not too far away is a family "factory" producing horses of many pieces of wood glued together. Even a horse 5 in (127 mm) tall will have a body with separate head, hind legs, 2-piece forelegs, tail and ears, apparently both to conserve wood and to spread the carving around among family members, the more competent carvers doing the more complicated portions. In that way, also, each person becomes very competent and fast in reproducing a particular shape. These carvings are also filled with gesso before sanding and painting.

What is gesso? It is simply plaster-of-Paris mixed with water. It has been used for centuries to make cheap copies of statuary relief panels, elements for interior architecture and so on. It can be carved, sanded, tinted and finished like wood, and it bonds well. With a sealing coat, it will not show noticeably, with a stain or varnish finish, or with oil and wax if carefully applied. Nowadays, art stores have a material called modelling paste, which is gesso mixed with marble dust. It comes ready to apply and easy to use. It will flex with the wood with change of humidity.

My own way of repairing minor checks and flaws is to cover the surface with glue, then to sprinkle with sawdust of the same wood, pressing the sawdust in when it has had a chance to be dampened by the glue. This operation is repeated as often as necessary to fill the flaw, plus a bit to be sanded off in finishing.

Usually, a patch such as this will shrink below the desired level in drying, so an allowance must be made for this when it is applied. Again, such a repair must be sealed before final finishing, except in very dark woods, because it will show darker than the adjacent wood. Any large flaw must, of course, be patched with a piece of the same wood, selected for color and grain, and glued and clamped in place. If you are adept at matching shapes, make such a filler block irregular in shape rather than rectangular or circular—the regular lines or a geometric shape are more difficult to hide.

Also, it is important to realize that if the wood is not kiln-dried, thus only fairly stable, any repair of a check or flaw may expose itself further as the wood dries out. Drying may cause widening of a check, and conversely, a check filled during dry winter weather may tend to split when the wood absorbs moisture in damp summer weather. All-in-all, it is much easier to learn not to be offended by checks; I have come to feel that they are a sort of indication that the carving is real and not a plaster copy. (Incidentally, a carving I bought hastily as a store was closing in Japan turned out to be a very clever fake. It was the right weight, felt and looked like wood, showing grain, saw marks on the bottom, and a rough spot or two. It turned out to be a careful casting, carefully painted! In fact, so much work had been done on it that I believe an honest carving would have taken no more time!)

While we are on the subject, it is only fair to point out that although the purist will not mix wood with any other material—and in fact, the oldtime true whittler wouldn't think of carving anything but a solid single block that could be held in the hand—today's pros will combine wood with whatever material they need to get a particular effect. Gardner Wood, for example, who carves synagogue doors of basswood, then ends up by gold-leafing and antiquing the surface, uses a variety of materials to get the surface textures he wants, to add strength, or just to save time. Thus, I have seen doors on which a dense Masonite or similar hardboard has been appliquéd instead of wood to provide

PRANCING HORSE
11 pieces - ears, head,
body, 2 hind legs, tail
2-part forelegs.
Mexico

Fig. 204

Fig. 205 (above). Constantino Calzada M has a family carving factory in Apaseo el Alto, Mexico. The factory is merely the central court of his house, and the product is prancing horses of all sizes, carved from various local woods, particularly palo santo, which is somewhat like balsa but harder. Horses are not monolithic (see sketch); they are assembled from as many as 15 pieces: three in each foreleg, two in each hind leg, body, head and neck, tail, and two ears.

Fig. 206 (below). Two small horses, one 5 in (127 mm) tall, the other 7 in (178 mm), are assembled in the factory just like the larger ones. These two are gessoed and sanded, ready for painting, which is done by the ladies of the family. I bought them unpainted, because they look like one-piece work unless closely inspected. The larger one is palo santo; the smaller is a wood I never heard of, but brown like cedar.

Fig. 207. Gardner Wood, of Albert Wood & Five Sons, Port Washington, NY, has carved a great number of doors for arks in synagogues. This pair, about 8 ft (2.44 m) tall, was finished recently for Ohel Yaacob Congregation in Diehl, NJ. The doors themselves are basswood, with carved elements of thinner wood appliquéd. The tree form is Masonite (pressed board) and some texturing is a metal spray. The finish is gold leaf, antiqued.

a surface design of constant and limited thickness. The synthetic board is thin, smooth, can be carved, and, of course, does not crack or chip as the wood might.

Also, other materials can be applied to provide textures not available otherwise. For example, there is a material called "Liquid Steel" or "Steel Patch," a mixture of metal grains with a chemical which is applied to fill dents in auto bodies. This material can be applied to wood as well. By spreading it with a spatula, for example, you can get a stippled effect that carving tools cannot achieve. Further, such materials stick well to wood and can be finished by gold-leafing or by conventional finishing. (The gold leaf itself can thereafter be "antiqued" by tinting desired areas or surfaces with "Rub'n Buff®," a heavy paste that is available in 18 tones of brasses, bronzes, copper and gold. This paste will also stick to any surface and can be applied by rubbing or, thinned with turpentine, by brush in difficult areas. Various tones can be applied one over another to get desired effects, and the more the surface is rubbed, the better the finish.) Incidentally, Mr. Wood spray-coats such surfaces with polyurethane gloss varnish if they are likely to be handled or touched constantly.

17

Time for a Little Relief?

SMALL, SPECIALIZED panels are in frequent demand. I have made them for commemorative purposes (see Chapter 3 on the V-tool), for nameplates, coats of arms, logotypes, trademarks, even breadboards, but the most unusual, I think, was carved from a towel as a model.

A friend wanted a Christmas present for his intended, who was born in a small Dutch town near De Wilt, which is well-known internationally for its long-established weather station. He had in mind a carving of the "Gemeentehuis," or town hall, a relatively modern building. He had no picture of it—just a depiction printed on a Turkish towel! The towel, 18 × 35 in (457 × 889 mm), was not too bad as a model, and I had a piece of teak just about

Fig. 208. A towel was the only available reference for a panel. Fortunately, the printing on it was quite detailed, and it was 18 × 35 in (457 × 889 mm).

Fig. 209. Teak panel is half the size of the towel, and by coincidence somewhat reverses the color scheme because of a light streak under the surface of the wood. Thus, it became a dawn scene. Note stylizing of the greenery and the incised (rather than raised) depictions of the metal-rail balconies and mullioned windows, a trick that fools the eye and is far easier on the carver.

Fig. 210 (left). A slab of spalted curly maple converted into a trivet 5 in (127 mm) square. The design is from an ancient Greek temple and is in low relief to provide a fairly flat surface.

Fig. 211 (right). Walnut plaque about 3½ × 5½ in (89 × 140 mm) is the logotype of an amateur theatrical group. The masks are copied from ancient Greek designs. Finish is oil and wax.

half that size. (The Dutch love of teak is a heritage of their former East Asian empire.) There was no further information, either from Dutch friends or printed sources, so I crossed my fingers—and carved.

So began the problems (or challenges) which are typical: The wood had a couple of small knots along what would be the building roof line. The three-story building apparently has a long gallery or balcony under the second-floor windows in the middle, and five circular balconies under third-floor windows, also in the middle. Balconies were wrought metal, not stone, and there was a small building attached on one side. Altogether, there were 40 mullioned windows, sloping tile roofs, even a small statue in front. (I guessed the latter to be some sort of weather instrument—which turned out later to be correct.) There was, of course, ornamental planting, and the main building projected ahead of the wings. And when I routed the sky area down ⅜ in (10 mm), I discovered a light streak in the wood, so the carving began to look like early dawn. But, "in for a penny, in for a pound," I decided I would carve a dawn view, with the skylight and the building relatively dark in silhouette—a reverse of the actual, because the building itself was of white stone. But this was once when somebody had to decide, and I had the artistic license.

A continuing series of other decisions

had to be made. What textures would suggest the greenery? How could the tiled roof be suggested? Could the greenery be stylized? (Yes!) Were the bulges at the ends of the wings, bays, or mistaken perspective? Could I crowd five different planes or frontal elevations into only ⅜ in (10 mm) of depth? (I had to!) Could the balconies be faked, or would they have to be added later of metal? (Better to fake.)

These examples are cited because they will face anyone undertaking such a project, and are typical of the problems of relief carving in general. Similar decisions must be made constantly when you convert from a two-dimensional photo or painting to a three-dimensional shape. And solving them is a great deal of fun and part of the challenge of progressing from simple in-the-round depictions to complex low-relief pieces.

Another example is the creating of a low-relief plaque from a pen-sketched letterhead—in effect, the carving of a logotype. A recent one was about 4×6 in (102×152 mm), in walnut, done for an officer of ACT (Amateur Community Theatres) in Cincinnati. The letterhead had rough sketches of the Greek masks of Comedy and Tragedy, which are so overused as theatre trademarks. It was possi-

Fig. 212

TWIN SWANS - Relief on horn

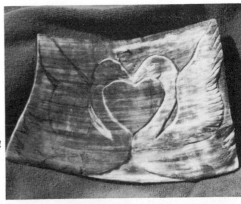

Figs. 213, 214. Cow horn can be flattened after boiling in a water-vinegar mix. The two samples (right) were carved in about an hour apiece with V-tool, small flat gouge, and knife for detail. Because the horn is laminated, it is possible to get a cameo effect in tones of grey and white, as shown at top right.

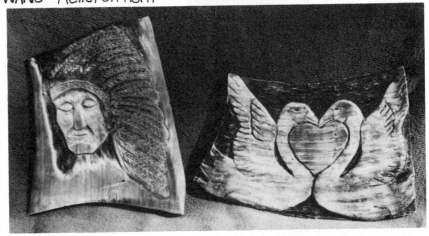

ble, with a bit of research, to find more elaborate ones to be grouped in an oval, with the name and location lettered on as well.

Odd pieces of nicely grained wood can be carved quickly and easily into coasters, paperweights, bases for art objects, or whatever. And larger pieces can be made into unusual and individualized bread-boards, pad holders or trivets. Simple examples are also shown here.

Fig. 215. Coats of arms are always popular. This one for the Carstens family carved by Herbert E. Blum of Neillsville, Wisconsin. It shows a half eagle on one side and two diamonds on the other, and is mounted with a raised-letter plaque reading "The Carstens Family History" as the cover of an album. I have my own arms in smaller size on the lid of a walnut mail-box and have made others with limited tinting as wall plaques.

18

How Deep the Ground?

"HOW DEEP shall I carve the background?" This is a constant question when I am teaching relief carving, and one that is difficult to answer exactly or convincingly. My tendency is to carve in very low relief, while many carvers tend to carve deeply. I tend to darken carved backgrounds and to break them up with a gouge pattern; other carvers smooth them out carefully and wouldn't consider tinting them—some even go over the entire background with a punch to create a pattern. (This is particularly true of carvers in India and Sri Lanka.) I don't like to carve formal patterns or connect relief elements with scrolls or vines or whatever; traditional European carvers did both, and many still do. I like to carve odd-shaped pieces, to "spill over" any framing, and on occasion to disregard scale; some carvers wouldn't think of it.

I mention these things so you can make allowances for any bias that you may detect in subsequent discussion. What I hope to do here is to provide a few starting rules and suggestions, then let you make your own decisions on your own panels—you will anyway, if it comes to that.

First off, the deeper a panel is carved, the more light and shadow it will show, and the more undercutting must be done, so, the more fragile it is. Further, the deeper you go, the more time it will take, of course. I have suggested to some of my students that the reason they carve backgrounds so deep is that they are subconsciously trying to avoid the necessity for shortening the third dimension, trying

Figs. 216, 217. Background and foreground are the same in these two panels, because the design is like scrimshaw—merely incising with a V-tool. At far left is a copy of a medieval etching of a woodcarver, at right a copy of a modern decorative "spot." After incising in walnut, both were sealed with matte varnish spray. Incised lines were enhanced with white pigment in oil and turpentine in one case and with black pigment in the other.

Figs. 218–220. These three panels were carved by my students in low relief, ground being lowered only about ⅛ in (3 mm). The dogwood blossoms (left) are in cherry and have raised branches; the stylized lily (middle) is in walnut and has incised stems. The madonna (right) is also in walnut, with normal modelling, and a random-gouged background. The cherry panel has been antiqued to bring out details and increase apparent depth—but this also shows up background imperfections.

in effect to carve half of an in-the-round piece against a background. This does solve a major problem in relief carving, that of trying to retain a third dimension in effect while cutting it drastically in actuality. The European masters did some remarkable work with principal figures actually carved in the round in front of the minor characters and background, almost as if the principals were actors before a diorama. And such pieces were usually monolithic—the foreground figures were carved from the solid! Contemporaries of Grinling Gibbons, in fact, criticized him severely by saying that some of his floral swags—which actually tremble as one walks by because they stand out so far from the background—were carved in-the-round, then mounted on a background panel. (Some of them *were* so made.) I go the other way so far that on occasion I can use the background as part of the picture, for example to depict the rigging on a ship or the veining of a leaf, or the needles on a pine. This would, I suppose, be considered to be the epitome of cheating by the purists, who would insist upon having a

vein, or a line, or a needle stand up clearly.

To show graphically the effect of depth of background, I have selected a series of pictures of work by students and others, except for a couple of incised samples—almost like scrimshaw—for which I have no other-carver equivalents. These range from incising to pierced carving—in which there is no background whatsoever until the carving is placed against one. The Japanese and Chinese make such carvings to act as screens which will admit air and some light, but interfere with view, flying birds and butterflies. Pierced carvings, however, can be extremely attractive as pendants against skin or fabric, or a wall.

Fig. 221. One of perhaps 100 hand-carved chair backs in an inn on remote Lake Pahoe, Patagonia, this hunting scene was carved by a local Indian. It is ⅛ in (3 mm) deep at most, so is comfortable to lean against, but the texturing gives it strength and definition. Each chair has a different scene.

Fig. 222 (above, left). Hal McClure, pro whittler, carved this frontiersman as his first major relief panel. Depth is about ¼ in (6 mm) and the panel is 7¾ × 21 in (197 × 533 mm). The irregular top of the panel was converted into a tree rather than being trimmed off into the usual rectangle.

Fig. 223 (above, right). Gardner Wood carved the panels of this teak buffet (only half is shown) about 40 years ago. Motifs are less than ¼ in (6 mm) deep, but crisp carving makes them stand out enough—and without becoming dust collectors.

Fig. 224 (left). Russian serfs did this relief carving over a century ago. It is ½ in (13 mm) deep or more, and very elaborate (see also Fig. 236). The building under this roof peak was probably just a log cabin.

Fig. 225 (above). This angle shot of a Spanish relief panel titled "The Moneylender" has the figures in very deep relief and the frame and background dropped well back, giving an almost 3D effect.

Fig. 226 (above). An African carving in ebony combines deep relief with a miniature mask. Fig. 227 (above, right). Clarence Whicher of Tilton, NH, does very deep grounding on his panels and trenches the figures. Mr. Whicher had a stroke ten years before he carved this, so must work with his left hand alone.

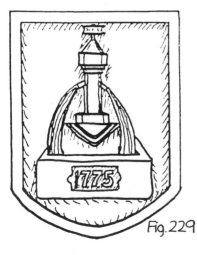

Figs. 228–230. Texan Gunther Goetz carved the coat of arms (above) in basswood, then inserted it ¼ in (6 mm) deep in the walnut disk. The two coats of arms at left were designed and carved by Herbert E. Blum, Neillsville, Wisconsin. The left one is for Mitlodi and the right for Haslen, both Swiss towns.

Figs. 231–235 (above and left). Typical of traditional European relief style are these five panel doors at the Chicago Athletic Association. They are carved in cherry and are part of a series, those above dealing with dining and those at left with Indians. Each is a pattern if you're ambitious.

Figs. 236, 237 (below). Serf-carved panels from old Russia, on exhibit at Zhagorsk. This carving is fairly deep and largely floral (see also Fig. 224). Sections of these pieces may be made into patterns.

Fig. 238 (above). This very high-relief panel is from Bali and depicts a scene from the Barong Dance, with musicians at lower right, dancers at left, and the Barong, a good demon, in the middle. His attendant monkey is below him. The panel is in mahogany, but others are in teak. It is 1¼ × 11 × 15 in (32 × 279 × 381 mm). The back is shell-thin because of the undercutting, which even admits light at top and sides. No two of these panels are ever exactly alike and size often depends on wood.

Fig. 239 (below, left). Pierced carving is the ultimate in background depth. These pendants were carved in dogwood and cherry by Jim Whiting and are about 2 in (51 mm) square. This is meticulous knife work. Fig. 240 (below). This scene from Java is about 10 in (254 mm) in diameter, and can be mounted against a textile or a plain wall with interesting results.

19

Flower Panels Can Challenge

FLOWERS CARVED IN RELIEF have been a popular subject since before the days of Grinling Gibbons in England, the master carver who made swags that have trembled for three hundred years. My friend Mack Sutter, of Portland, Oregon, has been teaching students how to make such floral panels for a number of years, and I am proud to own the one picturing pansies.

My carvings are much shallower than Mack's and undercutting in most cases is practically non-existent. This saves me tremendous amounts of time, but the carvings do not have the apparent fragility and more interesting shadows of Mack's work. You can elect to carve a panel like this as deeply as you choose, and with as much undercutting as you like and have tools to do. You can also work in a relatively hard wood, as I usually do, or in a softer one, as Mack usually does. But try it, and if you

Figs. 241–243. Depth of undercutting can vary, from the ¾ in (19 mm) of Mack Sutter's pansies at left and middle to the ¼ in (6 mm) of my gaillardia at right. The deeper the undercut, the more fragile and difficult the carving becomes, particularly in soft woods, but the delicacy of flower petals and stems is enhanced. Note that some of the pansy stems are free of the background and that the surface of the relief is less flat in appearance. However, more specialized tools may be needed and carving time is likely to be much increased. Mack's pansies are in basswood and my flowers in paulownia, an Oriental wood recently imported.

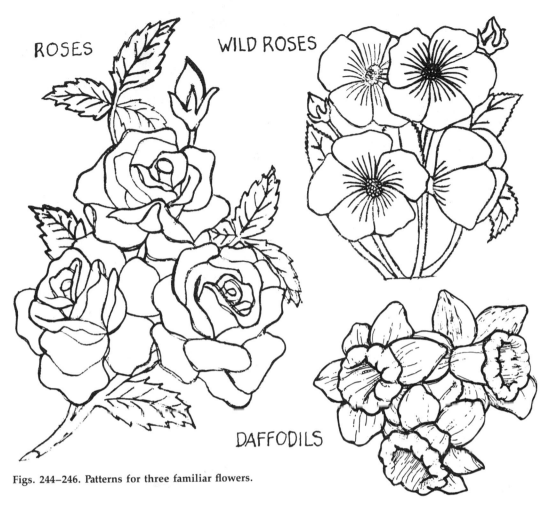

ROSES   WILD ROSES

DAFFODILS

Figs. 244–246. Patterns for three familiar flowers.

like it, you can find 21 more patterns in "Floral Wood Carving," by Mack Sutter (Dover ISBN 0-486-24866-6). The same publisher has several books of flower designs that may prove helpful if you want a particular flower—I used them for my carving designs here.

Start out with 8 × 10 to 10 × 12 in (203 × 254 to 254 × 305 mm) soft wood such as basswood or white pine, and have it over an inch (25 mm) thick if possible, because you may want to ground as deeply as ¾ in (19 mm), particularly if you plan undercutting. Select a simple design for starters, like the Jack-in-the-pulpit, and be sure that you have tools small enough for the job. You'll want something like the "thin tools" designed by Mr. Sutter, which have short handles. With such tools it's best to have a neoprene-coated light mallet to keep from shattering the handles.

Setting-in can be done with a ⅛-in (3-mm) firmer and equivalent gouges of appropriate curvature, and should be in a series of steps, each ¼ in (6 mm) deep at most. Setting-in can be done to the outline on flowers, but should be much more carefully done around thin sections, such as stems, of course. There I would suggest that you set-in to leave at least ¼ in (6 mm) of solid wood until grounding is complete; then you can go back and thin the section down by shaving off the side.

It is also possible to reduce the chance of breaking away wood on such thin sections by two other devices. One, which I use, is to set-in straight down on one side of a thin section, then to set-in with an *outward* slope (away from the design) on the other. The slope can be shaved vertical afterward, when the pressure represented by the waste wood is gone.

The other method, used by Mr. Sutter, might be called "stabilizing." He mixes a pound of shellac with three gallons of alcohol to produce what is commonly called #3 shellac. Then he thins that still further by adding one part of denatured alcohol to two parts of #3 shellac, producing what he calls #5 shellac. This is painted over the whole surface, immediately after a design is drawn, to keep the surface clean, and over carved surfaces after each carving session to preserve them. But, more importantly, he gives delicate areas a couple of soaking coats to strengthen them before he attempts intricate detail carving.

You can lower the background in various ways, removing it all to create a new background plane, carving geometrically to leave a frame all around the design, or trenching in from the edges, as shown here.

Modelling of most floral designs is fairly straightforward, unless the flower has elaborate petals or central elements. If the latter is true, you'd best work very carefully, and probably stabilize as you work. I do the petals and leaves and general outlines with small flat gouges, plus a V-tool for lines and accents, then do the really close work with a knife.

It is important to get such effects as overlapping petals correct, as well as curling edges or serrated leaves; otherwise, your flower will be unrecognizable—you'll have to try to excuse it by calling it stylized. I find the V-tool and small veiner invaluable for such work.

In addition to modelling, you'll have to do some texturing, like putting veins in leaves or petals, imitating the complex structure of some flower cores, showing the spines of a pine cone or a cactus, the roughness of some leaves, and so on. Undulations can be cut with gouges of appropriate curvature. I usually cross-hatch such an element as a flower core to suggest the flowerets; Mack stabilizes the core, then punches the surface with a punch filed down from a finishing nail. Hairs and fine projecting veins can be faked by inverting them—carving a V-groove to suggest each small ridge. When completed, it's best to coat the carving with varnish (matte spray if you follow my preference, shellac if you follow Mr. Sutter's) to protect it and strengthen it. Then, if you wish, you can color the flower with acrylics or pigments in varnish, as I did on the Oriental poppies. If your panel is at all thin, it will be advisable to coat the back and ends as well to seal them; otherwise the panel may warp with changing humidity.

Figs. 247, 248 (left). The Oriental poppy in white pine is 2 × 11 × 14 in (51 × 279 × 356 mm), with the background trenched down ½ in (13 mm) near the flowers, as at far left. V-tool outlining of petals has been begun—note fairing on lower bloom. Depth of grounding also permits indication of tilted leaves and curled petals. Detail lines and the frilly collar around the seed pod are put in with the V-tool, as are the antennaelike projections from seed pod.

Figs. 249 (below), 250 (right). This is a fairly complex design because of the folds in petals, leaf serrations, and thin projections, which do not show up without emphasis. As a consequence, I colored the panel as in the photo, using scarlet and green pigments in linseed oil and turpentine. The color was applied, then wiped down to avoid a "painted" surface. Thin lines on the bud and the like were emphasized with black on a very narrow brush; this you may prefer to do with a pen.

Fig. 249

Figs. 251, 252. Jack-in-the-pulpit is familiar in damp and woody areas of the Eastern United States. It is also called Indian turnip and bears its single flower late in May. The leaves are so large they dwarf the flower, so I carved only portions of them. This piece was in walnut, 1 × 8¾ × 11¼ in (25 × 222 × 285 mm), with about ⅝ in (16 mm) of framing on top and sides and 1 in (25 mm) at bottom. Grounding is about ½ in (13 mm) deep and level, after sloping in from the frame at about 45 degrees.

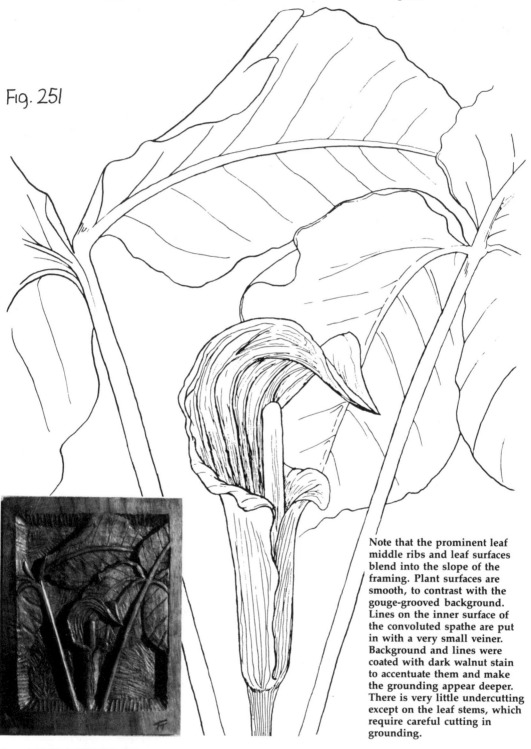

Fig. 251

Note that the prominent leaf middle ribs and leaf surfaces blend into the slope of the framing. Plant surfaces are smooth, to contrast with the gouge-grooved background. Lines on the inner surface of the convoluted spathe are put in with a very small veiner. Background and lines were coated with dark walnut stain to accentuate them and make the grounding appear deeper. There is very little undercutting except on the leaf stems, which require careful cutting in grounding.

Figs. 253, 254. The lady's slipper is an orchid that grows in swampy areas, so is now relatively rare except in florist shops. This carving is the show form, also called the moccasin flower, and is a complex bloom, the central element like a Dutch wooden shoe. A number of levels are involved. I carved it in walnut 1 × 8¾ × 13 in (25 × 222 × 330 mm). The frame is ⅝ in (16 mm) on top and sides and 1¼ in (32 mm) on the bottom. Grounding is ½ in (13 mm). Note that the design bleeds into the bottom margin and the background is random textured to break up light. The carving is antiqued with dark walnut stain.

Fig. 253

Figs. 255, 256. The pansy is, of course, a domesticated flower. Mack Sutter has carved it in several versions; this is the latest (1985), which I own. It is in pine, 1 × 10½ × 16 in (25 × 267 × 406 mm) and the background is lowered ¾ in (19 mm). Undercutting is almost so deep that the design is in the round (see Figs. 241, 242); stems are free of the background in various places. Note how effectively he has used various levels, V-tool lining, and small-gouge texturing to create desired effects, and how blooms are clearly separated from leaves behind them. Such carving requires many times the effort and care I put into one of mine. The result is one that the connoisseur will appreciate. Mack usually works in pine and rarely does any tinting or antiquing. If you have the time, the tools, and the skill, try it.

Fig. 256

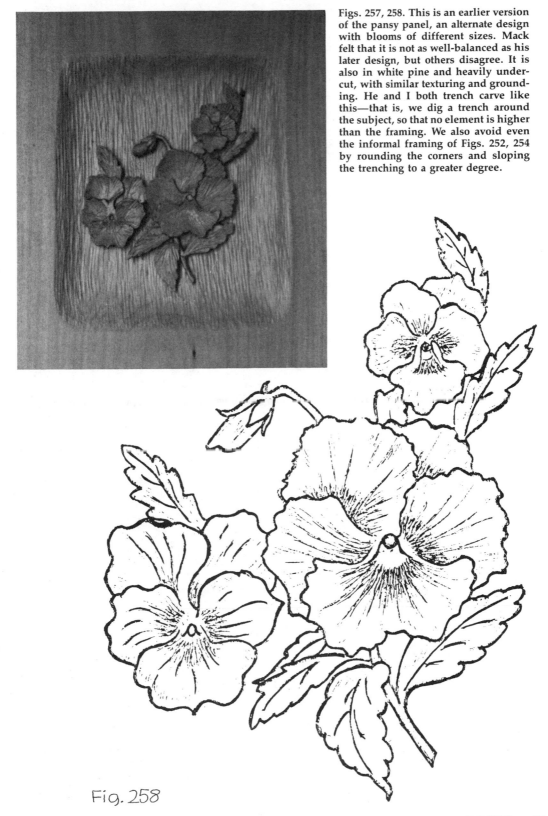

Figs. 257, 258. This is an earlier version of the pansy panel, an alternate design with blooms of different sizes. Mack felt that it is not as well-balanced as his later design, but others disagree. It is also in white pine and heavily undercut, with similar texturing and grounding. He and I both trench carve like this—that is, we dig a trench around the subject, so that no element is higher than the framing. We also avoid even the informal framing of Figs. 252, 254 by rounding the corners and sloping the trenching to a greater degree.

Fig. 258

20

Silhouettes—A Quick Story

THESE DESIGNS serve to show the variety possible in silhouette relief-carved panels. The first and simplest is a pair of kittens in mahogany, developed from the client's traditional "Krazy Kat" on his family's catboats, which was a mere outline. These figures are 8 in (203 mm) tall, of mahogany deeply modelled so they could be goldleafed and applied on opposite sides of the bow of a new plastic catboat named (of course) "Krazy Kat."

The second example shows how to combine a figure with a scene and still retain the silhouette idea. It is a bearded skater in 1890 costume (or even earlier), wearing a stovepipe hat with mistletoe, and skating along a frozen river or canal with a town in the background. I carved him in $1 \times 10 \times 10$-in ($25 \times 254 \times 254$ mm) black walnut, with pierced carving around the legs and skates, which are integral. His coat buttons are brass escutcheon pins set into holes.

Birds and fish, stylized or realistic, make particularly graceful silhouette panels, in my opinion. They can be silhouettes, modelled on both sides and hung singly or in groups as mobiles, or they can be placed against a wall or silhouetted in a window. As a very simple example of what can be done I have shown a Haida hummingbird. This was 8½ in (216 mm) long in pine.

Fig. 259a.

Support pin if stressed.

HANGING KITTEN

Mahogany or Holly—¾×5×8" Low relief

Bottom of figure

Figs. 259a (left), 259b (above). Completely modelled kittens were carved in mahogany to resist seawater attack. They were covered with gold leaf and flank the bow of a catboat. They are 8 in (203 mm) tall and 1 in (25 mm) thick. A brass pin supports the tail against possible stress.

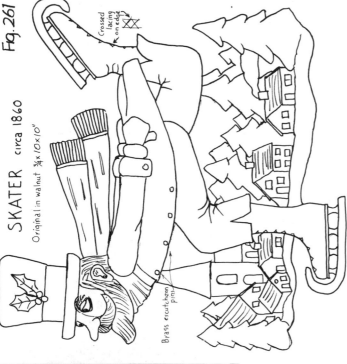

Fig. 261

SKATER circa 1860

Original in walnut 3/4 x 10 x 10"

Crossed lacing on edge

Brass escutcheon pins

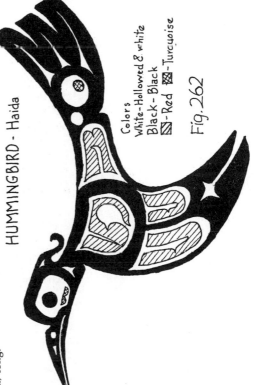

HUMMINGBIRD - Haida

Colors
White-Hollowed & white
Black-Black
- Red - Turquoise

Fig. 262

Figs. 260 (right), 261 (far right). This intent 1860 skater is 1 × 10 × 10 in (25 × 254 × 254 mm), and is passing a village beside the pond. Note pierced elements around upraised leg and on skates, which are integral. The buttons on his coat are brass escutcheon pins in drilled holes. The finish is oil and wax. This is a good exercise in modelling.

Figs. 262 (below), 263 (below right). Haida hummingbird is a very simple silhouette, relying on paint for most of its effect. The only carving is hollowing of white areas (see sketch). A design like this can be made double-sided and hung as a mobile. Mine was 8½ in (216 mm) long.

21

A Victorian Garden in Wood

MANY WOODCARVERS starting to do relief panels automatically make them rectangular or oval, thus reflecting the conditioning all of us have from framed paintings, photographs and the like, and our innate tendency to put a fence around everything. However, the Indians who painted on hides did not square up the hide. Central and South Americans who paint on bark do not square up the bark—until they learn that squared-up pieces are what gringos buy. But even those self-same gringos will buy an in-the-round carving that is not rectangular, and sometimes not even flat on the bottom. So why framed reliefs?

I realized some years ago that a relief carving could often be much more dramatic if the carving "broke the frame," just as theatrical directors have gone back to arena theatre by "breaking the prosce-

nium"—some actors enter the audience. In both cases, the work becomes more alive, more dramatic, doesn't convey that packaged feeling that everything manufactured has in this era of supermarkets. I have encouraged my students to carry a head or an elbow into the framing of an otherwise rectangular self-framed panel, or even to make the entire carving a silhouette. (If a purist later objects, the carving can always be mounted on a background of contrasting texture and framed.) Also, it is possible

Figs. 264, 265. Earlier figures carved in teak were intended as individual wall decorations, but can be grouped to create scenes, as pictured here. The Central Park skaters (left) range from 10 in (254 mm) tall downwards, and the Dutch children (above) are somewhat shorter. All have aluminum skate blades, and some have brass buttons made of set-in escutcheon pins. Skate designs suit site and period. Teak is 1 in (25 mm) thick.

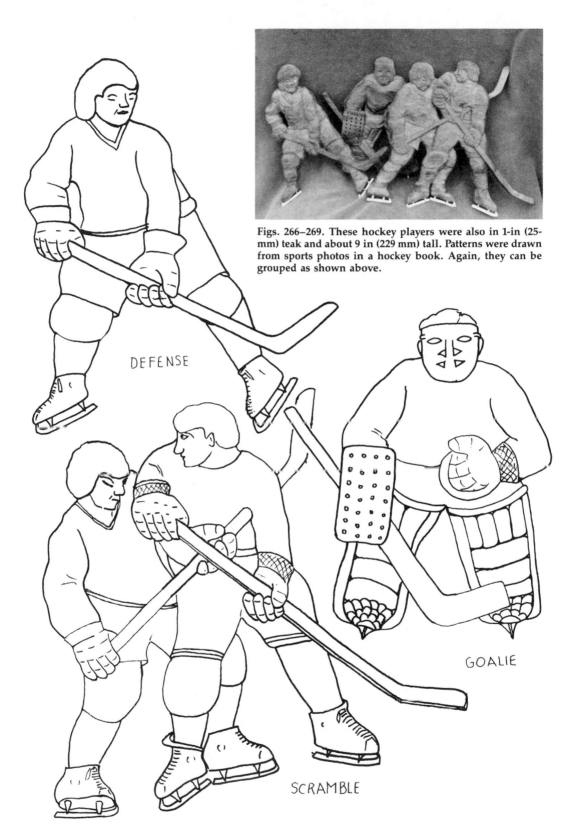

Figs. 266–269. These hockey players were also in 1-in (25-mm) teak and about 9 in (229 mm) tall. Patterns were drawn from sports photos in a hockey book. Again, they can be grouped as shown above.

DEFENSE

GOALIE

SCRAMBLE

to make pierced carvings which will let air or the color or texture of a backing show through, with very dramatic results. The Japanese are particularly adept at this in their painted wooden carved screens, and the Chinese have done it for centuries with ivory. Several of the present carvings have pierced holes.

Some years ago, I carved a series of skaters in low relief. These were in teak, because they were planned for the wall of a music room adjacent to the ice rink of a skating club, where dampness might well be encountered. The wall had an interesting rough texture, so I made a series of six silhouettes from 6 to 10 in (152 to 254 mm) tall. Three were in Victorian garb, three were Dutch children in traditional costume, for it was the Dutch who originated ice skates.

These figures were so successful that I was commissioned later to produce sets of six curling players and three hockey players—other activities of the same club. The client also remembered all these when she was planning a series of dinners for the garden club of a palatial estate converted into a summer-showplace county park. She suggested Victorian garden figures. With help from the local library, I sketched ten possibilities, from which I assumed she'd select six. She had also said that her first use of them would probably be as table decorations against greenery, so I made my designs so they could either be stood or hung. All would be 8 to 10 in (203 to 254 mm) tall. When I discussed my designs with the client (over the telephone, as it happened—she was too busy to see them), she suggested the addition of a tennis player, and I suggested a croquet player and London flower girl.

Thus I ended with thirteen rather than the expected six. There was a deadline as usual, so only seven figures made the first dinner, but they were so well received that there was no question about the others. Some of the latter, incidentally, included more than just a silhouette figure—actually silhouette scenes—one of two figures, one of three plus a goat and cart. This latter one required careful design so the wheels of the cart and part of the goat could be carved against the background created by

Figs. 270–272. These garden figures in 1-in (25-mm) bleached walnut or cherry can hang or stand. Standing figures are about 10 in (254 mm) tall. Tennis racquet is against dress to permit V-tooled "strings." Boy's hoop and stick are inserted music wire. Note proud lady's veil as a textured rear element only. Tea tablecloth includes a knot—use of otherwise useless walnut.

Figs. 273–276. Silhouettes play an important part in the effectiveness of these patterns.

1890's

1890's

1898

1898

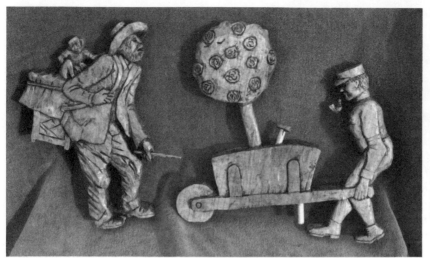

Fig. 277. The organ grinder with his monkey has a beard and worn clothes, so texturing and carved wrinkles are necessary. His stick, the gardener's pipe, spade handle, wheelbarrow support post are all inserts, and the trunk of the rose tree is reinforced by a headless spike pushed up through a hole drilled from the bottom.

the skirts of the two ladies. All this is evident in the photographs.

I had enough ¾-in (19-mm)-thick cherry for the expected six figures, but thirteen required some scrounging around. In desperation, I tried walnut, bleached after carving, and found that it looked quite well with the earlier cherry pieces, except for the occasional knot, which stubbornly stayed dark. Also, the walnut had to be matte-varnished to retain the bleached color. I also decided later to matte-varnish the cherry pieces, then give them a coat of dark-walnut Minwax®, wiped off immediately to leave the textured surfaces and carved lines darker than the body of the wood. The varnish is essential for this kind of "antique" finish, or the stain will bleed into the grain before it can be wiped away where not wanted. The varnish acts as a temporary seal, but the stain must be applied to, and wiped away from, relatively small areas at a time. The varnish also prevents faster absorption of the dark color in end-grain areas. This treatment makes carved lines appear deeper than they actually are by enhancing the contrast.

These designs were taken from a number of sources, some modified from costume drawings of the period, some originated to match. My wife, who has for some years been custodian of costumes for the local historical society, was very help-ful and originated some of the poses as well as the figures themselves. An unexpected side effect of all this was that I found that the figures could be grouped against a background to make scenes. So I borrowed back the skaters and the hockey players and made comparable scenes of them, as shown here. The Victorian figures were also used to create highly original stationery for the client to use in connection with garden-club activities, while the hockey-player group headed a card for casual skating-club correspondence.

Actually, design was the most difficult part of the commission. The designs could be cut out easily with a coping saw—which immediately established the over-all shape. Grain in all cases is vertical, and patterns were placed so that occasional knots in the walnut were isolated in flat areas, such as in the tablecloth between the two ladies at tea, or in the pot where the gardener is trimming an elephant-shaped topiary bush.

Several of the original designs had to be modified to increase strength or to reduce carving difficulty—which also reduced cost to the client. Thus, the tennis player has her racquet against her skirt rather than upraised, avoiding a fragile extended arm and making it possible to suggest the lacing with V-grooves. The croquet player also has her mallet against her skirt, while

Figs. 278–285. The two skaters (below) are patterns I have not carved, but are profiles to accompany the Victorian group shown in Fig. 264. The topiary elephant at right in Fig. 278 is textured all over with random diagonal lines both to suggest leafage and to make the clippers stand out. The patterns sketched below are for fairly complex figures.

1896

Alternate to hoop

1870 BOY

Stick & hoop are an inserted wire hoop

1894

"PARK" SKATERS
circa 1880

CROQUET PLAYER
1890's

1875

the ball, separately carved, is pinned to the mallet head. The boy's hoop and stick are a single piece of heavy wire looped through a hole drilled in his hand.

In the goat-cart group, one lady's parasol connects the two heads and protects the parasol handle, and the ladies' skirts provide a background for reins, cart openwork and wheel spokes. The long, thin, parasol handle is left thicker and, of course, connected at both ends. Goat horns, ears, goatee and forelegs are left thicker and run with the grain to make them stronger. The reins are music wire glued in and varnished to inhibit rusting, as is the wire supporting the bell at the goat's throat. The bell itself is the bronze tip of the pull chain on an ancient electric-light socket.

The gardener trundling the wheelbarrow has his pipe, spade handle and barrow leg separately carved and inserted, and the long trunk of the rose tree is reinforced by a headless steel spike inserted into a hole drilled from the bottom of the carving. Note also that the roses are carved oversize so they can be readily seen and the tree surface is left rough but not broken up by any effort to suggest leaves. (On the other hand, leaves are suggested on the elephant, partly in order to separate the trimming shears from the bush.) The proud lady and her daughter have es-

pecially frilly dresses, the lady's hat including a veil. At first I planned a veil of some kind of screening, but settled for the more durable suggestion of a veil on the back side of the hat next to the face. It is textured and looks less artificial than the screening would have, as well as being less rigid and fragile.

Tools and techniques for carving these figures are relatively simple, provided the wood itself is relatively hard, as are cherry, walnut and teak. I do rough shaping with a flat ½-in gouge, largely by hand, holding the work on a bench plate so it can be repositioned rapidly. Pattern lines for internal elements, such as dress frills, are drawn directly on the wood, and I cut them rather deeply with a ⅛-in V-tool driven by a plastic-faced mallet. This gives me close control of line direction and depth, and it is usually only necessary to precede the groove cutting with a knife or skew stop-cut when the line to be cut is running almost parallel with the grain. (It is essential that the V-tool be sharp and properly ground, as described in Chapter 3.) With some practice, it is possible to estimate correct depth and angle for the V-tool on the first cut. The first cut will drop the line almost the full depth of the tool; it should not be driven so it cuts deeper than that or it will dig in and snag off surface wood at the sides.

Fig. 286. These two couples offer a contrast, because one features sporting dress and the other formal strolling wear. Note the stick as well as the dashing cap and knickers ("plus fours") on the informal gentleman, and the top hat, tail coat, and spats on the opposite formal figure.

Figs. 287–291. The gardener with the rose tree in his barrow in Fig. 277 finds it a bit heavy. Although I hollowed out behind the foliage, he still does not stand very firmly. This is true also of the other gardener because of the bulk of wood high up and the limited support. If any of these four figures must stand free, it is advisable to mount it on a base, which can be a thin metal plate if you prefer, so it is not seen from the front. The couples can have a support block in back.

1890
GARDENER
& ROSE TREE

1897

1890
TRIMMING
TOPIARY

Texture to
suggest leaves

1896

Fig. 292. Most complex of the garden figures is this one. It has pierced carving around the parasol handle, as well as projecting goat legs and goatee—all of which should be left thick in depth. The cart wheels and rear goat legs are carved in relief against the skirts. Goat reins are music wire and the bell is the bronze pull from an ancient pull-chain light socket.

By "angle" in the preceding sentences, I mean the tilting of the V-tool to one side or the other so that one side of the Vee may be perpendicular to the surface of the wood, or almost so, while the other side cuts a long angle. This is important if the longer wall is to be faired away anyway and/or you want to make the side with the vertical wall appear to be above the adjacent one, or just to make the outline of an object more crisp. This sort of thing is best done with a V-tool having an included angle of 30°, or 45° at most—a wide-angle V-tool serves little purpose for me, so little that I don't own one. I also use the V-tool for putting in wrinkles and the like, unless the line being carved is to appear a bit softer, in which case the veiner is preferable because it does not leave a sharp line at the bottom of the groove.

To carve faces, which seem to be a bugbear for people who have learned to carve faces in-the-round, I start with a V-tool to establish the nose and eyebrow lines. Then with a small gouge, in this case about ¼-in sweep and fairly deep, I cut in the eye hollows and waste away the wood under the nose tip and at the sides of the mouth and chin, shaping the eye bulge at the same time. (A half-round or fluter works well too.) Details of the face can then be put in with a penknife or a small V-tool and

veiner. Such details as buttons require V-tool outlining and fairing around them as described above. I avoid some of that by making buttons of brass escutcheon pins in drilled holes, or brass decorative tacks driven in—they give a bright spot or two on the finished carving. Surfaces may be textured with the V-tool—as in the crosshatching of the veil on the proud lady—or they may be dotted with a punch made from a nail to a desired cross-section. Remember, however, that such a texture picks up dark stain and even dirt, so the textured area may be considerably darker than its surroundings. Insofar as it makes sense, I try to break up the plane surface of the original wood, which may be overly bright to the eye because it catches and reflects impinging light. Folds and grooves can be put in cloth, of course, as well as wrinkles when and where they are appropriate—as on the organ grinder. Also, the flat look of some surfaces may be removed by shallow scalloping with a flat gouge, which will serve to break up the light just a little. I intentionally leave tool marks in most cases, so no one can possibly mistake the finished piece for a moulding of one kind or another. The mentions of design short cuts and tool tricks here are intentional. Work like this must be done rapidly to keep the price within reason.

22

An Easel for Attention

A FREQUENT CLIENT phoned in high dudgeon. She's chairperson of the house committee of a nearby winter-sports club, and her announcements of events were not getting their share of the space on the club bulletin board! I must design her something appropriate and a bit "elegant" in time for the club opening ten days later. I proposed a separate easel, with "THE HOUSE COMMITTEE" carved in relief across the top and straddling the club logotype, plus some appropriate carving down the sides in low relief. Her posters were 22 × 28 in (559 × 711 mm), so we finally settled on 23 × 29 in (584 × 737 mm) for internal dimensions of the framed area, and a 5-foot (1.5 m) over-all height. I tried various hardwood lumberyards; they had only white oak. The local lumberyard had no suitable wood, but they did have 24 × 36-in (610 × 914-mm) corkboard for the framed portion. A hardware store had suitable brass chain. And a cabinetmaker had some Brazilian mahogany that could be milled to 1 × 3 in (25 × 76 mm) for the side supports and 1 × 4 in (25 × 102 mm) for the crosspieces. Sold!

From there on, it was all hand work. As shown by the sketches, I designed the crosspieces to lap over the uprights and project a bit at the sides to avoid a too rigid "look." I also wanted to carve the elements before assembly, to avoid working around a roughly 3 × 5-ft (914 × 1.5 m) frame. An added fillip was to carve the logotype medallion in ¼-in (6-mm) holly 2½-in (64-mm) in diameter and appliqué it as a high

spot. The lettering could be simple 1½-in (38-mm) capitals. Because the club is named after the former beaver dam where it is located, I put beavers at the top corners and at the lower ends of the carved side strips. The carving was designed to project up into the crosspiece, to be finished after assembly, with the theme of the history of

Fig. 293. This mahogany easel is 1½ × 5 ft (760 × 1520 mm), with 1 × 3-in (25 × 76-mm) side rails and 4-in (102-mm) crossrails. The rear legs are 2½ in (63.5 mm) wide and 4½ ft (1.49 m) long. The joints are half-lapped, and chains restrain the feet.

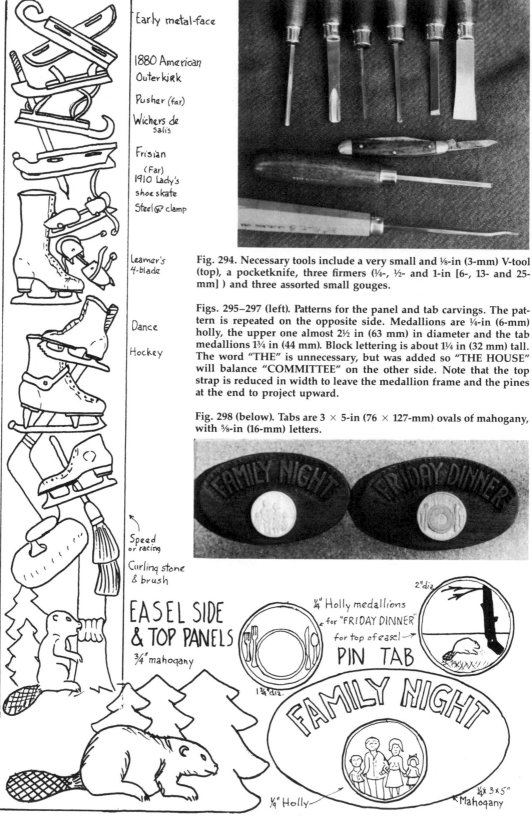

Fig. 294. Necessary tools include a very small and ⅛-in (3-mm) V-tool (top), a pocketknife, three firmers (¼-, ½- and 1-in [6-, 13- and 25-mm]) and three assorted small gouges.

Figs. 295–297 (left). Patterns for the panel and tab carvings. The pattern is repeated on the opposite side. Medallions are ¼-in (6-mm) holly, the upper one almost 2½ in (63 mm) in diameter and the tab medallions 1¾ in (44 mm). Block lettering is about 1¼ in (32 mm) tall. The word "THE" is unnecessary, but was added so "THE HOUSE" will balance "COMMITTEE" on the other side. Note that the top strap is reduced in width to leave the medallion frame and the pines at the end to project upward.

Fig. 298 (below). Tabs are 3 × 5-in (76 × 127-mm) ovals of mahogany, with ⅝-in (16-mm) letters.

skate design, plus modern skate types and a curling brush and stone, thus covering the major activities of the club. (The history of skating I had researched earlier in a friend's Dutch encyclopedia—for a group of carved 2 to 3-in (50 to 75-mm) Christmas-tree ornaments for the same client.)

Carving was only about ⅛ in (3 mm) deep and was "trenched"—meaning that the wood remained full width at the edges. The only extensive shaping of the mahogany was to cut the pine tree at the ends of the crosspieces, narrowing the top crosspiece to a bit over 3 in (75 mm) to allow the trees at the ends and the central-medallion backing to project.

The carving was set in with small chisels. Modelling was minimal, but did involve much use of very small (1/16-in) (1.6-mm) V-tool and veiner, as well as a pocketknife for close quarters. The finished carving was not sanded for fear of destroying detail, and the detail was accentuated by a process I call "antiquing" for want of a better term. I give the carved areas a spray coat of satin-finish varnish, then brush on a coat of a darker stain (like walnut Minwax®, for example) and wipe it down with a soft cloth, thus removing the stain from upper surfaces but leaving it in the background and carved areas and lines. The varnish prevents excessive darkening of cross-grain areas. When the surfaces are properly finished, the carving is thoroughly brushed (because of the wax in the stain), and the entire easel given a coat of satin or matte varnish. Then, instead of a conventional wax, which may show gray streaks in the grain of mahogany, as well as turning yellow eventually, I use Kiwi® natural shoe polish for final finish. This is a trick I learned from Balinese carvers fifteen years ago, and it works fine for any interior carving.

The easel turned out to be a tremendous success, but the client suddenly decided she needed something more. She had colored thumbtacks, but she had come to realize that some of her announcements, particularly for two regular events, the Fri-

day Dinner and the Family Night, were on 8½ × 11-in (216 × 279-mm) paper and were often delayed in order to apply some sort of decoration. Could I help? I provided two tabs appropriately lettered with ½-in (13-mm) letters and bearing 1¾-in (44-mm) carved holly medallions of identifying design on a 3 × 5-in (76 × 127-mm) oval of mahogany. A pair of 1-in (25-mm) brads inserted in the back and hand-filed to thumbtack-like points provided the anchor for a tab and announcements on the corkboard. Surely the most expensive thumbtacks I've seen!

Fig. 299. One side of the low-relief carving, showing how it extends across the lap joint. The motif is essentially the history of skates, as identified in the sketches, plus the beaver that identifies the club.

23

Let's Frame a Master

I WAS PACKING my suitcases for a month in Mexico in mid-winter when a regular client phoned. "Before you go, Mr. Tangerman, could you please go to New York? The Metropolitan Museum of Art has an exhibition of Dutch paintings that includes a Jan Steen. I have a similar one, also painted on wood, but the frame on mine is a gaudy gold-finished scrolled thing. I'd like you to carve a new frame for my Steen like the one in the Met, and the show will be gone before you return!"

So I went to the Met. I knew that no photography would be allowed, but I also found on arrival that sketching was not permitted either in that particular gallery, because the paintings were on loan from the Royal Collection in the Netherlands. Any effort to sketch would result in confiscation of the sketching materials. So I had to pass through the gallery, memorize as much as I could, then go out to another gallery where sketching was permitted and draw what I could remember. I made the circuit five times, because the cross-section of the frame was fairly complex and the carving was over 400 years old (Steen lived in Leiden from 1625 to 1679). The pattern was badly worn, but was a series of flowers, somewhat conventionalized.

I took my sketches to Mexico, where I hoped to find someone to make the complex frame at reasonable cost. (I had had the opportunity to see the painting to be framed so I could measure it. The frame, as I suspected, was gold-leafed hand-carved ormulu.) But San Miguel de Al-

lende is a small town with colonial status and carpenters and cabinetmakers have hole-in-the-wall shops. The only power woodworking machinery in town was owned by the casket maker, who speaks no English. It took three visits (with assistance from the English-speaking jeweller several stores up the street and from my wife, who speaks some Spanish) to arrive at the cross-section desired and agree on an available piece of Honduras mahogany. (The original was in oak.) On the fourth visit, I had a frame, exactly to dimension, although he worked in milli-

Fig. 300. Honduras mahogany frame, approximately 9 × 12-in (229 × 305-mm) opening, with design elements taken from a 17th-century oak frame for a painting on wood by the same artist (Jan Steen).

metres and I in inches. I went on to carve the frame with small tools I'd brought along, so it was still like the legendary postman's vacation.

I tell this story because, if you have any skill at all, you will be asked to repair or duplicate an endless number of pieces. Friends and family will assume that you know exactly how to do it, and you can't let them down.

Fixing is as much finishing as it is carving. Fortunately, a high percentage of the pieces you'll be asked to fix are in basswood, white pine, or some other relatively soft whittling wood. Often they are painted, so the job is largely one of rough-shaping missing parts, gluing them in place, and matching the painting. Even if they are in harder woods, you can usually work in pine or basswood—unless the finish is wax or clear varnish. Then you must match the grain of the wood adjacent to the repair, or retouch your addition so it looks the same. That tends to become an art job and you may need help from a painter. I have found, however, that I can usually get by, using oil pigments and varnish, lowering the gloss finish with fine steel wool if necessary.

The principal ingredient is not to be afraid to tackle the job. The owner has few alternatives: Where else will he (or usually she) find someone who can shape the missing pieces? If the carving is a fine one, you may have to do some research in art books to find out what a missing hand might have held, or a missing costume element might have been. Your local library can help on that.

Figs. 301, 302. Another view of the frame (above) shows the outer moulding or border more clearly. These mouldings must be designed to fit the space they occupy, to avoid a bad joint at the corner. Similarly, the floral units of the design must be adjusted to fit. Note that the sides of the frame are alike, merely reversed, as are top and bottom halves of the sides. But the top and bottom of the frame differ slightly in design at the ends because design units—the flowers—should stand upright in both. I adjusted partly by altering the width of elements and partly by shifting the morning-glory-like flower to the edge of greatest width.

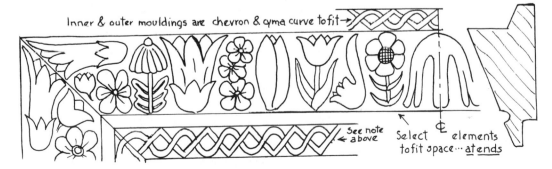

Inner & outer mouldings are chevron & cyma curve to fit →

See note above

Select elements to fit space···at ends

24

Signs that Sell

Fig. 303. A typical Bavarian maypole erected in Frankenmuth, MI. The silhouette figures were carved by Georg Keilhofer to show typical local crafts, plus the coats of arms of the city and of its sister city in Germany. Silhouette is important in such figures, which are usually carved on both faces and painted.

FOR SOME YEARS, shops in "restored" villages and period shopping areas, as well as other organizations, have been returning to the hand-carved signs which were once so common. Many of these are simply boards with lettering incised by machine, like the direction signs in state and national parks, but some include carved relief scenes, silhouette reliefs, or even in-the-round elements. I have known several carvers who specialize in such carving, some producing signs that are "antiqued" by scorching with a blowtorch and dented with chains. One carver who died recently spent years carving scenes in the oak ends of huge wine casks at a California winery, imitating the carving that can be found in *weinstubes* in such towns as Heidelberg and Oberammergau, Germany.

I have been approached on several occasions to design signs of this sort, and I believe the trend is just beginning. Therefore, I am repeating here a photograph from an earlier book, but adding a drawing which was omitted and which provides basic patterns. The photograph is of the Maypole in Frankenmuth, Michigan, as designed by Georg Keilhofer years ago and carved by him and his assistants.

Sketches show ten silhouette carvings of typical professions, any one of which could be the basis for a store sign. I have recently designed one that is similar in idea for a bakery headed by a young lady. For it I used a profile of the young lady in a long-dress period costume, with a baker's cap and carrying a cake. Beneath her on the sign is a golden pretzel 2 ft (610 mm) long, the symbol used on many German *bachereis*. Although she is Greek in origin, she liked the idea of the pretzel, knowing that in her community there are many people who will recognize the pretzel as a symbol at least as quickly as they will identify a baker profile almost 3 ft (914 mm) tall.

There is also, in the group of silhouettes, one for the City of Frankenmuth—another source of commissions, because most towns have coats of arms or logotypes and town halls where they can be hung. So do many local families and industries in these "root-conscious" days. Some carvers I know keep busy that way.

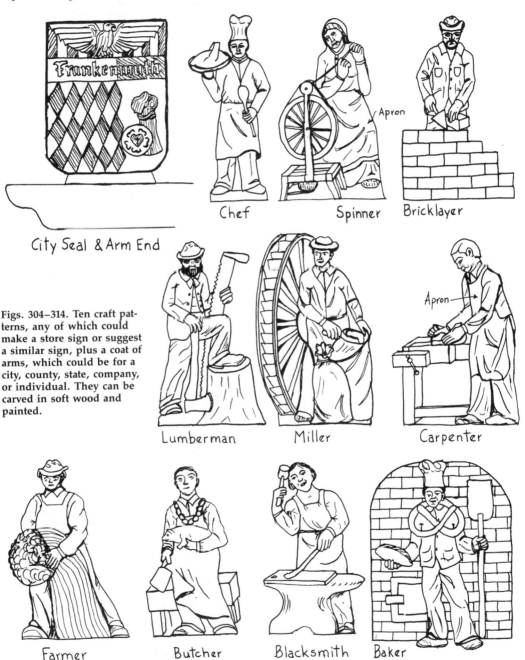

City Seal & Arm End

Chef   Spinner   Bricklayer

Figs. 304–314. Ten craft patterns, any of which could make a store sign or suggest a similar sign, plus a coat of arms, which could be for a city, county, state, company, or individual. They can be carved in soft wood and painted.

Lumberman   Miller   Carpenter

Farmer   Butcher   Blacksmith   Baker

25

Intaglio Is Inside-Out Carving

INTAGLIO is inverted relief carving—parts of the design which normally project are hollowed out, so that the completed carving becomes a mould. If dough or clay is pressed into an intaglio carving, it will emerge as a relief image. Thus intaglio is a good mental and physical exercise; the effort to think and do "inside out" is stimulating.

I have worked with intaglio on occasion, once to create a three-dimensional depiction of Escher's "Sky and Water I" as a teak fireboard and several times to make cookie moulds for special purposes. My friend, Ken Thompson, has made a "Madonna and Child" in intaglio and given me a lurid description of the work involved. But I suspect he enjoyed the challenge; I know I have.

Here's a typical case: Two local ladies operate a mail-order company that sells cookies and preserves. Their logotype is a sheaf of wheat. When they decided recently to sell an English shortbread, they wanted to reproduce their logo on top, so they appealed to me. I carved the sheaf about 4 in (102 mm) tall in rock maple, so it would be light-colored and long-wearing. I also made the mould 7 in (178 mm) in diameter so their baker could use it as the

Cookie-3"

1¼" Butter-Thistle
Cookie - Pineapple - 2½"

INTAGLIO MOULDS (Maple)

Fig. 315 (top left). Three moulds for a historical society, two for cookies and one for butter, the first depicting the namesake peninsula and the other two the pineapple. Fig. 316 (above). Mould for shortbread in rock maple. Patterns for the first three moulds are at left.

pattern for trimming the dough, and I put a suitable knob handle on the back. The design was carved entirely with small veiners and fluters so the dough would not "hang up" in it. After the first test, they found that the mould (or stamp) should be only 4½ in (114 mm) in diameter and also that a portion of the design "baked out," so it had to be deepened. (This was in the heads of the stalks.) With those two changes, the mould worked very well.

Fig. 321

MADONNA & CHILD

Fig. 320 (upper left). "Sky and Water I," by the late M. C. Escher, converted into a teak fireboard (fireplace screen). It is 30 × 34 in (762 × 864 mm) with the goose at top in ⅜-in (10-mm) detailed relief and the fish at the bottom in intaglio the same depth.

Figs. 321–324. A madonna-and-child design done in intaglio (left) and in relief (right) show the contrast. The relief is in American walnut, finished with neutral shoe polish, and the intaglio is in red willow, finished with oil. The intaglio is infinitely more difficult.

Fig. 324   Intaglio   Relief

Sections across Madonna's head

26

Marquetry Can Be Art

SIXTY-FIVE YEARS AGO, my parents bought a bed for their new house. It had fan-shaped marquetry panels on head- and foot-boards—some fifteen kinds of wood. My father was very proud of it; I thought it was gaudy—and I still do. Perhaps that will help explain my bias against much of the modern marquetry I've seen. It tends to be scenes copied from familiar sources and more suited to Ripley's "Believe It Or Not" or the *Guinness Book of World Records* than to display in an art show, because its principal claim to fame is usually the variety of woods included. It's a wooden version of "painting by the numbers," done from kits, and in many cases the cutting of the veneers is nowhere near being sufficiently accurate.

Perhaps we'd better explain a bit: *Webster*'s dictionary and Albert Constantine & Co., the American fount for equipment and materials for marquetry, say marquetry and inlay are the same. They're not, as the *Encyclopaedia Britannica* recognizes. They do have a tendency to overlap.

Inlay, primarily done on wood but possible also in other surfaces including horn, metals, bone and ivory, among others, is the placing of pieces of different-colored or just different material in shaped grooves that may be ⅛ in (3 mm) or less deep (or as much as 1½ in (38 mm) in some furniture) in a base panel. The inlaid pieces thus contrast with the color and texture of the base panel.

Fig. 325. "Hummingbird" won best of show in 1984. The wing is blue and bleached to get the translucent tones in the veneer. Either close up or from a distance the bird seems to be flying. It was made by Californian George Monks.

Fig. 326 (above). "Red Mill" won an honorable mention. By J. C. Robins of California, it is finely crafted and finished, but has so many veneers in the top that it throws the perspective off a bit. He also had trouble depicting water—as carvers do. Fig. 327 (right). "The Narrows," by Jeff Nelson of New York won third place. It is a bit busy with contrasting veneers.

Marquetry is the cutting of very thin veneers into pieces that are fitted together like a jigsaw puzzle, often with very hot glue so the glue oozes up between the pieces. (This is similar to parquetry, done with thicker pieces to make patterned floors, or to mosaic, the assembly of fitted pieces of stone, tile, glass or ceramic into an essentially flat surface with grout between. *Pietra dura* is the name for a mosaic of precious stones or finely cut semi-precious stones into a picture not necessarily flat on top. In metals, *niello* and *damascening* are respectively the equivalents of marquetry and inlay.)

Thus marquetry is a veneering process, while inlay is a laying-into-a-groove one. Inlaying was done in Egypt 4,000 years ago. Ulysses made a bed with gold, silver and ivory inlay. Pompeii contained furniture with gold and silver inlays.

Intarsia, developed in Italy, is basically inlay, but may include some marquetry. The earliest "modern" inlays and intarsia were made in Italy in the 14th century—wood into ivory boxes and later walnut into ivory or ebony and other dark woods, usually as arabesques, scrolls, or other patterns, but eventually including figures.

The French and Dutch later became very proficient at marquetry; much of the furniture in English museums and collections is of Dutch or French origin. The earliest French marqueteur of note was Jean Mace, who worked in the Louvre from 1644 to 1672. His daughter married Pierre Boulle, and André Charles Boulle succeeded Mace at the Louvre and became the greatest of the French. Many modern critics feel that the Boulles went too far, became too ornate and elaborate—too rococo.

Marquetry was not done in England until the Stuart period, and was almost entirely on furniture. By the late 18th century, marquetry became much shallower and solid inlay was done, but both were much more restrained than the French work. André Boulle, incidentally, was the man who figured out how to save money on marquetry by sawing sandwiches of two materials simultaneously, thus ending up with two products, one the reverse of the other.

There has been a considerable revival in marquetry in the United States in recent years—as a hobby—and there has been a sponsoring society for some time. Much of the work, however, has been the creation of scenes with various-colored woods, pri-

Fig. 328 (left). "Country Fiddler" by Ernie Ives of England won an honorable mention. It is an intricate monotone assembly almost like a pen sketch, an extraordinary exercise in silhouette, with some lines carefully omitted, yet so detailed that the fiddler's teeth show. Fig. 329 (above). "Variation I" by Gary Wright of New Hampshire won second place. It is a simple yet bold design, with each piece of veneer carefully chosen to suggest depth.

marily noteworthy for craftsmanship of execution and multiplicity and selection of veneers rather than art. It is a precise, meticulous, exacting craft, but the products too often are overly bright and tend to come on too strong. Colors are vivid and relatively flat over large areas, and sometimes the grain pattern or "figure" robs from the scene being depicted.

Marquetry has been a popular hobby in England, and this probably accounts as well for its popularity in Canada, Australia and New Zealand. One marquetarian, writing recently in a British publication, *Woodworking Crafts,* pointed out that differences have grown up between British marquetry and that of other countries, particularly the United States. The British marquetarian makes his work highly detailed and works to smaller scale, worrying over the technicalities of his craft. The over-all size of a British marquetry panel, as well as the size of its individual components, tends to be smaller than in American work. Part of the reason, he thinks, is the tendency of Americans to use veneers from 0.9 to 1 mm (0.040 in) thick, while British veneers are only two-thirds that: 0.027 in (0.6 mm). Thus theirs cut easily with a scalpel, while some of ours are safer

if fretsawed. The Australian veneers are also thicker, like ours.

Further, he points out that the British build up a complex design very slowly, possibly with an award at the National Exhibition in mind, while Americans and Australians in many cases work much more rapidly with sale of the finished work in mind. They try to make a work that is visually strong, and make it fast enough so that the price is not too high. (A similar comment could be made for much American woodcarving.) There are, of course, exceptions to these generalities—some American work is very painstaking and detailed, and some from both countries is rather awful.

British work also tends towards self-framing, so the finished picture is flat and smooth on top, while American and Australian work is put into the usual picture frames—the British emphasize the craftsman over the painter approach. This critic points out that George Monks's "Hummingbird" (see Fig. 325) is really a sort of amalgam of the two approaches; it is very effective at a distance yet can stand close-up inspection. (Monks was born in Britain and emigrated to U.S. years ago.) A British scene of badgers, for example, has individual hairs on the badgers made separately, which is only evident on close viewing. The tendency there is to use very small pieces; Americans use larger, more dramatically figured ones.

In addition to the American Marquetry Society and the British Marquetry Society, there are active marquetarians in Canada, Australia and New Zealand, among other countries. There was also the first International Creative Marquetry Show in Virginia in 1984, which emphasized original and creative pieces. Some of the winners in this show are illustrated in black-and-white here. The originals are in colored woods, of course, in some cases augmented or touched up with paint or colored pencils. The best-in-show piece of the hummingbird, for example, has blue wings which appear almost translucent. This was achieved by mounting the piece of veneer on a white card and drawing in details with colored pencils. Then each piece was cut out (from the front only) and bleached with household bleach (which proved better than commercial wood bleaches). After bleaching, the pieces were neutralized by running tap water over them, then sealed with a 2:1 solution of

Fig. 330. "Africa" is not marquetry, but a much easier overlay of glued-on walnut tree and satinwood-veneer giraffe. The background is an unretouched piece of grapefruit wood from a frost-killed Florida tree. The slab was 2 × 7 × 9½ in (51 × 178 × 241 mm) and I rounded the ends to suggest that the veldtlike scene continues.

water and white glue to prevent return to the original color. These pieces were edge-glued into place so as not to obscure the grain of the base which shows through.

My own efforts in this general field have been quite limited. I have done a great deal of inlaying of metal shapes in wood, eyes in birds, and the like, but recall only two or three close approaches to marquetry. One was in reality an overlay in which walnut and satinwood veneers, cut to shape, were glued to the surface of a slab of grapefruit. But the most elaborate is a tabletop in alternating pieces of ¼-in (6-mm) African mahogany and maple glued to a plywood back. The design was taken from M.C. Escher's "Persian Horsemen" sketch. Each horseman was actually modelled on top so

Fig. 331 (below). "Landscape" by Suzanne Cartwright of Virginia won an honorable mention. Backlighting made the design work, despite some cutting and finishing faults. Fig. 332 (right, below). "Ebony and Ivory," by Carol Teal of Canada also won an honorable mention. It includes ebony, ivory, and mother-of-pearl, but has some cutting and finishing faults.

PERSIAN HORSEMEN (Escher) Dark sections intaglio or other wood

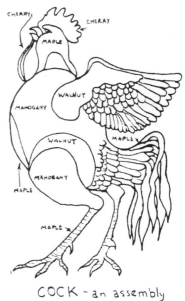

COCK - an assembly

Figs. 335 (above), 336 (opposite page). A cockerel, carved many years ago of several mahoganies, maple, and pecan on a walnut background, is about 6 in (152 mm) tall. It is similar to marquetry, but individual pieces are as much as 1 in (25 mm) and modelled to become a medium-relief carving. I called it "intarsia" for want of a better name.

FLYING HORSES (Escher) Cross-hatched

Figs. 333, 334 (left). These two designs are naturals for either marquetry or combined relief and intaglio carving, as in Fig. 320. As marquetry problems, they are repetitive—primarily jigsaw puzzles assembled of like elements. They are taken from sketches by the late M. C. Escher, and I did the upper one as an intarsia panel, as in Fig. 340, and the lower one as a combined relief and intaglio. Note that neither has any background as such—the elements interlock.

Fig. 336

it was a silhouette bas-relief, and the reins were of inserted copper wire for the maple horsemen and inserted silver wire for the mahogany ones. At the time I made this piece, my research indicated that this is somewhat different than marquetry, so for want of a name I called it "intarsia." I used the same name for another piece described in an earlier book, a cockerel about 6 in (152 mm) tall, made of modelled pieces of walnut, mahogany and maple on a walnut circle. These pieces were assembled before final carving, so the completed cockerel was actually a relief carving as much as 1 in (25 mm) thick in portions of the body.

SHELL-INLAY
PENDANTS
(Abalone in pitch)
Mexico

Figs. 337–339 (above). Mother-of-pearl-shaped pieces are inlaid in a pitch base to produce these Mexican pendants. The background wood forms a socket.

Fig. 340 (left). This is my version of Fig. 333. Maple horsemen going right interlock with African mahogany horsemen going left. It is 12½ × 18½ in (317 × 470 mm), and forms a table top. The pieces are ¼ in (6 mm) thick and modelled, with silver-wire reins inset on the mahogany and copper-wire ones on the maple.

MARQUETRY   121

27

Psychology, Expression, and Child Portraits

THERE CAN BE, and often is, a great deal of psychology in a woodcarving. The curled lip of disdain, the bared teeth of rage, the smile of friendliness, the threat of hooded eyes, the gestures with the hands, the pose of the body, the expression on the face—all of these telegraph emotions to the viewer. Many of them are older than man and are instinctive. Charles Darwin talked about them, as have his successors. The curled lip and snarl expose the canine tooth in a wolf or dog; we don't have the tooth in the same sense, but we snarl as if we did! The bristling of hair, the open mouth, the widened eyes and the look of disgust are other examples that probably date from a time when man was much more like the lower animals.

We also react instinctively to babies and children, and by extension to puppies, kittens and young animals and birds in general. Clever artists know this and have capitalized on it for centuries. Depictions of children and puppies have an inherent advantage in shows if the judges are at all human. Mexican pictures of wide-eyed—really overly large-eyed — children sold like hotcakes a few years back. Children are favorite subjects for mass-produced garden statuary. Ladies collect baby dolls. Among whittlers, another psychological characteristic has surfaced, accounting for the popularity of the cowboy caricatures of recent years. They are so ugly that we automatically consider them funny rather than repulsive, just as many children will develop a genuine affection for what we consider to be an ugly or repulsive fairy-tale giant or ogre. Consider the over-whelming popularity of the book on gnomes a few years back.

It pays to bear this in mind. I can perhaps make my point clearer by quoting the experience of Walt Disney studios with Mickey Mouse. In *Steamboat Willie* (1928), he was a rambunctious, almost sadistic, roughneck. He and Minnie played a chorus of *Turkey in the Straw* by squeezing a duck for a honk, cranking a goat's tail, tweaking a sow's nipples, hammering a cow's teeth to imitate a xylophone and playing the bagpipe on her udder. But as Mickey became a celebrity, audience reaction, watched carefully by the Studio, toned Mickey down into an almost straight man, no longer the teaser but the victim, deserving of sympathy. They introduced Mortimer to compete with him for Minnie's affections. They didn't stop there, however; they changed Mickey physically and made him younger! His head size was increased 50%, his eyes 30% (with pupils defined), his cranium 25%. By his 50th birthday in 1978, Mickey had come to resemble his nephew Morty. Mortimer, the rival, by the way, had a much longer nose than Mickey, 80% of his head length, was far taller, smart-Alecky, more "sharp" clothes.

Disney artists also shortened the beak on Donald Duck and enlarged his eyes, so he came to look more like his nephews, Huey, Louie, and Dewey. Goofy, the friendly hound villain, was drawn with a comparatively small head and overlong snout—like Mortimer. Mortimer's head was 29% of body length, Mickey's 45%. Mickey's snout is 49% of head length, and compared with Mortimer's 80% ratio.

Stephen Jay Gould, the evolutionary biologist, brings all this up in one of his essays in *The Panda's Thumb* (Norton, 1980). He calls the process of juvenilization "neotomy"—making Mickey younger as he grew older, so he'd appeal to the maternal/paternal instincts in all of us. We react to the oversize eyes, bulging forehead, receding chin and underdeveloped lower limbs of the child, and we carry this over into very sympathetic reactions not only to young animals, but to older animals with childlike characteristics, like the panda and the koala. Then there are the big-eyed animals like the deer, rabbit, squirrel and seal. We react negatively to the camel with his nose in the air and his turned-down lips, to the wolf with his slitted eyes— even to the legendary English lord with his nose in the air and his "Harrumph!" of disdain. We also do not like over-tall people, looming clouds, overhanging cliffs; they make us feel small and insignificant as well as insecure. It is no accident that the traditional policemen and guard troops are big, tall, beefy men. Or consider the thief and burglar, usually depicted as small men reminiscent in look and attitude of the weasel or ferret. Or remember cartoon depictions of the big businessman or tycoon and the little worker or consumer, the big king and the little peasant.

Face it: We humans react to stimuli just like other animals do, and the carver must never forget that fact if his work is to be effective. Remember the Hummel figures, the Teddy bear, the endless procession of baby animals and birds being cranked out in all sorts of materials and finishes for children and adults. Look at the sketches by Konrad Lorenz showing the difference in head proportions between adult and child; if the children don't twang your heartstrings, you have a problem. And if they do, you still have a problem that many primitive artists suffer from: how to make a child look like a child, not like a dwarf or an adult with cutoff legs.

My first remembered experience with

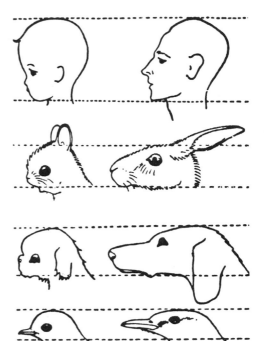

Fig. 341. Humans feel affection for animals with juvenile features: large eyes, bulging craniums, retreating chins, as in the left column. Small-eyed, long-snouted animals and adult humans, as in the right column, do not elicit the same response. (From "Studies in Animal and Human Behavior," Vol II, by Konrad Lorenz, 1971. Published by Methuen & Co., Ltd., London.)

portraiture was more than fifty years ago, when I decided to carve the head of our son, then age two. I got well into it one evening, and could see the likeness emerging. But then I'd remove another shaving, around the mouth, for example, and the whole face would freeze. Hour after hour went by and both baby and mother were increasingly fretful; I kept insisting that another few minutes would see it completed. Eventually, it was, but not without threats of divorce. When I had the pine head properly mounted on a walnut plaque, I took it in to my employer's studio to be photographed. The company art director was aghast. "Don't you know," he shouted, "that it is impossible to make portraits of children in wood? They have no lines in their faces, no character showing. All there is is softness and roundness and fleeting expression!" I've never forgotten his comments and have tried to avoid child

Fig. 342
Hawkins head
(life size)

Hawkins & my early imp
heads compared.   Fig. 343

Six typical Hawkins designs

Fig. 344

Fig. 345   Fig. 346   Fig. 347   Fig. 348   Fig. 349

Figs. 342–351. The secret of the lovable Ruth Hawkins carved face, as compared with a normal one, is sketched at upper left. With it are six of her patterns for children. All but the imp are carved in thin holly; he is appropriately in walnut. At left in the photograph are four Hawkins figures, and at right my imp in walnut compared with one of her figures. The face seems somewhat similar.

portraiture ever since—indeed, portraiture of any kind, like Mark Twain's cat who burned himself sitting on a hot stove and thereafter never sat on a stove again, hot or cold. When that self-same son carved his daughter at age two, he did too well; he showed her with a habitual pout. She has

never liked the portrait as a result of that.

I'll admit that I've never really learned the lesson either—until now. My recent cross has been the child figures carved by Ruth Hawkins of Brasstown, North Carolina. They started out as Christmas-tree decorations, but in recent years have become strictly collector items, and Ruth has expanded her designs to more than 40. All are small figures, children or angels, carved as silhouettes in holly about ³⁄₁₆ in (5 mm) thick. All have angelic faces. I've described them in a couple of my books and admitted that I had difficulty in copying the faces. Mine just lacked the spirituality, the piquance, the twang of the heartstrings that hers evoked. As time went on, I learned that at least a dozen other carvers shared my frustration—including some who'd taken lessons from her.

There's more than that to the story. Ruth is now a senior citizen. Five years ago I glimpsed a unique piece she'd carved for a friend. It was still cherubic and spiritual-looking (believe it or not!) but it was a satanic imp, in walnut rather than in holly, but with a holly pitchfork! The friend would not allow me to copy it.

Just this year, I discovered that Ruth had carved not one, but two imps! And the second one I was allowed to borrow long enough to get a pattern and memorize the modelling, but not to make a photograph. Since then, I've carved four in walnut and one in cherry. The first four were attractive imps, very nice if you'd never seen the original. But they had mature Satanic faces that belied their wings. The devil was in them, but the imp was gone.

Konrad Lorenz' sketch of a child, reproduced here, has I think solved my problem. I have just finished the fifth try, and he has the face of a sleepy imp! The answer lies in the proportions of the face. Note, in my sketch, that the proper face has a very long forehead running down into a short, tip-tilted nose, and that forehead and nose are one and a half to two times the distance from nose to chin. I've unconsciously been putting adult proportions into the child face, forgetting that the small child has a large cranium, but very small features, scrunched down near the bottom of its face. The cheeks are pudgy and the chin recedes, the lips project, the eye is not strongly defined. The ear is bigger proportionally than it is in adults. So— try it; you may like it.

While I'm talking of facial expression and Satan, I thought I'd include a unique piece of several years ago, when Mt. St. Helens erupted. The natural color of the old cedar contrasts with the grey of the overheated piece. Further, it gets the psychological reaction which I was seeking, and reinforces my initial remarks about the importance of facial expression in getting a reaction to carvings like portraits and caricatures of both humans and animals.

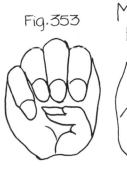

Figs. 352, 353. Cedar, greyed by the Mount St. Helens eruption, provides the 1 × 5½ × 10-in (25 × 139 × 254-mm) background and volcano of this composite panel, while 8,500-year-old Virginia cedar (still reddish) makes the inserted hands and head of Satan. Thus we have "Mount Satan." Cedar tends to crush unless tools are very sharp; the features were whittled, the background socketed and carved with chisels.

MT. SATAN
Head & Hands

Fig. 353

28

To Get Ahead on Heads

FEW CARVERS can produce likenesses and ordinary faces rapidly and with little apparent effort. Many can whack out a standardized version of a face or head in fairly fast time. And almost anybody can caricature a head. But most of us have trouble carving heads to look like they should, whether of humans or of animals. Thus I find myself carving heads and figures on scraps to "keep my hand in" when I'm not busy on a major carving. I recommend that you do the same. Here are several recent examples, just for example, mostly carved in "given" woods.

Fig. 354 (above). Janus, Roman god of doors and our source for "January," is a two-faced god stylized here in an ash fork. About 2 ft (610 mm) tall, he is a pedestal in Massachusetts. He provided excellent practice in carving hair.

Figs. 355, 356 (left). A walnut stump about 4 ft (1.2 m) tall provided space for more than a score of faces of men and animals, ranging from formal to caricature, from Thomas Jefferson (copied from a nickel) to a horse. Mounted on a black plastic base, it was entered in a local art show, and sold to the chairwoman.

Figs. 357, 358 (above). Harold Enlow sent me a piece of sassafras from his home in Dogpatch, Arkansas. To check it out, I carved this little bearded Russian with hands behind his back. His furry hat and his beard are the original bark.

Figs. 359, 360 (right). Several Mexican sculptors swear by palo santo as a carving wood. It is a bit harder than pine, with more figure. One gave me this 30-in (762-mm) log, which I covered with faces much simpler than those in Figs. 354, 355. Two central faces of men and monkey dominate the piece.

Fig. 361 (right). A local friend brought me this weather-worn locust stump. Inverted, it suggested blowing hair, so I added an old man's face to make it into a garden ornament. It is about 18 in (457 mm) tall. A similar piece with a crude face has since won top honors in a big county art show—but not for me.

Fig. 362 (bottom right). Ponderosa pine bark is frequently carved by the Tarahumara Indians in northern Mexico. While there, I practiced on it with these heads, which took less than a half hour each. The middle one is the previous Pope, wearing a Oaxaca feather headdress, as he did on a visit in 1979.

Fig. 363 (below). Lest your forget, hands are also difficult and require constant practice. This fist I carved from roadside scrap while waiting for a bus in Guatemala.

PILLAR of HEADS - Palo santo

Fig. 359

29

The "What Shall I Carve?" Syndrome

IN A SURPRISING number of ways we convince ourselves to postpone a selection of a carving subject—or actually start on one already selected. One excuse is the lack of exactly the right piece of wood, another the availability of the exact desired design, still another the necessity of waiting for an auspicious day upon which to start. I'm quite familiar with all of these, particularly the last, which perhaps is an outgrowth of

my fascination with so-called "primitive" cultures. (Many are as advanced culturally as ours, or were until we ruined them, but their traditions and thought processes give different results.) I remember a very competent billboard artist who used to hide under his Pierce Arrow car, allegedly fixing something, to keep from starting the next stage of doing the art, already contracted for, that earned his rather plentiful

Figs. 364–366. Three answers to the title question, all from similar blocks of cherry roughly 8 × 8 × 16 in (203 × 203 × 406 mm). "Eternal Question" (far left) is intentionally blocky to emphasize the hairdo question mark. "Answer Man" (near left) is Sherlock Holmes with deerstalker cap and meerschaum pipe. "Laughing Dwarf" (opposite page) has decorative brass nails for buttons, and leans well back on his base "rock."

daily bread. His wife said she spent half her time arguing with a pair of feet sticking out under the running board. I am afflicted with the same ailment, but I can report some of the palliatives I've used.

The greatest incentive to start is to leave an attractive piece of wood in the way: on the workbench, visible on the terrace, even on desk or table in living areas. Sooner or later, your mind will suggest a suitable project just to get the wood out of the way. And I often find that a project so generated creates a great deal of interest—even sales—among viewers.

Take, for example, the 2-ft (610-mm)-diameter cherry tree that I had taken down. It had been dead for a year or two, and dead cherry cut to fireplace length and near the ground will dry-rot with surprising speed. So it behooved me to split it, and in the process I salvaged five blocks about 8 × 8 × 16 in (203 × 203 × 406 mm), each split off-center to reduce checking. Standing on the terrace and visible from the dining room, those blocks

haunted me until I have now reduced their number to one. An early casualty in their ranks became two pieces, one a rather ordinary commission, the other the pumpkin described elsewhere in this book.

The other three were knocked off one after the other by three ideas that crowded one upon another. The first was a bust of Sherlock Holmes, triggered by my reading a "biography" of him that included a couple of pictures that could be put together to give the familiar deerstalker hat, big nose, and meerschaum pipe. In the midst of that carving, I had an idea for a female head with her hairdo forming the "Eternal Question" mark. And coming close on the heels of that one is the annual domestic question: "buy or make" a Christmas present for the lady of the house. This time I elected to make—an enlargement of a laughing dwarf that I saw originally as a salt shaker in Sweden 25 years or so ago. And on this one, the wood caught up with me; that cherry fought me every step of the way, with wavy grain, tendency to splinter, funny spots in texture—you name it. Besides, I'd elected to carve the figure across the corners of the block, so I had some tricky modifying to do in the design around the thighs and feet. And of course the wood splinters most where I have too little for the design anyway.

However, I am providing photos and patterns of all three of these figures here, in case you want to duplicate them in any size. Also, I took step-by-step photographs of the Sherlock Holmes carving, to indicate the method of attack on a relatively complex design including several delicate areas like the hat bill, the hand and the pipe. The Polynesian lady of "Eternal Question" is by far the simplest of the three, because her hair is stylized and she is quite blocky to emphasize the question mark. Also, her eyes are closed, which avoids *that* hurdle. But she has a face and an ear that will require some care and skill.

These carvings, incidentally, were finished in different ways. The lady was simply oiled and waxed, to preserve the orange-red color of the wood, while Sherlock and the dwarf were both antiqued to emphasize the detail and texture. This is evident in the photographs.

Of the three pieces, I enjoyed most carving the laughing dwarf. In the first place, he is a humorous piece, and that raises the spirit of the carver—or should. In the second place, he furthers a point I have tried to make in talking and writing about carving—that how the piece will be viewed is important. A carving to go high above eye level must be done with upper surfaces projecting beyond lower ones, and a carving to go below eye level must be done the opposite way. Also, the typical in-the-round figure is carved to be viewed straight on, and so needs to be at eye level. This may be inconvenient for the owner

Fig. 367 (right). My dwarf was simply an enlargement of this Swedish salt shaker. Figs. 368, 369 (below). Holmes was fitted to the available block, which permitted his cap bill and pipe, but had no stock for a left arm. The girl has no arms.

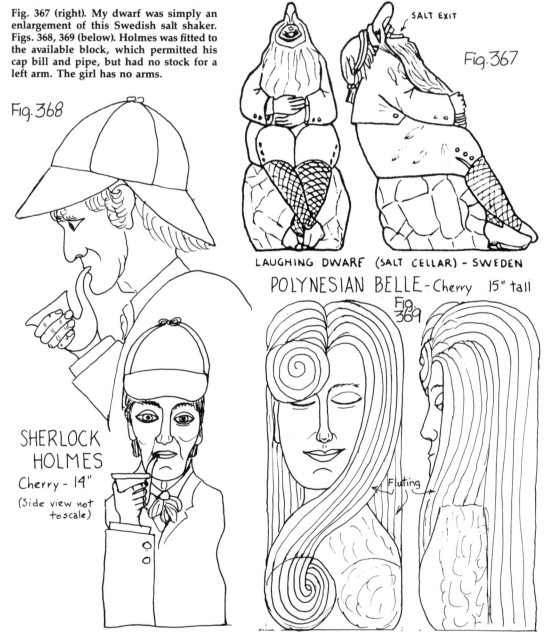

SALT EXIT

Fig. 367

LAUGHING DWARF (SALT CELLAR) - SWEDEN

POLYNESIAN BELLE - Cherry   15" tall

Fig. 369

Fig. 368

SHERLOCK HOLMES

Cherry - 14"

(Side view not to scale)

Fluting

Fig. 370 (right). To retain the back squareness of the girls' head, the hair is carried straight down from the swirl at the top. This also leaves wood for the modelled ear. No neck is indicated, and the bottom of the question-mark swirls over one breast while the other is merely suggested.

Fig. 371 (far right). A side view of the original salt shaker shows a different foot placement; mine was adjusted to available wood—as usual.

Fig. 372. These figures do not require many tools. Those used for the laughing dwarf were: three gouges, a firmer, two V-tools, and a knife. The V-tool is a long-bent ¾-in (19-mm) heavy-duty tool, as is the 2½-in (64-mm) flat spade gouge. The others are a ½-in (13-mm) firmer and a conventional-sized flat gouge. A ⅜-in (10-mm) spade firmer and a ¼-in (6-mm) round gouge, both short tools and two weights of plastic-faced mallet complete my set.

who has neither a grand piano or a series of pedestals, as well as being unnatural for some carvings. I have, through the years, carved several almost-life-size dogs to be placed on the floor or used as door stops: I learned as a child that dogs should not be allowed on the table. The same goes for sleeping cats. So, several years ago, I carved a 16-in (406-mm) bear cub in cherry. He sits on the ground and looks up appealingly. I did a 24-in (610-mm) Mexican peon in mesquite who has his sombrero pulled down over his eyes and has huge bare feet—he is a shy floor-stander too.

When I was carving the laughing dwarf, I kept track of the time per step. During most of the early work, I used only a saw and a 2-in (51-mm) flat gouge. To make the enlarged drawing by the point-to-point method took 1½ hours. It took two more hours to get the block ready and make a rough transfer of my enlarged sketch—which was a bit small for the block—and to round up the top as shown in Step 1. Locating the nose precisely, as well as the kneecap, back of the head, meeting of buttock and rock top and cutting away some of the waste wood took three hours more, Step 2. The face of Step 3 took another three hours and required a V-tool and large roughing gouge (1-in or 25-mm). From there on, it was heavy work. Shaping the body took about 10 hours and details and finishing about 8, for a total of about 28 hours.

Step-by-step instructions for Sherlock Holmes on next page.

CHERRY FIGURES   131

CARVING SHERLOCK HOLMES STEP BY STEP

Fig. 373 (left). Step 1. The split-out block was not exactly rectangular, so the wider end was used for the cap bill and pipe. The side view has been sketched and top handsawed to rough outline.

Fig. 374 (right). Step 2. Further sawing and chisel work clears the cap bill and locates pipe and projecting hand. Some hat modelling is done and the width of head determined. Note that the face has been sketched in.

Fig. 375. Step 3. The cap is now largely completed, nose rough-shaped, plus hand and pipe. The ear is located. Hairlines are drawn and being worked with smaller tools.

Fig. 376. Step 4. The face contours in and hair outlined with ear lobes shaped. The pipe is being separated from chin so neck can be formed. The hand and wrist are being shaped.

Fig. 377 (left). Step 5. The cheeks, eyes, jutting chin are rough-formed, as well as the hand. The hand is slightly small for the face, I think, despite careful measurement. Small flat gouges and a V-tool do most of this work.

Fig. 378 (right). Step 6. The big pipe is now shaped, but still anchored to the chin for security. The hair and neck contours have been worked out, but ear lobe and collar with Windsor tie have yet to be drawn.

Fig. 379 (left). Step 7. The face is shaped and eyes opened by delineating lids and pupils, using small veiner or fluter, flat gouge and V-tool, with light mallet. Cherry is tricky; note knot at lower right.

Fig. 380 (right). Step 8. The body is thinned beneath shoulder on left side to suggest usual bust form. Lapels, tie, and fingernails are carved. Ears are shaped. Chisel marks are left, but are smoothed, and directed.

NOTE: The completed figure was sprayed with matte varnish, then given a coat of dark walnut stain, applied in small areas and immediately wiped off, to leave some color in cut lines to accentuate them. After thorough soft-brushing, it was given two coats of neutral shoe polish and brushed each time.

SHERLOCK HOLMES   133

THE LAUGHING DWARF
STEP BY STEP

Fig. 381 (left). The projecting corner of the rough block was an opportunity to extend the feet a bit, so the pattern was applied across corners. Shaping the face has begun. The near corner has been cut off to the chin line.

Fig. 382 (right). Further cutting makes the nose project. The features are sketched in around it. The arms and hands have also been located so wood can be cut away around them. This block is big and heavy enough that cutting can be done without holding.

Fig. 383 (left). The face and beard are now defined, as well as cap and shoulders. Work is done largely with a flat 2-in (50-mm) gouge, with heavy mallet. A V-tool and ½-in (13-mm) firmer and light mallet develop the features. The arms and hands are defined further.

Fig. 384 (right). When the head, shoulders, and arms are shaped, balance can be determined readily. Tilt the piece back until it is just short of tipping over backwards, mark the base parallel with the ground, and saw the block off as shown. Then the hips and rock top can be located.

Fig. 385 (above). Because of the narrow point and limited stock, I decided to cross the feet, which I like to do anyway. The knees had to be close together because of lack of stock. Note hand positions—the white is, of course, a knot, also knee breeches, cross-hatched stockings, jacket projection.

Fig. 386 (upper right). Shaping was intentionally left somewhat crude and bulky, in keeping with the subject. The shoes are heavy and the beard is profuse and coarse. The teeth are very large in an oversized mouth, but the figure inspires laughter.

Fig. 387 (right). Stripes are carved around the close-fitting stocking cap and the tassel is defined. The hair and beard are not detailed to the limit, and the rock is merely rounded to look like a rock rather than a box. (You may prefer the multiple planes of the original—see Fig. 371.) Brass upholstery tacks can be driven in to serve as buttons flanking the openings at the sides of the jacket tail, at the knee split, and on the cuffs and pockets. Finish can be antiquing as described for Sherlock Holmes on page 133.

30

Hands and Faces

DR. W.L. COLLETTE of Burnsville, North Carolina, is a graduate of the University of Florida in science and got his doctorate in veterinary medicine at Auburn. He was in practice for a busy 25 years in Florida and still has varied business interests there. Since retirement, he has taken various drawing and painting courses and his teacher, Mrs. Timberman, has criticized his drawings and been a major influence.

As a carver, he is mostly self-taught. He came into my class at the Campbell Folk School three years before these pictures

were taken, never having done any relief carving. His first panel was a vegetable polyglot, and I told him it was not so hot. He told me at the time that he had memorized most of my books and those of Harold Enlow, and I believed him after a week of his quoting me back at myself. Since then he has carved up a storm. He sends me Polaroid® shots of his latest carvings. I criticize and he rebuts loudly. But he has learned to draw and to study art—the advice he gives to anyone who asks, and some who don't. His wood is usually "tulip poplar," also called yellow poplar or tulip tree. (He does *not* carve the common poplars, but does do some work on red

Fig. 388 (above). "The Misanthrope" and Dr. Collette, giving some idea of the size of these panels. Fig. 389 (right). His lion is overly human, particularly in the eyes. It shows the variation in board color before stain and antiquing.

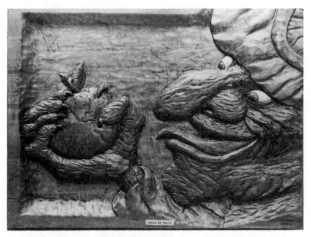

Fig. 390 (above). "Trick or Treat" is a take-off on Rodin's "Hand of God." The wormy apple is the earth. Fig. 391 (right). "Voodoo" shows fervor, accentuated by tinted eyes and teeth.

and white oak and black walnut.) Ordinarily, he buys 8/4- (50-mm) kiln-dried rough wood by the truckload and cuts it into 8- to 10-ft (2.59- to 3.05-m) lengths. He planes and edges it, then glues it with Elmer's Carpenters Glue® into roughly 36 × 48-in (914 × 1,219-mm) panels. Ends of joints are cross-dowelled with ¼-in (6-mm) dowels "just in case."

He has had one-man shows at various libraries and schools, won top honors in relief carving in the only show he has entered—and hasn't sold a piece despite tempting offers. And he has become a carver of hands and faces to emulate.

How does he do it? He thinks first of a theme: thinker, alienation, religious fervor, Hand of God. Then he makes several sketches to depict the theme—what he calls "thematic art." From these, he selects one to develop. Almost everything he does currently has to do with human emotions, and he feels that most of the body language is expressed in faces and hands. He actually gets a feeling of awe as a face emerges in his carving, and the awe shows when he is done.

These are obviously big panels, so they give Bill scope. After he transfers the drawing to the wood, he drills negative spaces with a drill that has a stop collar. This provides a depth gauge when he grounds out the panel. He actually grounds quite deeply, sometimes almost through the panel, so he has freedom to model his subject(s). The pictures tell that story. He may use paint to emphasize an eye or whatever.

The finished carving is coated with a water-based stain of German origin (the Beiz stains to which I've often referred, available from Georg Keilhofer, (976 S. Main St., Frankenmuth, Michigan, 48734.) Oil-based stains proved unsuitable for poplar. Final finish is three to five coats of clear wax, buffed with a fibre wheel in an electric drill. Then he uses my "antiquing" method, with a walnut oil stain. (The stain will darken any wax it coats, so the antiquing must be carefully done.) He paints carefully with a small brush into the edges of depressions and wipes off any excess at once with a clean rag. (I had suggested Krylon® spray satin finish for a sealer, but this did not work well on yellow poplar.)

Bill is by no means solely a relief carver, nor even a hand and face carver. He has more than 30 in-the-round carvings of all sizes, including the usual cowboys, Indians and dancing girls. And he has big horse carvings as well.

Fig. 392. "Full Circle" contrasts a gnarled old hand with that of a child.

Fig. 393. "Hard Day" is a good study of work-worn hands and face. The eyes add to the feeling of tiredness and almost despair.

Fig. 395 (below). "Three Generations" stresses the mother and papoose, with the grandmother subdued. Fig. 396 (bottom). "Partners" contrasts men and horse heads at close range.

Fig. 394 (below). This is an interesting untitled study. Viewed as shown, it can indicate religious fervor, while viewed as a horizontal composition it suggests a beggar and could be titled "Alms."

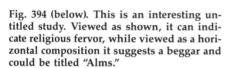

Fig. 397. "Tenza's Neighbors," echoes "Fiddler on the Roof," is active and alive, and "breaks" the frame very well. The perspective suffers a bit on fiddles and belt lines.

Fig. 398. "Albert E" is, of course, a giant portrait of a giant intellect—Einstein. The eyes are tinted to strengthen them. The hair and moustache treatment is fine.

Figs. 399, 400 (below). "Lifeline" catches desperate action, strengthened because the background is simple texturing rather than a scene. The sketch is my effort at a pattern from this panel.

Fig. 400

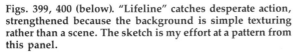

Fig. 401. "Emperor" breathes smugness, but threatened stiffness is broken and fatness and smugness emphasized by the hands "breaking" the frame.

31

Stylizing by an Expert

SETH M. VELSEY was a Midwestern sculptor who worked in the Twenties and Thirties. I became familiar with his work and kept these photographs of some typical pieces because of his ability to stylize, which I do *not* share. I wish I did. He worked in both wood and stone, either in-the-round or in relief, depending upon the planned use of the sculpture. Thus he made a series of interesting yellow-poplar panels 3½ × 6 ft (1067 × 1828 mm) for the then-new post office in Pomeroy, Ohio (see Chapter 3 on V-tools) which are really polyglot assemblies or montages. The pieces shown are all in-the-round, and vary from attentuated figures to blocky ones. They do, however, give some idea of the sorts of stylizing that can be accomplished, as well as being prime examples of good stylizing as opposed to some of the crudities which are masked by being called "styled." Stylizing should have a purpose, and be consistent within itself. Above all, it should make sense. These pieces do.

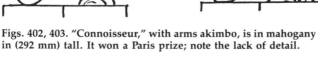

Figs. 402, 403. "Connoisseur," with arms akimbo, is in mahogany in (292 mm) tall. It won a Paris prize; note the lack of detail.

Fig. 404 (above). "Elinor" is a 15-in (381-mm) bust in Carrara marble, with simple lines. Figs. 405, 406 (right). "Slav March" is in Austrian mahogany 29 in (737 mm) high. Fig. 407 (below, left). "Gothic" is a 3-ft (910-mm) mahogany figure against a gold-leaf back panel. Figs. 408, 409 (below, right). "Man and Dog" is a 12-ft (3.66-m). work in buff oolitic limestone.

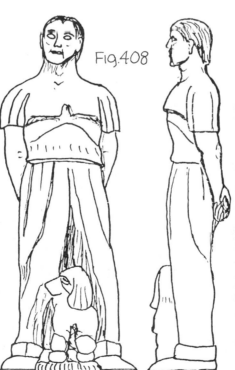

Fig. 408

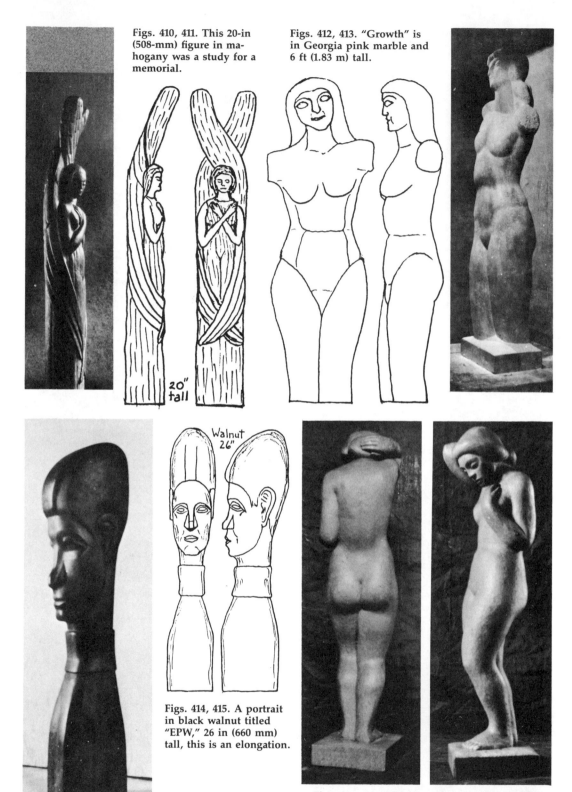

Figs. 410, 411. This 20-in
(508-mm) figure in ma-
hogany was a study for a
memorial.

Figs. 412, 413. "Growth" is
in Georgia pink marble and
6 ft (1.83 m) tall.

20"
tall

Walnut
26"

Figs. 414, 415. A portrait
in black walnut titled
"EPW," 26 in (660 mm)
tall, this is an elongation.

Figs. 416, 417. "Eve" is only 14 in (356 mm) tall in
mahogany. It is relaxed and not aggressively
female.

32

The Homesteader's Axe

MY FIRST "editorial" in wood—after hundreds in words—was the result of a chain of circumstances. I had been reading about the white man's treatment of the Indians, then and now. I saw a sketch in *The New* York Times by Peter Kuper that showed a series of Indian heads on a totem pole being chopped down by pioneers. And I had a slab of black walnut about 1 × 15½ × 28½ in (25 × 394 × 724 mm), slightly warped but an interesting shape retaining most of the bark on one sloping edge and rounded on top. These three coincidences resulted in "The Homesteader."

The heads are, from the top: a Great Plains Indian (Sioux) flanked by clouds, a Mesa Indian (Hopi) flanked by buttes, a mountain Indian (Paiute) with a panorama of the Rockies, and a forest Indian (Iroquois) flanked by pines. The side panels suggest the wings projecting from birds topping some totem poles, but are framed at the side to hold them together and tie them to the bottom scene of the bearded homesteader chopping down the pole to use its wood in his partially built cabin.

Because the elements are all large, I set-in the background almost ½ in (13 mm), routing the sky areas to save time. The background was later textured with a flat gouge, simply to contrast it with the modelled heads and scenes. It was also darkened with dark-walnut stain to make it recede still more.

It seemed appropriate to have the large

Fig. 418. "The Homesteader" is carved on a 1 × 15½ × 26½-in (25 × 394 × 724-mm) walnut slab, leaving the bark and irregular edge along one side and extending this into an irregular top line. Grounding is ½ in (13 mm), quite deep, to create shadows. This is not a picture, but an editorial— a political cartoon, if you will.

heads with closed eyes, suggesting shame or resignation. Opening the eyes would suggest inattention at least, and be more derogatory to the red men, at least in my opinion. Also, I accentuated the high cheekbones and angular faces, and turned down the lips in disdain or disapproval, because the Indian did not destroy the forest and its wildlife—he lived with them.

A panel with a story or thought expressed in it is considerably different from a simple scene. It requires some of the kind of thinking that is done by a political cartoonist. It must speak for itself when viewed, must have a message that is readily understandable. This is much more dif-ficult than composing a simple scene, but the result can be much more pertinent as well. Also, the treatment can be less formal; in fact, it can be pure caricature if that makes the point better.

This particular carving turned out to be a splendid exercise in working out faces at varied angles, as well as in developing expression. The facial planes are more accentuated than usual, and there is some irregularity and detail in the silhouettes. Also, it provides an opportunity for a subliminal suggestion in the irregular background shape—the suggestion that rigor and squareness replaced freedom when the whites took over.

Figs. 419- 425

HOMESTEADER

MOUNTAIN INDIAN

FOREST INDIAN (Iroquois)

← MESA INDIAN (Hopi)

PLAINS INDIAN → (Sioux)

CABIN SHELL

Fig. 426 (left). Step 1. The ground was routed to ½ in (13 mm), then cleaned and textured with a flat gouge. Also details of the silhouettes were cleaned out.

Fig. 427 (above). Step 2. Modelling is lengthy. Here the headdress is partly done with a V-tool lying over to create steps. The face and clouds are also outlined.

Fig. 428 (left). Step 3. The top Indian, clouds, and birds are complete. The hair on the mesa man was done with a small V-tool, leaving one loose lock. The eyes are underlined to age him.

Fig. 429 (below). Step 4. Three-quarter profile requires deeper lines and setting back on left side, long slopes on right.

Fig. 430 (left). Step 5. I usually complete modelling as I go, for the pure pleasure of seeing some part of the panel finish-carved. I have tried to distinguish one Indian from another by slight differences in facial characteristics and dress to suit tribal custom. Here the roached hairdo of the Iroquois (specifically the Mohawk) is defined with a V-tool, and the background has been scalloped with random flat-gouge cuts. Because the cabin area offers some problems in perspective, I worked on that next, to put in stumps and part of a log cabin.

Fig. 431 (below). Step 6. Note here how the V-tool is used to suggest pine trees (along the top of the picture) and how the two smaller stumps are cut back toward their bases so the latter will almost merge with the ground as they should. (The larger stump runs into the border, so needn't be cut back.) The pioneer is intentionally much smaller in scale because a relatively few pioneers soon destroyed the hunting grounds of a great many Indians.

33

History Hidden in a Panel

A POLYGLOT PANEL can be decorative yet include history, or perhaps other hidden elements. A case in point was the commission that was open-ended—"for one of your panels." Alice, the client, had tried twice to embroider pillows showing her husband Fred's many and interesting avocations, but the pillow designs had not hung together. She was willing to accept anything from a simple depiction of a sailing dinghy to a complex record—something that "will be interesting to others."

Fortunately, I know Fred quite well. It occurred to me that perhaps the best solution was a polyglot panel in which his special interests could be "hidden" among images of birds and flowers that would give the panel general decorative value. I had a length of ¾ × 9¼ × 16-in (19 × 235 × 406-mm) Thai teak, longer in proportion than the usual. This, with a ⅝-in (16-mm) border, would give an effective area of 8 × 14¾ in (203 × 375 mm). If I made the units

somewhat smaller than usual, I could include a considerable number, enough to hide the 16 personal elements that Alice and I put together. In this instance,. most of the bird and flower designs could be taken directly from field guides, size for size, making the copying much easier. The special elements were picked up largely from memory or description—the only source material I had was a sketch of the Cornell

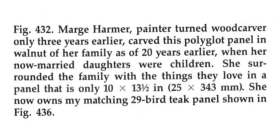

Fig. 432. Marge Harmer, painter turned woodcarver only three years earlier, carved this polyglot panel in walnut of her family as of 20 years earlier, when her now-married daughters were children. She surrounded the family with the things they love in a panel that is only 10 × 13½ in (25 × 343 mm). She now owns my matching 29-bird teak panel shown in Fig. 436.

Figs. 433–457. Sixteen items of personal history of the owner of this panel are hidden among 50 common flowers of the Eastern seaboard, the leaves of 42 trees and bushes, a dozen of their flowers and fruits, plus a Monarch butterfly and a tree frog. This ¾ × 9¼ × 16-in (19 × 235 × 406-mm) panel is Thai teak and contains 119 units. The hidden history includes six bust depictions of the owner's roles in amateur theatre, a sailing dinghy, part of a piano keyboard, a trumpet, a tennis racket. There are also a pair of choristers, the male wearing a Marine cap, the elongated Alice in Wonderland by John Tenniel (his wife is named Alice), the sugar maple (New York state tree), live oak (Georgia state tree), dogwood (Georgia state flower), and the violet, his fraternity flower. Readily visible is the old library tower of Cornell University, his college.

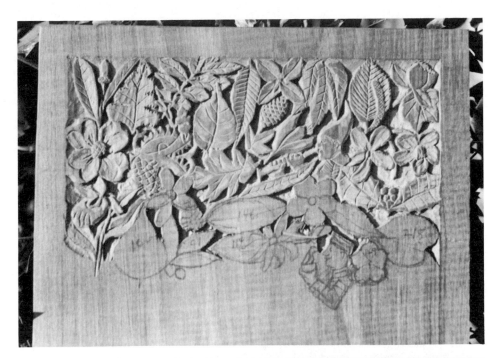

Figs. 458 (top), 459 (bottom). The beginning and ending of panel carving. Patterns are sketched in as needed, just ahead of grounding. I also model immediately to reduce confusion in relocating references and for the satisfaction of seeing part of the panel finished. In Fig. 458 (top), the dragon and Pied Piper can be seen carved, and convict with snake is sketched below. In Fig. 459, the piano keyboard, sailboat, tennis racket, and Alice are carved. Fig. 459 may "invert"—appear to be in intaglio—because our brains tell us that shadows should be beneath bulges. If your brain tells you this, look at Fig. 459 upside down.

Fig. 460. Also in teak, this very simple polyglot panel depicts 29 birds of America. It is 10 × 13⅜ in (254 × 340 mm) overall and is carved relatively shallow, the background and modelling being accentuated by "antiquing."

University Library tower, which I planned to include to suggest his college. Fred had acted with me or for me (as director) in half a dozen plays, and the other avocations were somewhat familiar shapes.

Carving was begun in the upper left-hand corner, with a live-oak spray and a dogwood flower, respectively the state tree and flower of Georgia, where he courted his wife. Elsewhere on the panel are the violet of his college fraternity, and the sugar-maple leaf of New York State, where they now live.

These are easy, of course, because they blend with the principal design of the panel. As the carving progressed, however, I could work in a dragon head, a Pied Piper with recorder, a prisoner, a king's head with crown, a pirate head and a Satan head—representing six amateur theatrical roles. A trumpet, a section of piano keyboard, a tennis racquet and a sailing dinghy cover other hobbies. His enjoyment of singing and his singing in choirs (that's how he met his wife) were combined with his Marine Corps background by showing the two singing as choristers, he wearing a Marine cap. His wife, Alice, donor of the plaque, is depicted in the lower right-hand corner as the familiar elongated Alice drawn for *Alice in Wonderland* by John Tenniel. (She carries a valentine with his name, "Fred," on it.) Also shown is the tower and roof of the old Cornell library, his college. Thus there were about 13 very personal elements hidden in a decorative panel which also includes 50 common flowers, 42 trees and bushes (with 12 flowers or fruits), a tree frog and a butterfly—all told 107 separate pictures.

This appears to be a monumental undertaking at first glance, much more difficult than a single subject, but this is not entirely true. Because the individual subject

Fig. 461. Many of
these silhouettes
are single-bird pat-
terns; the panel is
multiple-numbered
to suggest their
use in that way.

is quite small (each is about 1 sq in) (625 sq mm), detail can be reduced and only the silhouette remains vitally important. Further, the carving can be quite shallow—under ⅛ in (3 mm) deep, so no undercutting is required, and for much of the work only a single setting-in is enough. Also, depth of background can vary somewhat and background sections need not be extremely smooth nor carefully patterned, because they will be covered by a dark stain ultimately anyway. So the work can go quite rapidly; this entire panel took less than 50 hours to complete.

Tools included ⅛-, ⅟₁₆-, and ¼-in (3-, 1.5-, and 6-mm) firmers, ⅟₃₂- and ⅟₁₆-in (0.8- and 1.5-mm) veiners, ⅟₁₆-in (1.5-mm) V-tool, and small gouges of varied sweeps, mostly ¼ in (6 mm) wide. Designs were set-in without previous outlining, taking care to angle cuts on the second side of narrow sections across grain.

34

Character from Hands and Faces

A most famous and competent wood sculptor of only a half-century ago was Ernst Barlach (1870–1938), yet he is relatively unknown today. His graphic work and sculpture were frequently exhibited in the United States, and he was described as a "carver of wood inspired by Gothic wood sculpture" who sought "the evidence of the inner man." He was actually more than a sculptor; like da Vinci and Michelangelo he was a draftsman, lithographer, woodcut maker, playwright (eight plays), author and essayist (three books)—in other words, he was an all-around artist and his work is worthy of study.

Barlach was born in the little town of Wedel on the Elbe, now a suburb of Hamburg, and lived there until he was 40, when he moved to and remained in Guestrow. He travelled little, but did go to Paris and Florence, as well as to visit a brother in the Ukraine. This latter visit was very important; it brought him into contact with the short, squat, round-headed, flat-faced, and slit-eyed people who became his characters and established his style.

Barlach began his work in ceramics, but he found wood better for his purposes, and only occasionally used clay or bronze in his later works. His favorite wood was oak, although he also carved walnut, beech, linden, lime, and teak—whatever was available in large, weathered blocks. He did on occasion laminate his wood, but the result still appears to be a single piece, with limbs close to the body and the general effect one of lumpiness. He left tool marks and did not camouflage or overpower the surface of the wood or change its color. Most of the character of his figures is portrayed in faces and hands, because he covered the rest of the body with voluminous, loose-fitting clothing (except for Christ on the cross). Many of his works were unfinished in back—even flat—probably because the usual Gothic figure stands against a wall, a pillar, or is in a niche. The figures rest heavily on their integral bases and are usually single subjects, rarely in motion. Thus he adds a feeling of loneliness to works uniformly free of sentimentality. He often pictured the misery and humiliation of poverty, illness, grossness, terror, or doubt. His figures are not idealized; they are usually old, blind, crippled, fat, or otherwise deformed, but they are never caricatures. He felt very strongly the injustices that beset man, and was very strongly pacifist. Thus he was banned by the Nazis, who called him an expressionist and pacifist and removed his anti-war memorials one by one. He died a virtual outcast in his own country, but has now regained renown there. His works are included in some museums and private collections and he is again becoming recognized as the master he was. A 1911 figure, 31 in (787 mm) tall, was sold to a collector in 1972 for $110,000, for example, and a number of galleries and museums have staged commemorative exhibitions. The works pictured here are photographs loaned by the German Information Center, New York.

Fig. 462 (above). "Monks Reading," 1932, in wood. Fig. 463 (top right). "Shivering Girl," done in 1917, is 760 mm (30 in) tall. Note the scalloped texturing that suggests the title. Fig. 464 (right). "The Suspended One" symbolizing the peace of the dead, is in Antoniterkirche in Cologne.

Fig. 465 (top left). "Old Woman Dancing" was done in 1920. Fig. 466 (above). "Shivering Old Woman" was done in 1937. Fig. 467 (far left). "The Lonely One" was done in 1911. Fig. 468 (left). "Crippled Beggar" was done in 1930. Note that none of these is a "pretty" sculpture; all deal with real people.

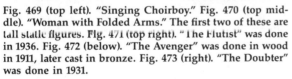

Fig. 469 (top left). "Singing Choirboy." Fig. 470 (top middle). "Woman with Folded Arms." The first two of these are tall static figures. Fig. 471 (top right). "The Flutist" was done in 1936. Fig. 472 (below). "The Avenger" was done in wood in 1911, later cast in bronze. Fig. 473 (right). "The Doubter" was done in 1931.

Fig. 474 (top left). "Blind Man" is again narrow and tall, and shows Barlach's ability to capture an idea simply. Fig. 475 (center above). "The Reunion" was auctioned in Cologne in 1961 for 20,000 marks, but is much more valuable now. Fig. 476 (above). "Moses" is again simple and strong. Fig. 477 (left). This detail is from a larger work called "The Dead Man."

35

Those Famed "Limited Editions"

In 1937, a chemical engineer and lawyer, George Robinson, 45, who was director of the Robinson Galleries in New York City, had begun to experiment with inexpensive reproductions of sculpture in plaster, cast stone and wood. His first pieces were sold for $10 to $97, and include some shown here. In 1939, he showed larger pieces which began at $500—but for both shows his artists were among the best known of their day. At that remote date, I couldn't have afforded any of the pieces, but I did afford these photographs which have been in my files ever since. I think they are worth reproducing because they show the best sculpture in wood of fifty years ago, reproduced by Mr. Robinson in his "Limited Editions." These sold very well and brought good sculpture within the price range of many people. They popularized sculpture. I have drawn patterns of several to show how you can use them.

Fig. 478 (below). "Paul Revere's Ride" is by Warren Wheelock, carved in 1935. It is much more stylized than . . . Fig. 479 (right). "The Mayor" was also carved by Warren Wheelock in walnut in 1937. It is, of course, a stylized portrait of the beloved "Little Flower," Fiorello LaGuardia, who gave his name to an airport, was honest, and read the Sunday comics to children over the radio during a newspaper strike.

Fig. 480 (right). "Hand Stand," by Chaim Gross, is 5 × 6 × 15 in (127 × 152 × 381 mm) in walnut and typical of his bulky figures.

Figs. 481–484 (below). Alice Decker is renowned for her simple animal figures, of which there are three in this group. Her "Sleeping Kitten," just below, for which I have sketched a pattern, is in mahogany 4 × 5 × 8 in (101 × 127 × 203 mm), while her "Curled Sleeping Kitten," below it, is in walnut 4 × 6 × 5 in (101 × 152 × 127 mm). Her "Penguin" (lower right) is in teak, 4 × 5 × 9 in (101 × 127 × 229 mm).

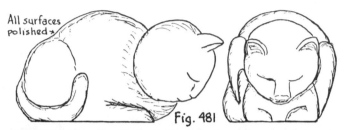

All surfaces polished →

Fig. 481

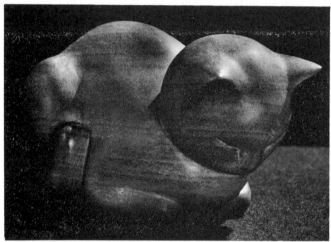

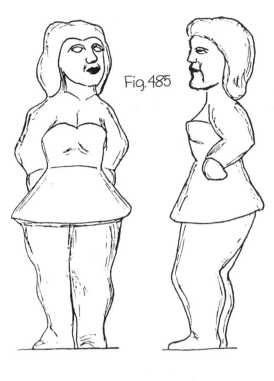

Fig. 485

Figs. 485, 486 (left). "Circus Girl," also by Chaim Gross, again shows his penchant for stubby figures. It is in mahogany, 3 × 4 × 13 in (76 × 101 × 330 mm). I have provided two views if you wish to try it.

TORSO - Oronzio Maldarelli   Fig. 487

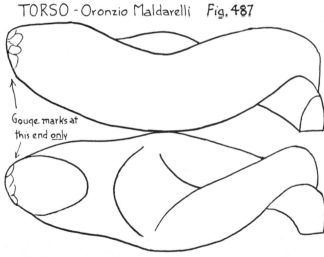

Gouge marks at this end only

Figs. 487, 488 (left). "Torso" by Oronzio Maldarelli is smooth all over except at the base of the neck, where he left gouge marks which can be seen clearly at bottom left.

Fig. 489 (below). "Child Drinking," by William Zorach, was originally in mahogany. It is 4 × 6 × 9 in (101 × 152 × 229 mm).

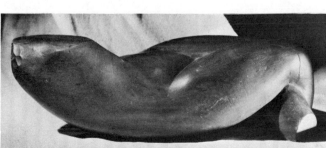

A CLOSER LOOK AT WHEELOCK WOODCARVINGS

Fig. 490 (right). "Morgan" was carved in satinwood and finished in natural color. It referred to J. Pierpont Morgan, financier alive at the time. Fig. 491 (far right). "Sanctuary" was carved in 1930. This is a detail. Fig. 492 (below). "Eve" is in teak, about 2 ft (600 mm) tall. Fig. 493 (below, center). "Pugilist" is a rare relief, in oak about 3 ft (915 mm) tall and 25½ in (650 mm) wide. Fig. 494 (below, far right). "Madonna and Child" was carved in mahogany in 1923. This is a detail.

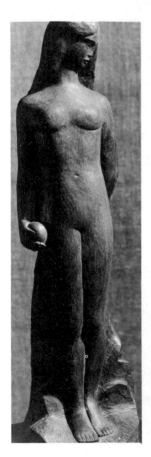

Figs. 495, 496 (right). "Black Dancer" is in ebony, carved in 1930. Figs. 497, 498 (below). "Little Girl" was carved in mahogany in 1935. It is 3 ft (915 mm) tall. Fig. 499 (below, far right). "Meditation" is in walnut, carved in 1935 and shown four years later at the Museum of Modern Art.

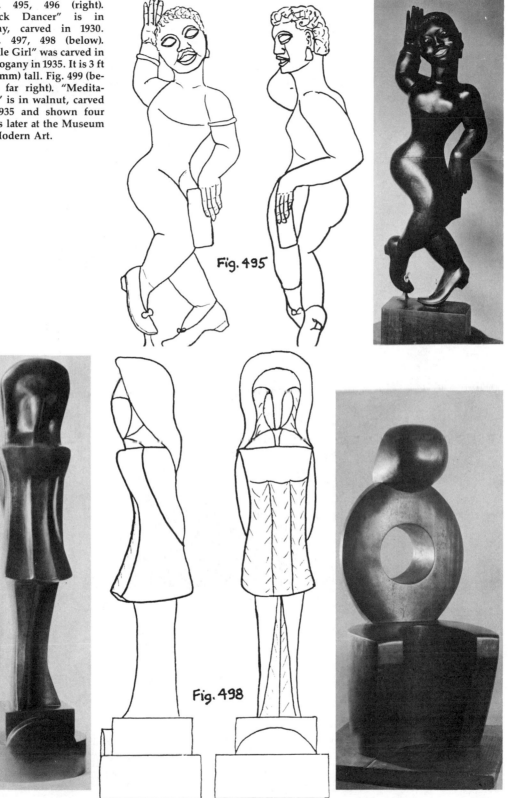

Fig. 495

Fig. 498

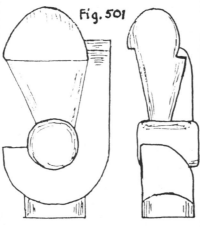

Fig. 500 (left). "Venus of the Wave" was carved in teak in 1923. Figs. 501, 502 (below and right). "Mother and Child" is an abstraction in mahogany, carved in 1928.

Fig. 501

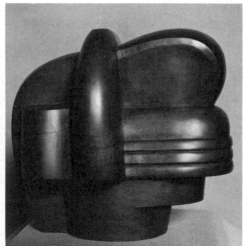

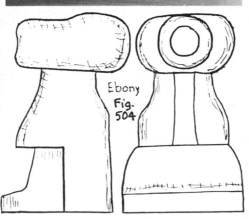

Ebony
Fig. 504

Fig. 503 (left). "Embrace," carved in satinwood in 1932, is an excellent abstraction. Figs. 504, 505 (below). "Spiritual Singer" is another abstraction, carved in 1930 (before Snoopy). Wheelock died in 1960, but his work lives on in museums and collections. It is well worth study for design ideas.

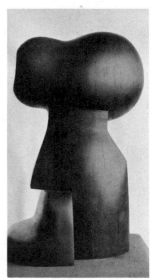

36

Fairy-Tale Panels Make Rackham 3D

PREVIOUS POLYGLOT PANELS of mine have had unit subjects; each element was independent. Rarely, I had a lady gnome picking flowers, or a frog seated on a basswood leaf, or a fish spitting at a bug, thus making a very small scene. However, this series of panels actually presents miniature scenes in polyglot fashion, although each panel has an identity, as does the group in a panel. The idea originated from my long-term admiration for Arthur Rackham (1867–1939), the famous English illustrator—a sort of British equivalent of Norman Rockwell in the United States. Rackham earned a tremendous following for his illustrations, both pen-and-ink and color, for fairy tales and fantastic stories. As a matter of fact, his books are still being reprinted, as well as biographies and bibliographies, because the younger generation has taken him up in the last ten years or so. I discovered his work in the Thirties, and collected such copies of his books as I could find and afford.

I first decided to carve selected illustrations done by Rackham for *Aesop's Fables*. I had a walnut panel of suitable size. Following my usual practice of selecting illustra-

tions, or portions of illustrations, I fit the spaces in the panel as I went along. (Rackham obviously had to design his illustrations to fit a particular format, so many were of the same shape and size, which would have led to a rather dull panel layout. By selecting a portion of some illustrations, I could get considerable variety into my adaptation, usually without changing dimension.) In a sense, these panels differ from earlier ones in that there is some background, some scene. This

Fig. 506. This partially carved Aesop panel illustrates the approach to design. Several new units have been drawn in at lower left to be certain the panel "comes out even" at the bottom. Designs must be added before grounding out previous ones to insure that necessary wood is not cut away or possibly needed overlaps left unresolved. This may require changing the scale of a particular design or omitting a portion, without, of course, omitting the major elements. Note that some of the top scenes are just blocked in, others completely modelled.

Fig. 507 (left). Aesop's fables in a walnut panel, 1 × 13 × 21 in (25 × 331 × 533 mm). The 28 scenes are adapted from Rackham drawings in a book of the same title.

Fig. 508 (right). Hans Christian Andersen's fairy tales are the basis of this 1 × 13 × 21-in (25 × 331 × 533-mm) walnut panel to match the Aesop one. This one required 23 scenes. Panels are carved to edge—there are no frames.

Fig. 509 (left). Grimm Bros. fairy tales are depicted in this walnut panel, 1 × 10 × 23 in (25 × 250 × 576 mm). There are 20 scenes.

Fig. 510 (right). Familiar fairy tales from various works make up this walnut panel, 1 × 10 × 23 in (25 × 250 × 576 mm). (Photography narrowed the panel bottom.) There are 21 scenes taken from Rackham drawings in various books.

Fig. 511. Here a single Rackham full-page illustration has been adapted to fit a slab of paulownia wood roughly 1 × 9½ × 11 in (25 × 225 × 280 mm), left as cut with the bark on one side and unsquared edges. The original drawing was longer at top and bottom to fit a book page, so upper tulips and the foreground stamp had to be slightly closed in. The original sketch depicts a dwarf in Kensington Gardens so startled by the flying arrival of Peter Pan that he has dropped the postage stamp he has been reading. Paulownia is a Chinese wood brought to the United States about half a century ago as a flowering tree of considerable beauty. The wood has a fairly strong grain, as can be seen. The carving was trenched from the edges.

Carving was done with a relatively small number of small "thin" tools, now readily available in the United States and easier to handle for close work of this kind than standard-length chisels. (See Chapter 2; they're also much cheaper to buy!) In most cases, I set-in the edges of a design with an ⅛-in (3-mm) firmer or equivalent flat small gouges to fit the contours, usually without preliminary outlining with a V-tool. (The outlining can be skipped in a case like this if the edge of the subject is to be modelled later anyway—modelling will remove any bruised surface fibres and the small thin tools don't bruise fibres to any extent anyway.) The background was set-in only a bit over ⅛ in (3 mm), so could be done in one step. Grounding was done with the small gouges leaving a scalloped surface. Modelling was also done with the small gouges and a small V-tool, assisted by my pocketknife, of course, because some details are quite small, and walnut must be treated with respect. For some lines, a small veiner gives softer effects. Finishing was two coats of sprayed matte varnish, followed by "antiquing" lines and background with dark-walnut Minwax® brushed on and wiped off the surface at once to leave stain in the lines and on background. Final finish was a coat or two of Kiwi® neutral shoe polish. With walnut, it is inadvisable to finish with oil because it makes the wood even darker, and it becomes necessary to exhibit the panel in very strong light.

When the first panel was finished, I was so taken with it that I decided to make a diptych (two panels side by side), so I did Andersen's fairy tales, again selecting from Rackham books. Then I was due to go to Mexico on vacation, so I took along several books and two walnut panels of a different size. Thus, we now have four, including one of the Grimm Bros. fairy tales and one of a mixed group. The panels have not been assembled, but hang individually. They do, however, occasion more comment when exhibited than have any of the earlier simple polyglot panels.

makes it necessary in some cases to "bleed" the edges of a particular unit—to make it disappear at the edges into the background. This is not always necessary; many Rackham pen-and-ink illustrations are already odd-shaped self-contained units. When it was necessary to change size of a unit, I used either the method of squares or point-to-point drawing. This might be easier by pantograph, if you have one, and can be done also by photostating. Incidentally, to keep from damaging a book in copying, it may also be advisable to photocopy—Xerox or whatever—an illustration rather than to attempt to trace it from the book. Same-size sketches were transferred to the wood usually by carbon paper from a Xerox.

III
Carvings from
Round the World

37

What Head Hunters Carved

"THE WILD MAN OF BORNEO"was a child-hood sideshow attraction, so I visualized Borneo as a very primitive place. There *were* head hunters there a few generations ago, and the country is still rather wild, but oil and timber are rapidly changing all that. It is practically impossible to move around inside the country except by boat, but the natives wear Western clothes, their dugouts now have outboard engines and the larger towns have electricity and radio. Borneo, the third largest island in the world (bigger than Great Britain and surpassed only by Greenland and New Guinea), is now divided between Malaysia, which has the old British protectorates of Brunei, Sabah and Sarawak, while Indonesia has the lion's share of the island, now called Kalimantan. There are about five million people in the Indonesian area, which is just below the Equator, the lowest population density in the world, although the civilization there is older than that on Java. About two million of the people are Malays, Chinese and other foreigners living in coastal cities and for short distances upriver. The Dayaks—the original "wild men"—live up the rivers and just inland from them in the jungle. They are of Mongol origin. They retain some of their original culture, despite district schools and changes in living standards, all with the help of the Indonesian government. Many still live in longhouses, supporting 100 families or more. Most villages are not visited by tourists, so carvings are not turned out for sale. In one village, which had not had white visitors in the dozen

years of its existence along the Mahakam river, we were actually initiated as Dayaks—I think largely to give their chiefs and medicine men practice. Examples of craftwork shown here I bought from the makers in most cases, and in a half-dozen or more remote villages to which we got by taking a river "taksi"—six of us, with our

Fig. 512. Three Dayak weapons, two swords and a wavy-bladed kris. Each has a carved-wood sheath, that of the kris also having dog-tooth dangles. The swords have deer-horn handles, carved and often decorated with hair. Their sheaths have a second sheath of light-colored fibre on the inner surface (visible at left), which houses a short knife with a long handle (left and right) used in carving.

Fig. 513 (above left). A closer view of the swords and sheaths shows the carving. The swords are hand-forged and sharpened on a stone, but very effective.

Figs. 514–516 (above). Miniature shields show typical tribal designs. On full-sized shields 5 ft (1.5 m) long, these designs would be carved before painting.

Figs. 517, 518 (left). Two female ancestral figures inside a medicine-man's necklace, with small ancestral carved figures separated by beads.

Figs. 519, 520 (below). Rice is harvested with a crescent-shaped knife held in a slit midway of a handle like this, carved to placate the rice god.

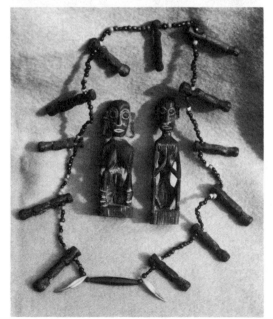

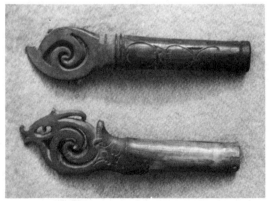

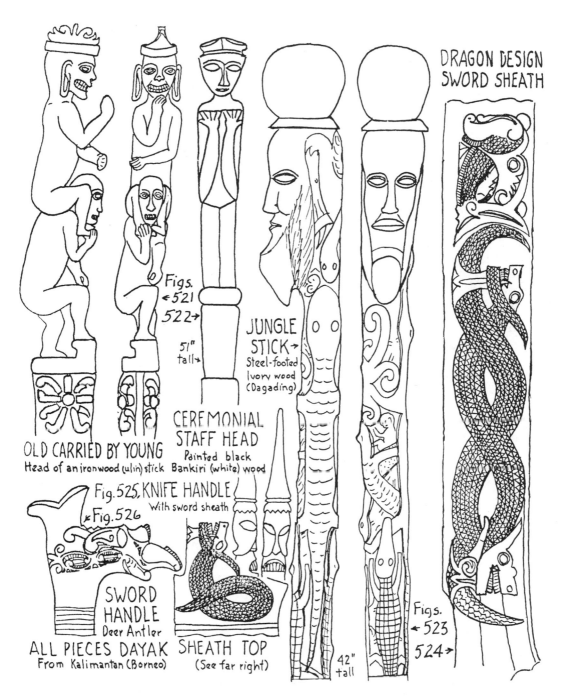

DRAGON DESIGN SWORD SHEATH

Figs. ←521 522→

51" tall→

JUNGLE STICK→
Steel-footed
Ivory wood
(Dagading)

CEREMONIAL
STAFF HEAD
Painted black
Bankiri (white) wood

OLD CARRIED BY YOUNG
Head of an ironwood (ulin) stick

Fig. 525, KNIFE HANDLE
With sword sheath
←Fig. 526

SWORD
HANDLE
Deer Antler
ALL PIECES DAYAK
From Kalimantan (Borneo)

SHEATH TOP
(See far right)

42" tall

Figs.
←523
524→

guides and the crew—for a week of sleeping on the crowded deck, without anything but mats under us. The food was heavily Indonesian but very good, bought along the way and cooked aboard—nobody got sick. Incidentally, once we'd been initiated, they showed us how a village lives, including planting and other ceremonies, as well as dances, so we got our share of anointments with river water, rice paste and chicken blood, especially about the face.

The men apparently do not use the bow. They carry a 6-ft (1.8-m) blowgun made from a straight hollowed branch and heavy enough also to be the handle of a spear—

Fig. 527 (above left). A chief's stick carved with interlaced crocs (Fig. 523), a house post of ulin showing age riding on the shoulders of youth (Fig. 521), and an elder's staff of soft wood, carved with a human figure and blackened (Fig. 522). Fig. 528 (above). Two ancestral figures, 10 in (254 mm) tall. The male has a crocodile carved on his back and the highly valued female carries a child and wears an earring of aluminum, probably a later addition. Fig. 529 (below left). The two sides of an antique spirit board (Fig. 532), which tells the owner when to travel, fight, hunt, or go head-hunting.

Fig. 530 (below). Spirit whistles of "lion" (puma) teeth are for animist medicine men to call animal spirits. Tooth is bored so blowing across the top makes a high-pitched sound. Top has scrimshawed motif.

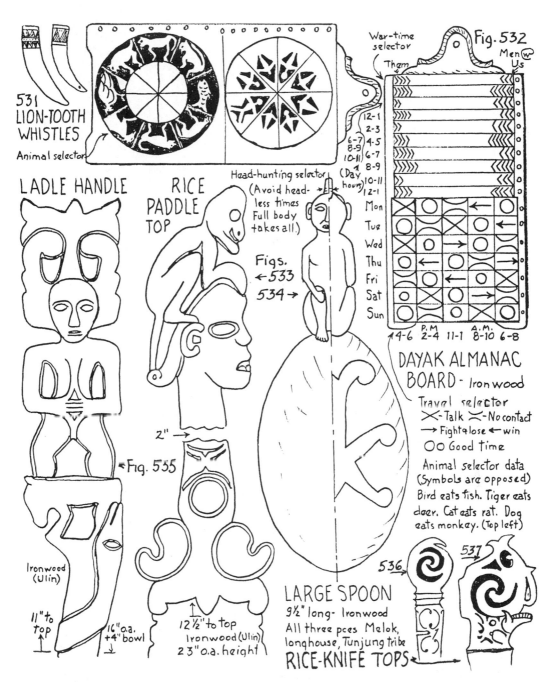

531 LION-TOOTH WHISTLES
Animal selector

War-time selector
Thom
Men Us

12-1
2-3
6-7
8-9
10-11
(Day hours)

Fig. 532

LADLE HANDLE

RICE PADDLE TOP

Head-hunting selector
(Avoid headless times. Full body takes all.)

Figs.
←533
534→

12-1
Mon
Tue
Wed
Thu
Fri
Sat
Sun

P.M. 4-6 2-4 11-1 8-10 6-8 A.M.

DAYAK ALMANAC BOARD - Ironwood

Travel selector
✕- Talk ✕- No contact
→ Fight & lose ← win
OO Good time

Animal selector data
(Symbols are opposed)
Bird eats fish. Tiger eats deer. Cat eats rat. Dog eats monkey. (Top left)

2"→

←Fig. 555

Ironwood (Ulin)

11" to top

16" o.a. +4" bowl

12½" to top
Ironwood (Ulin)
23" o.a. height

536

537

LARGE SPOON
9½" long - Ironwood
All three pces Melok, longhouse, Tunjung tribe
RICE-KNIFE TOPS

sort of like our rifle and bayonet combination. They also carry swords in elaborately carved sheaths. On the inner face of the sheath, there is a second, smaller sheath for a knife with a blade about 4 in (102 mm) long and a twig handle about ½ × 15 in (13 × 381 mm). They do their carving with the latter, putting the carved head of the handle into an armpit, holding the blade in their fingers, and *moving the wood under the knife*. It seems awkward at first, but the blade is rigidly held by the extended handle, and the carving is as intricate and well done as we can do by our reverse method. I watched a medicine man carving a sheath like one sketched, and am still amazed.

174   BORNEO

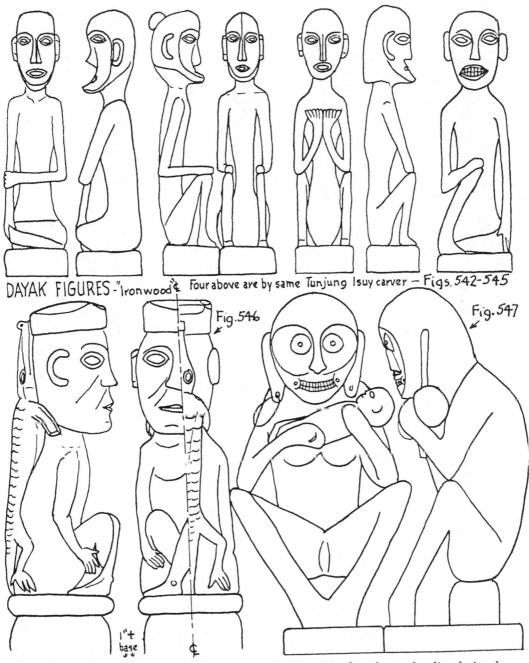

DAYAK FIGURES - "Ironwood" Four above are by same Tunjung Isuy carver - Figs. 542-545

Fig. 546

Fig. 547

1"+ base

¢

Figs. 538, 539 (opposite page, above left). Most Dayak ladles have single ancestral figures for handles, usually in the round. However, the one at top right has a woman with child, flanked by a monkey and a bird, in pierced low relief, and a decorated edge—it is more bowl than ladle. The three at lower right, Fig. 541, have figures facing in opposite directions. (Figs. 539 and 540 were photographed through glass in museum cases, hence suffer in clarity.) Fig. 541 (far left) is an assembly of house posts.

The Dayaks formerly lived in longhouses, some several hundred feet long, up on stilts above the ground, and consisting primarily of a long gallery with a series of cells off it, each cell housing a family. Some longhouses are now being abandoned, which explains how I obtained some of the old carved ladles and posts, pictured here.

Fig. 549 (above). A small ladle with seated figure for a handle (see Fig. 534). Figs. 548, 550, 551 (left). Ancestral figures, all with sketched patterns at right or in Figs. 542–545 on page 175.

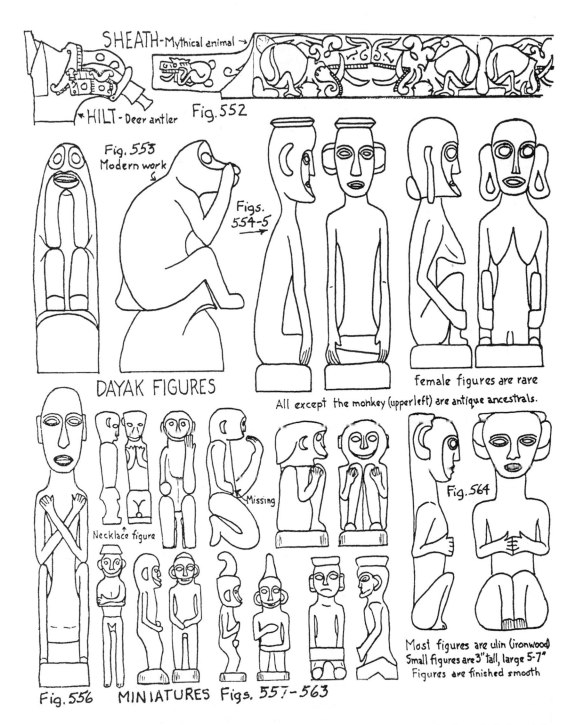

SHEATH—Mythical animal →

*HILT—Deer antler   Fig. 552

Fig. 553
Modern work

Figs.
554-5 →

DAYAK FIGURES

female figures are rare

All except the monkey (upper left) are antique ancestrals.

Fig. 564

Necklace figure

Missing

Most figures are ulin (ironwood)
Small figures are 3" tall, large 5-7"
Figures are finished smooth

Fig. 556   MINIATURES Figs. 557-563

NOTE: Ancestor worship is a major element of the traditional Dayak religion. Not only are ancestral figures in houses (in the longhouse, each family has a room off a frontal porch or corridor), but also small ones are carried for good luck and necklaces with ancestral figures are worn by medicine men. Older people are also venerated by the young. The religion is animistic, involving veneration of the crocodile, the hornbill, and other animals and their spirits. Usual images are carved in ulin (local word meaning iron-wood because of its hardness), which is also used for the large guard posts at entrances to houses (Figs. 527 and 540). Men's houses are decorated with the elaborate carved and painted scrolls shown on shields of Fig. 518 that identify the tribe, often combined with mythical beasts.

38

Bali—Where Carving Is Beauty

EACH TIME I go to Bali, I am impressed all over again by the variety and uniqueness of its art. Much of the present-day work is cranked out in factories for the tourist trade, but it is still distinctive and very well detailed, and the better pieces are still in good wood although most of it must be imported. Bali must depend on the tourist business for its very life; there is little there to export. It is a Hindu island a short distance from far-bigger Moslem Java at its closest point. And on the other side there are also Moslem and Christian islands. Bali's five million people live a life separate from the rest of Indonesia, and always have, for even their Hindu is a very special brand. The story is told that when a Dutch war yacht pulled into Bali in the late 16th century, the entire crew jumped ship and it took the captain two years to round them up and re-sail. Many people since have also considered Bali a sort of heaven on earth.

The tourists, who are usually there for short periods, never get to the back country, where much of the carving is still done. But because of them, Bali produces several distinct types of carvings. One is the traditional images of gods and demons, ornate, over-detailed and complex, like the Barong, silhouetted female heads, and bone carvings. Another type consists of floral and animal panels like the nameplates, the picture frame and the recorder. A third consists of quite modern items like the frogs and birds. A fourth includes very distinctive three-dimensional sculptures of people and gods, some attenuated, some fat and squat.

Much of the carving is done in macassar ebony imported from the Celebes, now called Suluwesi. Other woods include black ebony, a light-colored wood resembling maple and a native dark red wood. A peculiarity of the island appears to be that almost every male can carve, and a high percentage of the compounds have carved wood and carved stone (lava) in them. The women weave beautiful things of reeds and grasses, as well as textiles, and assist in finishing wood carvings, while the sexes collaborate in making elaborate temple displays.

Even in 1970, when I first visited Bali, the economy was poor; I bought a 9 × 15-in (229 × 381-mm) pierced panel there for less than $10, while the same-size Maori panel in New Zealand cost ten times as much—and it was not pierced. Today, prices have risen, but are still very low to the well-heeled tourists, so Balinese carvers stay reasonably busy, but don't make much. Their work is hawked on the beaches and in town by skilled salespeople. The result of all this is that even in the so-called "factories" the carvers sit on the floor and hold the carvings with their toes, and the finish-sanding and polishing is done by women and children—or even by the beach peddler as he waits for business. Kiwi® shoe polish is the universal finish, and the typical carver has a few long thin tools without handles and a club whittled into a mallet. Carvers never seem to be

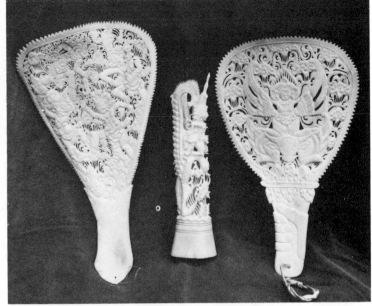

copying a pattern, although they obviously have a design in mind as they work. It is obvious that many of the carvings are adjusted to fit the available wood, so pieces tend to have triangular bases—as split from a log—rather than the rectangular bases ours have because we start with a plank. They achieve incredible detail, as shown above.

Figs. 565, 566 (top). Cow bone is a traditional carving material in Bali. The two at left are antiques, a goddess and a demon, while the one at center right is an image of Siva. The two fans are delicate pierced work from cow shoulder blade, now rare and expensive. They depict scenes from the Ramayana, because Bali is strongly Hindu. Figs. 567, 568 (above). An elongated dancer (pattern on next page) 18 in (457 mm) tall, in macassar ebony, and a high-relief teak frame are typical modern carving. Time is unimportant to the Balinese carver, who delicately uses small chisels to produce pieces like these.

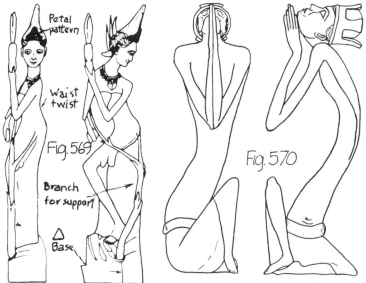

Petal pattern

Waist twist

Fig. 569

Branch for support

Base

Fig. 570

Fig. 569 (far left). Dancer pattern for Fig. 567. Figs. 570 (left), 573 (center, below). A priest figure, 16 in (406 mm) tall, in a light-colored wood, is again attenuated. Figs. 571, 572, 574 (left, right). Antique spoons from the countryside are not ebony but stained to look like it.

SPOON TOPS
Bali - Antique
Black.

Black areas are pierced

Fig. 575 (left). The Barong, a good demon depicted in a familiar dance, is a stylized lion played by two men. His elaborate costume, full of detail, is meticulously copied in this 5-in (127-mm) macassar ebony figure. Fig. 576-577 (above). These unusual frogs are new designs, highly polished. They are by Ida Bagus Tilem, premier Balinese carver, who also designed the frame of Fig. 568.

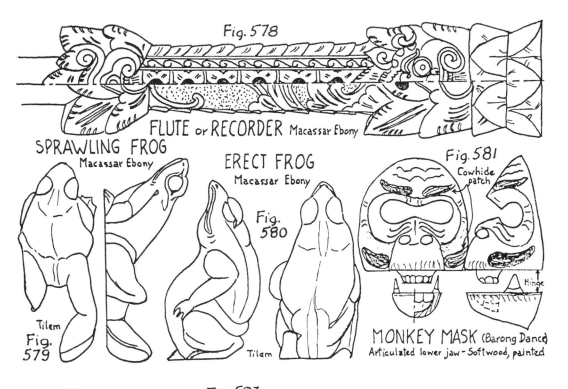

Fig. 578

FLUTE or RECORDER Macassar Ebony

SPRAWLING FROG
Macassar Ebony

ERECT FROG
Macassar Ebony

Fig. 581

Cowhide patch

Tilem

Fig. 579

Fig. 580

Tilem

Hinge

MONKEY MASK (Barong Dance)
Articulated lower jaw - Softwood, painted

Fig. 582

Fig. 583

FEMALE HAND Macassar Ebony & BARONG (Good Demon) - Black Ebony. Traditional pieces contrast

Tilem

Fig. 584 (right). Almost a foot (305 mm) long, this flute or recorder is another floral design (see sketch above). It is produced in quantity (but still by hand) for tourists.

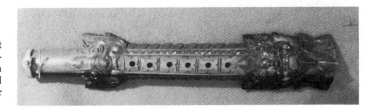

HIGH-RELIEF CARVINGS *from* BALI

Fig. 585 - PICTURE FRAME - Teak - 1⅛ x 9¾ x 10¾"

NAMEPLATE - Black Ebony - 14" long

Fig. 586

csscaȼ

TANGERMAN

Tilem

LOW-RELIEF CARVINGS *from* BALI

Note differences be-tween these two

9" tall
¾" thick
⅞@ back

Figs. 587-8

9¼" tall
⅝" thick @ back

Fig. 589

13" tall - ⅞" thick

Fig. 590 (left). Tropical countries, in particular, have trees subject to parasites that distort growth. Here are three such sections, carved into a frog, a fantail gold-fish, and a cock. The fat little owl is also Balinese.

Figs. 591, 592 (above). Even a common design will be changed by particular carvers. There goddess heads are good examples; study details in these two photos and in Figs. 587–589, which are patterns for them. All are in quite low relief and in macassar ebony: the one at left is ⅞ in (22 mm) thick, 13 in (331 mm) tall; the pair at right is ⅜ in (10 mm) thick, 9 in (229 mm) tall. Note that the pair don't match. Fig. 564 (right). This ebony nameplate, 14 in (356 mm), is massive, with raised lettering and requires about three days to carve. Figs. 594, 595 (right). The garuda is a legendary bird that carried Vishnu, thus a good-luck symbol. Here are two versions; the left one in unpainted ebony, the right one in painted soft wood. Note the extreme detail.

Fig. 596 (right). Small Balinese duck. Fig. 597 (below). Sketched in Fig. 607, this feeding scene illustrates the way in which carvings are reinforced. Note the several branches that support the heavier bird. Fig. 598 (center). The two flanking birds are typical modern designs, while the center one is a more elaborate older one, a complex feeding scene patterned in Fig. 605. These birds are in ebony with triangular bases with rounded corners. Fig. 599 (center, right). These birds are in a hard light-colored wood about like our maple and again have triangular bases. All these birds are about 8 in (213 mm) tall.

Fig. 604 (right). The rural landscape of Bali in rice-growing areas has many flocks of ducks like these (Fig. 596 also). They are herded out to the paddies in the morning and back at night like sheep, and earn their keep by eating bugs. These are small figures, only 2–3 in (51–76 mm) tall and relatively simple carving projects, but make attractive shelf spots.

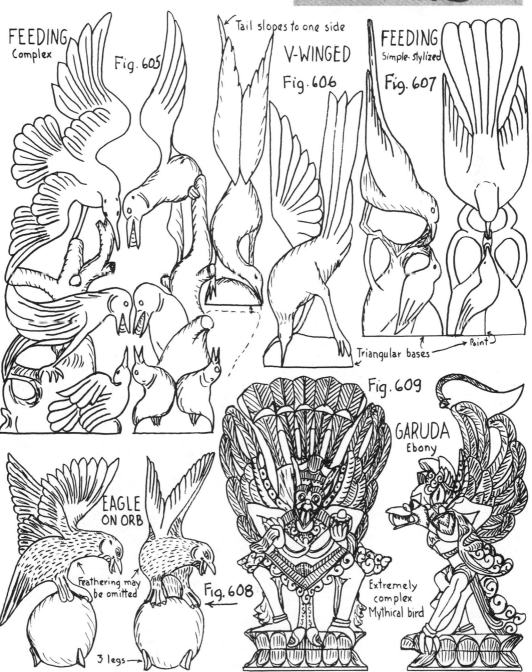

FEEDING
Complex

Fig. 605

Tail slopes to one side

V-WINGED
Fig. 606

FEEDING
Simple-stylized

Fig. 607

Triangular bases   Point

Fig. 609

EAGLE
ON ORB

Feathering may
be omitted

Fig. 608

3 legs

GARUDA
Ebony

Extremely
complex
Mythical bird

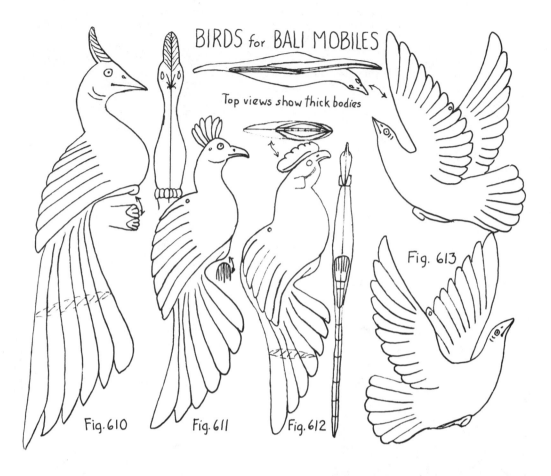

BIRDS for BALI MOBILES

Top views show thick bodies

Fig. 610

Fig. 611

Fig. 612

Fig. 613

Figs. 610–615. The Balinese carve a variety of birds in thin sections of macassar ebony or lighter-colored woods, usually designed to be single-unit mobiles. Those at lower right are softer wood and painted, but most are simply polished. I have grouped them in 6- or 8-bird mobiles very successfully.

39

Where Sandalwood Is Carved

NUSA TENGGARA is the collective name for the southeastern islands of Indonesia. They are little known and infrequently visited today, and the only one to be mentioned in the Western press is Timor, where Indonesia is still trying to bring under control the former Portuguese eastern portion. Other major islands in the group are Sumba, Flores, Sumbawa and Lombok, all but the last much larger than Bali, which is better known as a tourist haven.

In the group also is the natural-preserve island of Komodo, where the giant lizard called the Komodo dragon lives, and influences some of the local art even as far away as Timor. These islands were all important trading locales several hundred years ago.

Fig. 616 (right). A mythological lizard is carved in high relief on this 7½-in (191-mm) sandalwood panel from East Timor. It is obviously based on the Komodo dragon, which can reach lengths of 12 ft (3.66 m). Fig. 617 (far right). Sandalwood forms this modern copy of an old East Timor design. It is 20 in (508 mm) tall and depicts a Komodo dragon standing on the shoulders of a squatting man, with two caricatured heads between theirs. Workmanship is excellent, and sandalwood is expensive, as always.

There are only seven million people, and one and a half million of those live on Lombok, next to Bali and are influenced (one time largely governed) by it. These islands tend to be mountainous at one end and grassy at the other, with long and definite dry and wet seasons. In many respects, they are a hundred years behind the more familiar islands in development; roads and communications are sparse and very poor. Back-country travel, where there are "roads," is by horse, truck or jeep, and there are still villages of almost aboriginal natives in the mountains.

Yet Timor was once famous for its sandalwood, as was Sumbawa. Together, they exported sandalwood to China and India for more than 300 years. Timor got so much gold from China for the wood that Portuguese and Dutch invaders scoured the island to find the mines. Kupang, capital of Timor, was a famed whaling port early in the 19th century, stopping place for British and American whalers, and the port where a very disgruntled Captain Bligh finally landed, 6,500 km (4,000 mi) after the mutiny on the *Bounty*. Nowadays, Kupang is thriving again; there is some oil on Timor. The Indonesian government is pushing handicrafts, including woodcarving—and in expensive sandalwood. Yet Kupang didn't get street lights until 1971! We had a suite in a *losmen* (inn) filled with fancy West Sumatran carved furniture, but electricity only in the evening (and not reliable then); we had to go out for food. Timor's present population is about 900,000, its principal products cattle and maize (corn). It took some searching (we were not permitted in East Timor), but I did find modern woodcarvings—some of which are copies of traditional ones—and several antique pieces, including a horse that shows Chinese influence although this island, and adjacent Sumba and Flores, raise small horses for export. These three islands are mainly Christian, and the missionaries discouraged traditional woodcarving which depicted idols. Sumba is very Islamic—a girl who appears there in halter and shorts may be stoned—many women there still wear the veil. But Hin-

Fig. 618 (below, left). The knife at left was probably Dutch-made, but has its handle carved into an ancestral figure on Sumba (see Fig. 625). The tobacco box in center, 1½ × 3½ × 4 in (38 × 89 × 102 mm), has top and body each monolithic, with triangles of darker wood inlaid on the box. The top is decorated with beads and held with a carrying cord. The fly whisk is deer horn and horse hair and comes from the Batak of North Sumatra. Fig. 619 (below). This caparisonned horse from East Timor is one piece including the base (Fig. 620), 10 in (254 mm) tall.

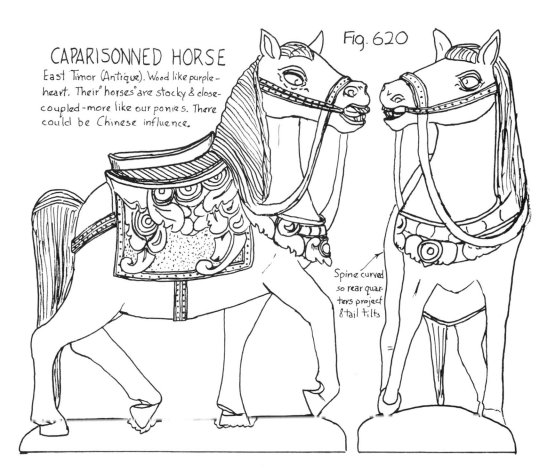

CAPARISONNED HORSE

East Timor (Antique). Wood like purple-heart. Their" horses" are stocky & close-coupled—more like our ponies. There could be Chinese influence.

Fig. 620

Spine curved so rear quarters project & tail tilts

duism encourages woodcarving and depiction of gods—the reason for so much carving in Bali and to a lesser extent in Lombok. Sumbawa, incidentally, was practically wiped out by a volcanic eruption in 1815; its population has now recovered to 320,000 and it exports sandalwood—and horses.

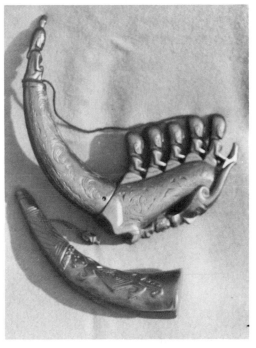

Fig. 621 (right). The water-buffalo horn at bottom has been carved and converted into a container with a wooden head for a stopper, the Timor equivalent of our powder horn and possibly as old. It has a dragon lizard on one side, as sketched in Fig. 624. With it, for comparison sake, is the much more elaborately carved and mounted medicine horn of the Batak of North Sumatra (see Chap. 40).

MOTIFS from a TOBACCO JAR
Sumba Island (Antique)
Hard, dark-red wood

BOX & CAP (below)-Lombok
Deer antler, hollowed - Antique.

Fig. 622 & 623 →

Cap →

Note: This figure represents the family. Ovals may contain faces.

Note: Warriors have spears & parangs, wear sarongs

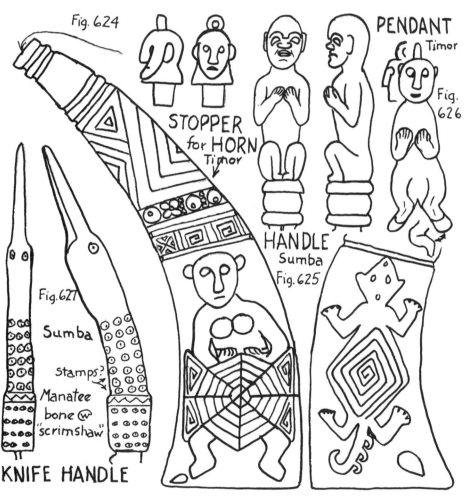

Fig. 624

STOPPER for HORN Timor

PENDANT Timor

Fig. 626

HANDLE Sumba Fig. 625

Fig. 627

Sumba

stamps?

Manatee bone @ "scrimshaw"

KNIFE HANDLE

Fig. 628 (below). In a heavy dark wood, this antique tobacco jar was carved in Sumba. It is 11½ in (292 mm) tall, with the top laced to the bottom by a carrying cord. The head is crude, but the relief carvings are not (see Fig. 623).

Fig. 631 (lower left). At left in this group is an antique and unusual carved bone box from Lombok, 1½ × 2½ × 4½ in (38 × 64 × 115 mm), with tight-fitting top. The design looks Balinese (see Fig. 622). Beside it is a dagger from Sumba with a shaft of carved and scrimshawed manatee bone! Beside it is a bone case from Timor, sketched at right in Fig. 630. The figure and mask next to them are deer horn, made by the Batak of North Sumatra. Figs. 629, 632 (below). Carved horn, with an ebony and horn top. This box comes from Lombok. The relief carving on the side is a serpent. It is 2½ × 5½ in (64 × 140 mm).

LIME BOX
Bone & wood

wood

Scrimshaw   Bone / Timor

wood

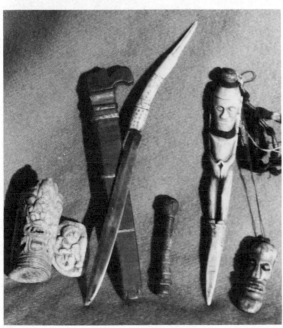

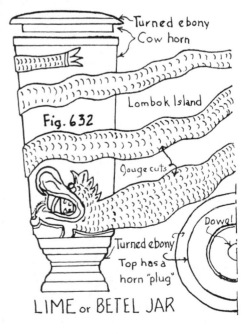

Turned ebony
Cow horn

Fig. 632

Lombok Island

Gouge cuts

Dowel

Turned ebony
Top has a
horn "plug"

LIME or BETEL JAR

40

Sumatra and Java Patterns Change with the Tribe

INDONESIA is a country of more than 13,600 islands in the Southeast Pacific, freed in 1948 from the Dutch. It has almost 140 million inhabitants and includes half of New Guinea, world's second-largest island (Greenland is bigger), the third-largest—Borneo, and the fifth-largest—Sumatra. The islands stretch over a distance equal to the width of the United States, and total 5 million sq mi in area, only 25% of which is land, ranging from 5,000-metre (16,000-ft) mountains in Irian Jaya to steamy jungle swamps in Sumatra. Some 400 volcanoes, 70 to 80 still active, are strewn over its length. There are about ten major eruptions in an average year; they provide the lava rock that Hindus on Java have carved for more than 750 years. The population is in 366 ethnic groups including emigrants from China, India, Mongolia, Arabia, Polynesia, Portugal and Holland, among others. With such diversity, crafts are similarly diverse.

Jakarta, the capital, is on Java, which is a relatively smaller island and very densely populated, but Sumatra, with only 21 million, seems to have been the source of its original culture. It is about a third central swamp, yet has mountains to 10,000 ft (3,000 m). It was sending gifts to China as early as 441 A.D. and was visited by Marco Polo. There is some vestigial woodcarving being done on Java, but not much by comparison with Sumatra, where two areas are still very active, producing totally different

kinds of work although they are relatively near each other. One is the Batak country around Lake Toba, and the adjacent mountains of northern Sumatra, now rapidly deteriorating because it is overrun by tourists; the other is the Minangkabau area of West Sumatra. The Batak were once the cannibals of Sumatra, although they ate enemies only for ritual. Their religion was animist, and they still retain elements of that belief overlaid with Christianity. The

Fig. 633. The entrance ell of the Bukit Tinghi "town hall," typical Minangkabau, with all vertical surfaces covered with carved and painted scrollwork panels.

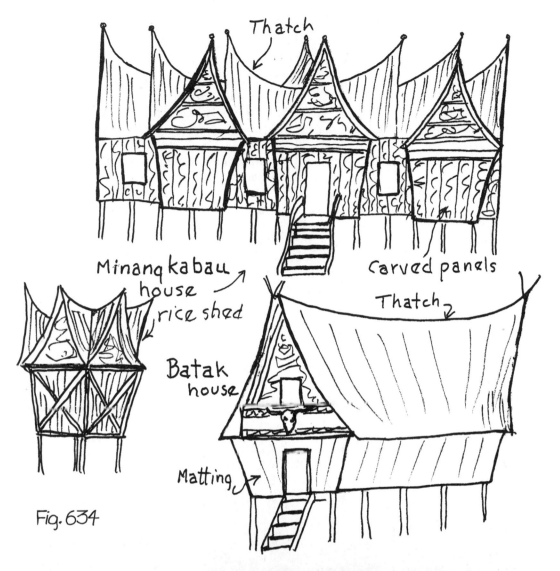

Thatch

Minangkabau house

carved panels

Thatch

rice shed

Batak house

Matting

Fig. 634

Figs. 634 (above), 635 (right). Minankabau and Batak houses are very different, although they are on the same island—the first being elled, multi-peaked, and faced with panel carvings, the second having a single swayback roof and a frontal gallery. At right is a Batak house front with gallery, showing more limited designs. The cylinders at left are drums of a gamelan orchestra—one player's head, visible at right, gives scale.

society is patriarchal and patrilineal, fiercely so. The Minangkabau, on the other hand, are Islamic, matriarchal and matrilineal—women own all the property and inherit it, although Islam is strongly patriarchal.

The Bataks are mountain men, farmers and fishermen; the Minangkabau basically rice planters. The Bataks are of proto-Malay origin (they come from the border between Burma and Thailand); the Minangkabau are Malay. Strangely, both areas are strongly democratic. There are about 600,000 Bataks, 20% living on one large island, Samosir, and in Lake Toba, now the goal of tourists. There are about five million Minangkabau (one quarter of the Sumatran total). "Batak" is from the Malay word for robber (because of their fierceness); "Minangkabau" means victorious buffalo, and from their language has grown the present national language of In-

donesia—an effort to establish communication among about 750 dialects differing so much that villagers in adjacent towns often cannot talk to one another.

Both of these groups can read and write, but their woodcarving has developed very differently, the Batak being what Westerners would call tribal and primitive, while that of the Minangkabau is quite formal and sophisticated, classical in form. Most Batak art consists of small, three-dimensional utilitarian objects, such as staffs, pots, medicine horns and sheaths, while that of the Minangkabau includes relief and pierced panels intended usually for house and furniture decoration.

Both cultures have been influenced by Oriental and Indian cultures, but have re-

Figs. 636, 637. Pierce-carved elements for shutters that replace glass in a Minangkabau palace. They are painted in pinks, blues, yellows, and greens. The one at right can be adapted for narrower shutters by dropping the side panels. They may be 3 ft (914 mm) tall.

tained their individuality in myth and form. The Batak carve recognizable human and animal forms, while the Minangkabau content themselves with floral variations. The Batak combine wood with horn, hide and other materials, while the Minangkabau work almost exclusively in wood. There seem to be no large figures.

Both cultures have houses raised above the ground on posts as much as 10 ft (3 m). Both had thatched roofs (now changing to corrugated terne plate.) Both house as many as 40 or 50 people. But the Batak house has a single ridgepole and rises at the ends in an arc, as do houses among the Tarajas in the Celebes and in Thailand, said by some to originate from the shape of

Fig. 638 (right). A double picture frame 8 × 11 in (203 × 280 mm). Figs. 639, 640 (below). These two panels are carver's samples, thus unpainted, although the one below has a darkened background. They are about 7½ in (191 mm) wide, with carving about ⅜ in (10 mm) deep. They are typical of the floral scrollwork carved for house faces and shutters.

Fig. 641 (left). Elaborate floral letters like these are a Minangkabau standard. They are made in various sizes and finished in color like panels. These are about 3 in (76 mm) tall. Others may be 2 in (51 mm) to 6 in (152 mm) or more. Sketches below show the pattern applied.

642

TYPICAL CARVED LETTERS- West Sumatra

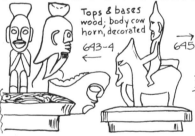

Tops & bases wood; body cow horn, decorated

693-4 ←   → 695

LIME JARS-Tops & motif- N.S.

696

Fig 651

BETEL JAR

Bataks of N. Sumatra scratch designs like these on bamboo or horn sides of cylinders. See also above right.

LIME BOTTLE   647 & 648

LIME-BOTTLE TOP- Incised Wood Batak - N. Sumatra (Bottle at far left)

Fig 649

650

BEAST of MYTH
Both designs from Sultan's Palace, Tenggarong, Kalimantan (Island of Borneo)

DRAGON MOTIF

Fig. 652 (right). This oval panel is in suriana wood like the others, and is 10 × 18 in (254 × 457 mm). Most of the designs pictured are traditional, but they are adapted to fit space or even modified on occasion, and they may be sold to other Indonesian islands thousands of miles away.

the horns of the water buffalo, which is both a working and a worshipped animal. The Minangkabau house has multiple roof points rising along the ridgepole, and may have ells off it with similar peaks. The Batak house is entered from the end and is without side windows, while the Minangkabau is entered from the side and usually has window openings as well as doors, so is much lighter. The Batak house has a gallery over the entrance, which may be both decorated and trimmed with a mythic protective figure, water-buffalo horns,

or a carved buffalo head. However, this decoration does not begin to compare with that of a Minangkabau house, which will have all vertical surfaces carved and painted in scroll-like patterns in organized panels. The Bataks carve scrolls as well, but on small objects and more nearly as scratching.

This is, I am sure, more than you wanted to know about the background of these two cultures, and more than I wanted to say, but it is essential in comparing the woodcarving of the two and the

Figs. 653, 654. Batak lime boxes can be complex combinations of wood with bamboo, horn, or leather, or they can be gourd with a carved wood top. The motifs on these are sketched in Figs. 643–649. Scrollwork is shallow and filled with color. The rider on horseback as a top is common. The gourd carries the Batak calendar—which was good.

Fig. 655. Quite unusual are these two Batak carrying cases. They are wood cylinders with ends of leather and horn, plus thin bamboo jackets that are scrimshawed with mystic scrolls. The taller has a carved wooden cap and is 4 in (101 mm) tall.

Figs. 656, 657 (below and center). Two Batak fiddles and their carver. They are one piece except for the top face (see Fig. 664) and have old Dutch coins inlaid. A closeup of the fiddle head and a ceremonial staff, 4 ft (1.3 m) tall, shows similar design. Note the seated top figure. The staff is supposed to have magic power. Fig. 658 (right). These shorter magic wands or batons (upper ends only shown) are 24 and 28 in (610 and 711 mm) long, and depict a series of men riding horses, some of the horses having snake-like bodies. They are dyed black, polished, and carried only by chiefs.

reasons behind it. Woodcarving is like other crafts concentrated in villages or areas, the best known being Pandi Silkat in West Sumatra, which exports decorative panels to a wide market, particularly in the East. Almost all work is done by hand and the craft is passed from father to son and by the apprentice system. Tools nowadays are all of steel, but are limited in number and jealously guarded. The work area may be a table or bench for relief carving, with the carvers seated on stools or benches, or it may simply be the floor, with the carver using his legs as a vise as they do in Bali. Tools tend to be very slim and long and have no handles. They are driven by what we'd call a small club. There are no dust collectors or other amenities; light may be very poor, so the workday is dawn to dark. However, in Pandi Silkat, all carving shops seem to have dressed lumber to carve.

Earlier carving by the Batak was done in hard woods like ebony, but now is often in softer woods painted black—tourists don't know the difference. A common wood in both areas is suriana, something like our white pine, but harder. Paints were originally earth and vegetable dyes like those

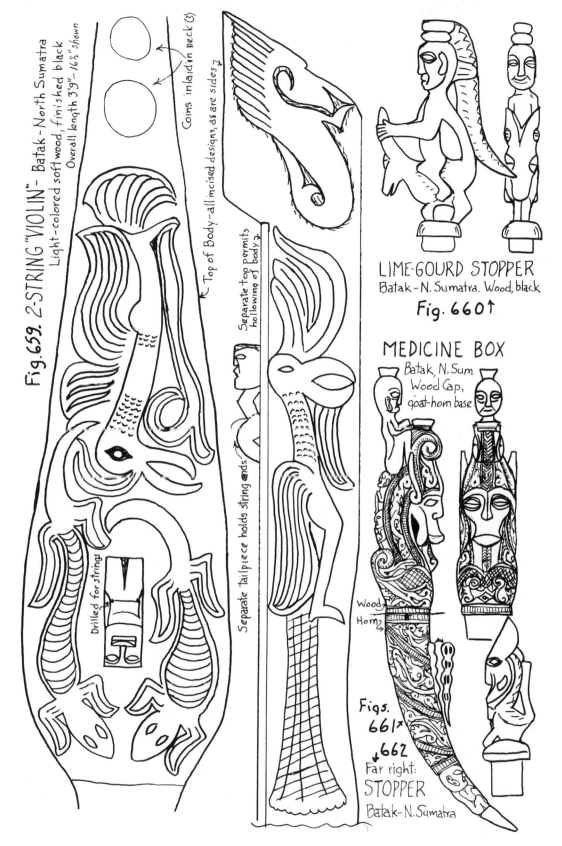

Fig. 659. 2-STRING "VIOLIN" - Batak - North Sumatra
Light-colored softwood, finished black
Overall length 3'9" - 16½" shown

Coins inlaid in neck (3)

Top of Body - all incised designs, as are sides

Separate top permits hollowing of body

Separate tailpiece holds string ends

Drilled for strings

LIME-GOURD STOPPER
Batak - N. Sumatra. Wood, black
Fig. 660 ↑

MEDICINE BOX
Batak, N. Sum.
Wood Cap,
goat-horn base

Wood
Horn

Figs.
661 ↗
↓ 662
Far right:
STOPPER
Batak - N. Sumatra

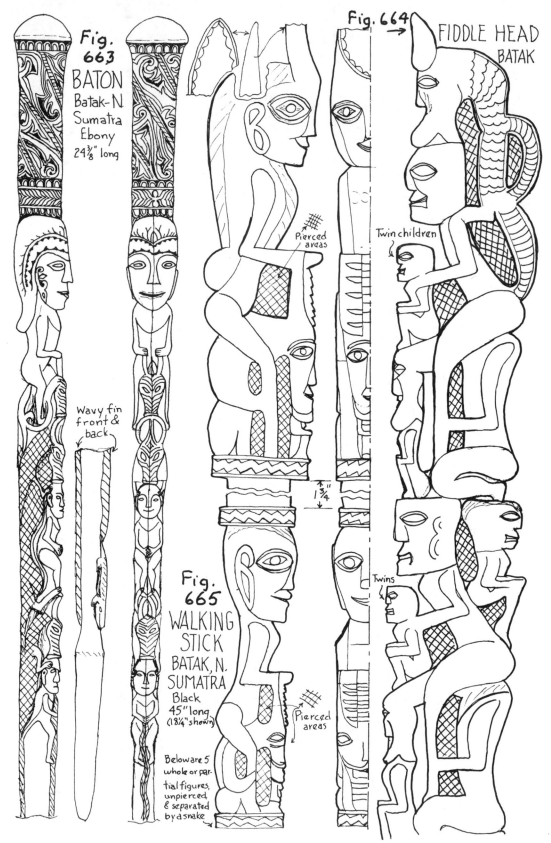

Fig. 663
BATON
Batak- N.
Sumatra
Ebony
24⅜" long

Wavy fin
front &
back

Fig. 664

FIDDLE HEAD
BATAK

Twin children

Pierced
areas

1¾"

Twins

Fig.
665
WALKING
STICK
BATAK, N.
SUMATRA
Black
45" long
(18¼" shown)

Below are 5
whole or par-
tial figures,
unpierced
& separated
by a snake

Pierced
areas

for textiles, but are now commercial colors, which tend to be brighter. Earlier finishing methods have yielded to sandpaper, commercial finishes and Kiwi® shoe polish. Some shops even have planers and power saws, although they must be big shops or co-ops to share the cost. There may also be local factors who handle export sales, and of course the better salesmen handle the business even in small shops. And the craft is losing recruits, particularly in West Sumatra, where the matriarchal society offers less incentive for aggressive younger men. They migrate to Java or big cities.

Examples of West Sumatran designs shown here are in some cases unpainted because I bought what were in effect a carver's trial or pattern pieces. Some of these would normally be repeated on a much larger panel or incorporated in a door shutter (common instead of glass). Variety is almost endless, but these convey

the idea. Also, I have not sketched the Minangkabau designs because they can readily be copied from head-on photographs and enlarged to whatever size you may prefer. However, on the Batak designs, I have tried to detail the elaborate scroll patterns, which in some cases are so shallow that they do not photograph well.

Jakarta, like most major cities, is overcrowded, hurried, and dirty, despite modern buildings and hotels. It has, however, a flea-market area that is like a Near East casbah in the variety of merchandise offered, particularly in woodcarvings, not only from Java but from the rest of Indonesia and who knows where else. Some of the items I bought there are pictured here, with my guess as to their origin when I found the seller over-willing to assign any origin I seemed to want. The point is that the pieces were of interest for their design, so let their ancestry remain clouded.

Figs. 666, 667. Batak medicine boxes are composites of buffalo or other horn and carved wood. The horn carries scratch-carved mystic scrolls (see Figs. 668, 669) and is pegged to a complicated carved wooden head. (There may also be a figure of wood inserted at the small end of the horn.) The two parts are also connected by a carrying cord. Heads depict men riding in boats. The three-head one is 13 in (330 mm) long, the five-man one 15 in (381 mm).

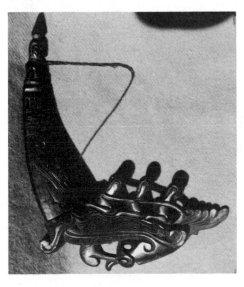

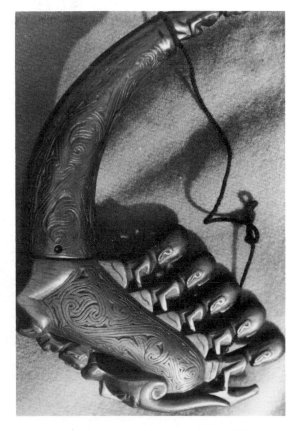

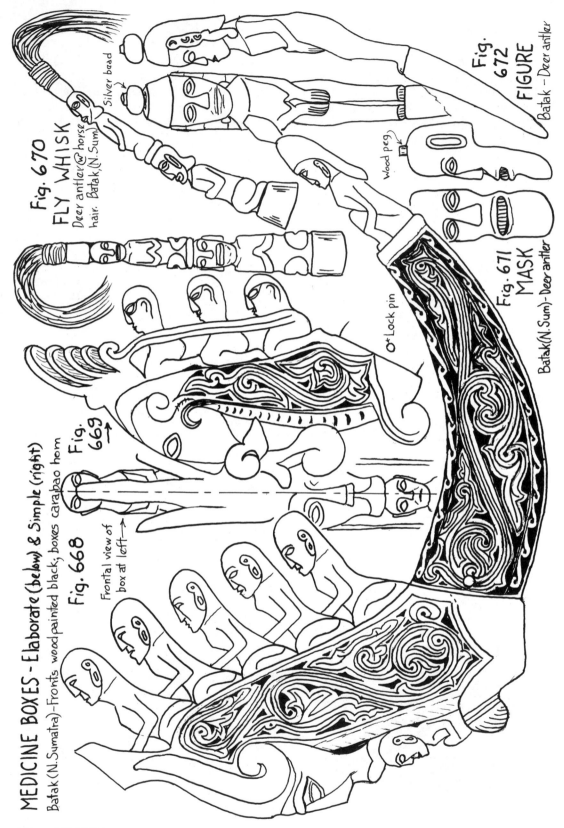

MEDICINE BOXES - Elaborate (below) & Simple (right)
Batak (N.Sumatra)-Fronts wood painted black; boxes carabao horn

Frontal view of box at left→

Fig. 668

Fig. 669→

♂ Lock pin

Fig. 670
FLY WHISK
Deer antler @ horse
hair. Batak (N. Sum.)

Silver bead

Fig. 671
MASK
Batak (N.Sum.)-Deer antler

Wood peg

Fig. 672
FIGURE
Batak - Deer antler

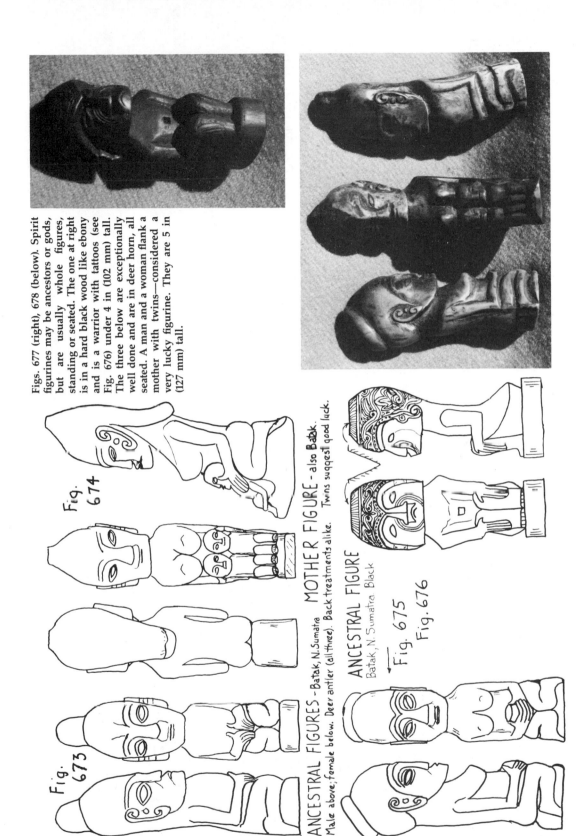

Figs. 677 (right), 678 (below). Spirit figurines may be ancestors or gods, but are usually whole figures, standing or seated. The one at right is in a hard black wood like ebony and is a warrior with tattoos (see Fig. 676) under 4 in (102 mm) tall. The three below are exceptionally well done and are in deer horn, all seated. A man and a woman flank a mother with twins—considered a very lucky figurine. They are 5 in (127 mm) tall.

Fig. 674

Fig. 673

ANCESTRAL FIGURES - Batak, N.Sumatra
Male above; female below. Deer antler (all three). Back treatments alike.

MOTHER FIGURE - also Batak.
Twins suggest good luck.

ANCESTRAL FIGURE
Batak, N. Sumatra. Black

Fig. 675

Fig. 676

SOME CARVING DESIGNS FROM JAVA

MEDALLIONS
Java-Teak
Med. relief

Figs. 679-81

BIRD PANEL Fig. 682
Java-Teak
Pierced relief

Figs. 683-4

TURTLE CHARM-Fig. 685
Java Mac. Ebony

KRIS HANDLE-Sumatra
KRIS HANDLE Sumatra

SPOON HANDLES
Java - Pierced cow horn

KNEE-HEAD Sumatra

Fig. 688

Deer antler

Deer antler

Fig. 689

Fig. 690

MASK PENDANTS
Java

686-7

VISHNU
& jewels

Fig. 691
Puppet head of
Bandung, Java

Fig. 692
BUST
Irian Jaya
Ebony
10" tall

Fig. 693 (left). Three small
medallions from Java (see also
Figs. 679–681) are carved in
teak about 2 in (51 mm) square.
They are reminiscent of West
Sumatran floral work but not
as elaborate.

Fig. 694 (top left). Vishnu puppet from Bandung is almost 3 ft (914 mm) tall. The head rotates and arms are articulated. Fig. 695 (above). Theatrical masks, at left a monkey from Bali with articulated jaw (see Fig. 581) and the other a demon from Bandung with very red face.

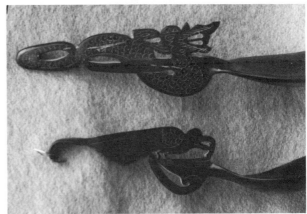

Fig. 696 (above). Kris handles of deer horn like this pair (see also Figs. 689, 690) are now collector's items. They depict a bird atop a monkey and a fisherman with his catch between his legs.

Figs. 697 (middle). Horn spoons with silhouette handles are inland Javanese carvings. One is a dragon, the other a bird (see Figs. 683, 684). Fig. 698 (above). These teak silhouettes are for wall decorations.

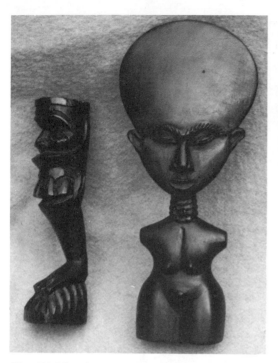

Fig. 700 (above). Monkey and demon heads, turtles and other small figures are carved in ebony in Java for watch charms, key chains, and knicknacks. These are typical. (See Figs. 685–687).

Fig. 702 (below). The smaller Batak medicine box (see Figs. 661, 666, 667) is made with a goat horn and carried vertically rather than horizontally. It is only 11 in (280 mm) long. With it is a water-buffalo lime horn from East Timor (see Fig. 624), also an antique but much less sophisticated in design.

Fig. 699 (above). Unusual carvings are from the flea market in Jakarta. My guesses on origins are in Fig. 688 and 692. Fig. 701 (below). Two carved buffalo-horn birds are from North Sumatra and beautifully done.

41

Southern Asia Carves to Sell

INDIA (including Kashmir), Sri Lanka (formerly Ceylon), and remote Nepal (including Tibetan refugees) are all major producers of woodcarvings, but, except for Indian pieces exported to America, relatively little of their work gets to the United States. However, carvers there have a number of designs and ideas that are vastly different from the more familiar work from Europe, China and Japan. Sri Lanka and Nepal are still relatively undeveloped countries, so woodcarving there ranges from a cottage industry to a "factory," even a town, industry. The carving factory there is not like anything I've seen elsewhere, except possibly Mexico. The factory is merely a work place, with an owner who acts as a factor or seller for the work produced. There are few or no machines, inadequate work areas (by our standards), primitive lighting at best. Mostly they produce tourist items; these men do not carve for pleasure. But there is a great range of designs, and two pieces ostensibly of the same design are likely to vary somewhat—there are no pre-sawed blanks. Further, as in Bali and other low-income countries, a design may be adapted to fit the available wood. One village may specialize in carving in-the-round figures of ebony, another may carve low relief in other woods, a third may specialize in carving masks, or furniture. There is much freedom in design, actually.

Tools are limited, each worker usually having his own, often homemade. The work area may be a crude bench, or in Nepal often the floor. In carving villages, there may be apprentice schools; I found one far up a dirt road in central Sri Lanka. There were about fifteen boys who went to public school from seven to noon, then worked at least eight hours afterwards in the shop, with minimum tools and inadequate light in the evening. Apprenticeship usually lasts eight years, from age 12 to 20, and is taught by a nearby skilled carver. Students make their own designs.

Most intricate of the carvings are statues of gods and goddesses, mostly Hindu, from all these countries, and masks from Sri Lanka. Figures of Buddha are also common in Nepal and Sri Lanka, and are quite cheap. Sri Lanka is also a source of carved taborets that can be folded for carrying. Woods don't seem to matter much; all carvers use chisels and club mallets anyway. Some mahogany is carved in Sri Lanka for furniture; the pieces I saw from Tibet were mostly walnut. Ebony was relatively rare and used for in-the-round figures. The wood for masks seems to be a balsa-like wood called *nux vomica*, which has a poisonous fruit used in pharmaceuticals. I was surprised to find, in one Nepalese shop, samples of available woods on display—the shop was offering to make quantities of carvings in whatever wood was desired, on commission.

Some of the pieces pictured here have been shown in photographs in two of my earlier books, (also published by Sterling Publishing Co., Inc.) "Carving the Unusual" or "Relief Woodcarving," but the

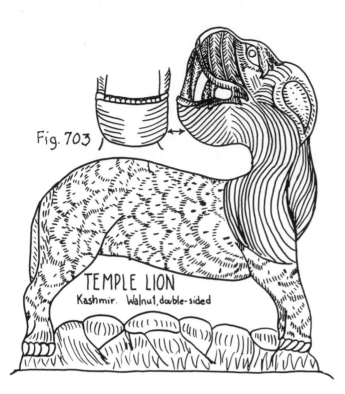

Fig. 703

TEMPLE LION
Kashmir. Walnut, double-sided

Figs. 703, 704 (left and above). Temple guardian "lion" from Kashmir is in walnut, 10 in (254 mm) tall, drilled through the neck for a lamp cord to a bulb in the hollowed mouth. The eyes are semi-precious stones. Note the pelt technique.

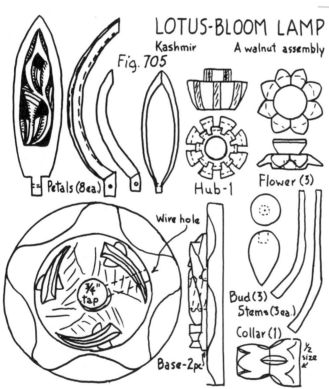

LOTUS-BLOOM LAMP
Kashmir   A walnut assembly
Fig. 705

Petals (8ea.)   Hub-1   Flower (3)

Wire hole

¾" tap

Bud (3)
Stems (3ea.)
Collar (1)

½ size

Base-2pc

Figs. 705, 706 (above). This walnut lotus-bloom lamp from Kashmir is an ingenious assembly of carved elements (see Fig. 707).

sketches were omitted, so no patterns were provided for copying. The exceptional pieces, therefore, have been repeated here, together with a majority which have not previously been described.

It is interesting to compare the designs in terms of source. Tibet, Kashmir and Nepal have designs somewhat similar, perhaps because all three are mountain fastnesses remote from other influences. Sri Lankan designs are somewhat like those of India, but again reflect the fact that this island was developed differently than India, from which much of its population was originally derived. However, India is by no means a country of like peoples, as current political unrest proves. Tribal differences are very important in the differences in art—in fact, are the major factor in determining whether there is any traditional art at all, and if so what it shall be. It is easy to say that woodcarving is to be expected only where there is wood, but even this is by no means a general rule. Why were the woodcarvers among American Indians confined largely to the Pacific Northwest? Why were Germany, Switzerland and Austria (before the Tyrol was lost to Italy) traditional woodcarving producers, while other countries were much less so? Why did Italians carve for Spain and Dutchmen for England? Yet within the carving countries, there are limited areas, tribes, towns, or whatever, with the traditions and skill to do woodcarving. The same thing is true in southern Asia. Among the teeming millions of India, there are only isolated groups that do carving of any sort. Further south and east of this part of Asia, the Polynesians were highly skilled woodcarvers, and spread their knowledge as they journeyed and populated added islands, like the Trobriands, Hawaii, and New Zealand, while the Melanesians on nearby New Guinea had a much less refined culture. The same is true in southeast Asia, for carving villages and "factories" and colonies are often the result of the idea of one or two men, whose apprentices, students and/or helpers eventually go to work on their own, forming a carving colony.

Fig. 707 (below). As the corolla collar of the lamp is rotated, the petals open and close because of a thread on the hollow stem, which carries a light cord to the lamp in the blossom. A collar lower down has three buds and three flowers on individual stems. Total cost was about $6 American!

Figs. 708–710 (below). From Tibet comes this prayer wheel. A wooden collar with raised lettering bears four mantras (prayers—two versions sketched) to Buddha on a metal spindle with cap and handle. A weight on a chain helps rotation when the piece is swung in a circle.

Figs. 711–715 (left and right). These horn figures are from India. Boiling in vinegar softens the horn so it can be shaped, then cut to suit. Figs. 716, 717 (below). Sketches of the Tibetan folding server and card box.

Fig. 713

Fig. 712

ivory inlays

Fig. 714

HORN FIGURES India

Fig. 711

Fig. 716

Designs mate with those on box sides

Top

Floral pattern of inside dishes. Surface modelled.

Leg pattern – incised.

Design & carving somewhat random.

Fig. 717 – CARD BOX

These two walnut pieces are from Tibet. Box at right has rounded corners, is carved as an assembly

FOLDING SERVER

Fig. 720 (above). The Tibetan walnut cardbox has an intricate floral motif that extends from the top down the side, over the joint. The flowers are simple forms.

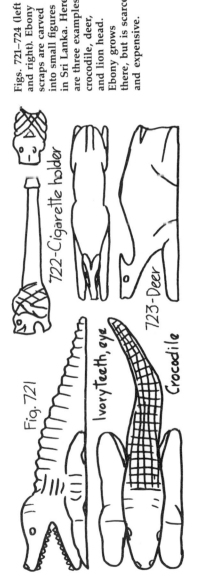

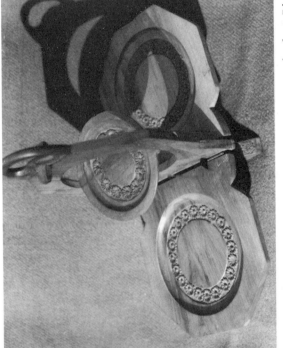

Figs. 718, 719 (left and above). The server is two octagons of walnut, 7 in (178 mm) on a side, hinged to a middle section with tripod base. Each octagon is a small tray inside with floral carved rim, and a like tray folds out of the middle section as shown above.

Figs. 721–724 (left and right). Ebony scraps are carved into small figures in Sri Lanka. Here are three examples, crocodile, deer, and lion head. Ebony grows there, but is scarce and expensive.

722-Cigarette holder

723-Deer

Fig. 721

Ivory teeth, eye

Crocodile

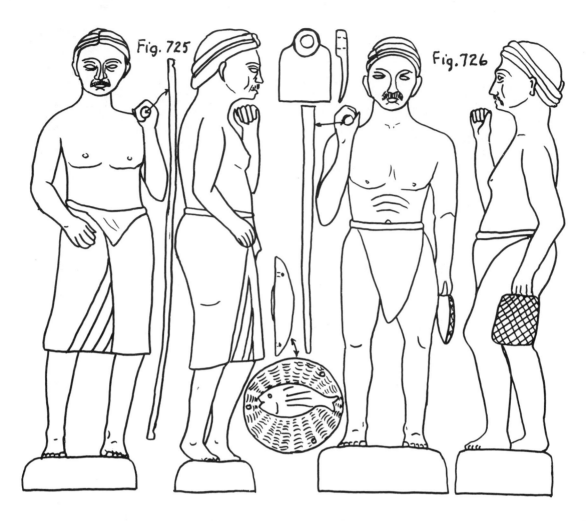

Fig. 725

Fig. 726

Figs. 725–728. Ebony figures are produced in one Sri Lankan town, and apparently only there. The two pictured here are typical (as are the two on page 213). About 10 in (254 mm) tall, they include a carrier with a pingo (shoulder yoke) carrying fish and a farmer with his mattock. They are both integral with their bases. The carrier's pingo and farmer's mattock are separate assemblies inserted in hand holes.

Fig. 729

Copper

Lotus

Fig. 730

Pole slightly longer than man

Figs. 729–732. A rather portly queen carrying a lotus for a temple offering and a Hikkaduwa fisherman. The queen's skirts make a base unnecessary. Queens were distinguished from their attendants by being bare-breasted. The fisherman sits on a bar he lashes to any of a number of posts he plants in shallow bay water—his pole is a separate assembly.

SACRED GOOSE Sri Lanka Fig.736
Lotus border as above; ball divider as below left

FABLED BIRD or BEAST Sri Lanka-Fig.739

Background dot-stamped

PIERCE-CARVED TABORET
Sri Lanka - ¾" Mahogany
Top 11"dia.; 3 legs 11¼" long
Fig. 735

Leaves hollowed
Round edges

Gouge fluting

Hollow leaves slightly
Round edges

DEATH (Maru)

Figs. 737-8
RAKSHA
MASKS
Sri Lanka

COBRA
(Naga)

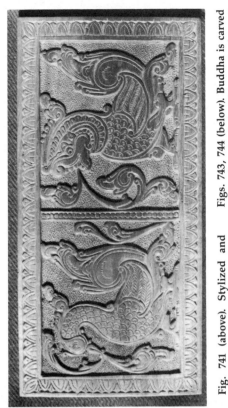

Figs. 743, 744 (below). Buddha is carved everywhere in Asia. This one is ebony 4 in (102 mm) tall, and from Sri Lanka. The hand positions are very important in depictions of Buddha, and feet are shown top down, as sketched. There are also statues of Buddha reclining, heads, busts, and panels showing events in his life.

Fig. 741 (above). Stylized and decorated animals are carved on this Sri Lankan panel of light-colored wood, 7 × 14 in (178 × 356 mm) (see Figs. 736, 739). The Hansa or sacred goose is at left, a mythical beast at right. The carving is about ⅛ in (3 mm) deep. Note the punched background.

Fig. 744

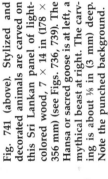

Figs. 740 (above), 742 (left). Pierce-carved foldaway taborets are made in Sri Lanka. This one is of ¾ in (19 mm) mahogany, with top 11 in (279 mm) in diameter carrying a sacred-goose design. Three legs are hinged together and are 11¼ in (285 mm) long (see Fig. 735).

Figs. 745, 746 (above). The Taj Mahal in Agra, India, is justly famous for its inlays in marble of many-colored semi-precious stones from far away—Persia, Russia, Africa. This design is taken from the Taj and done in a tray of the same translucent marble with similar colored stones. It is about 10 in (254 mm) tall.

Figs. 747–750 (right and below). It is interesting to compare design and workmanship of these two 6 in (152 mm) tall household goddesses. Lakshmi is from India, carved in one piece of sandalwood, with a separate turned base. The Nepalese piece is more intricate, mounted against a separately carved background, and vastly cheaper.

LAKSHMI India Sandal

Fig. 747

Adina cordifolia wood

Fig. 748

ZOGINI Nepal

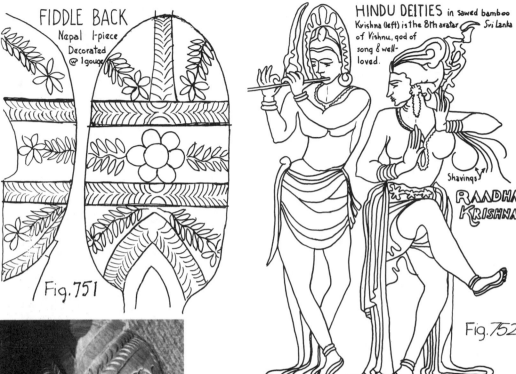

FIDDLE BACK
Nepal 1-piece
Decorated
w/ 1 gouge

Fig. 751

HINDU DEITIES in sawed bamboo
Krishna (left) is the 8th avatar — Sri Lanka
of Vishnu, god of
song & well-
loved.

Shavings

RAADHA
KRISHNA

Fig. 752

Figs. 751, 753 (above left). The carver of this Nepalese fiddle apparently had very few tools. The workmanship is crude, and all the carving seems to have been done with two tools, a veiner and a large gouge. The body is one hollowed-out piece, and keys are merely whittled branches.

Figs. 752, 754 (right). Fret-sawed bamboo pieces, carefully selected for appropriate curvature, make up this Sri Lankan panel depicting Krishna and Raadha (Hindu god and consort) in figures about 12 in (305 mm) tall. The assembly is surprisingly resistant to breakage and has dramatic shadows. It could be done in sections of branches.

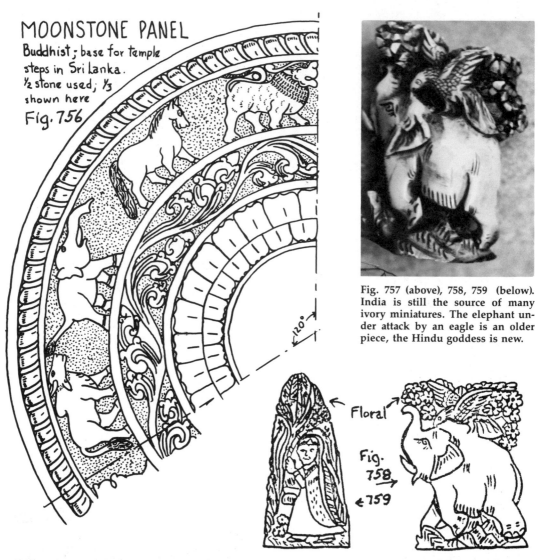

MOONSTONE PANEL

Buddhist; base for temple steps in Sri Lanka. ½ stone used; ⅓ shown here

Fig. 756

120°

Fig. 757 (above), 758, 759 (below). India is still the source of many ivory miniatures. The elephant under attack by an eagle is an older piece, the Hindu goddess is new.

← Floral →

Fig. 758 →

← 759

Figs. 756, 760 (left). Buddhist temples often have a stone threshold, a semi-circle of the moonstone, showing the way to Nirvana. This is a depiction of the stone in wood, showing only five of the seven steps. (Sacred geese and one flower ring are missing). Mine is 14 in (356 mm) in diameter, a complete circle.

FABLED LION Sri Lanka Yellow hardwood ⅜" thick

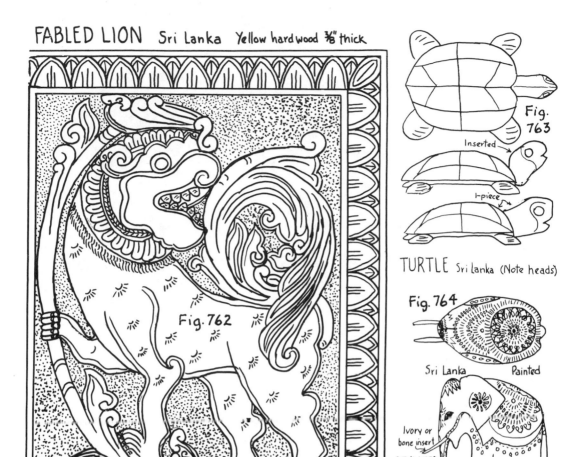

Fig. 762

Fig. 763

Inserted

1-piece

TURTLE Sri Lanka (Note heads)

Fig. 764

Sri Lanka   Painted

Ivory or
bone insert

STYLIZED
ELEPHANT

Figs. 762 (above), 765 (lower right). Highly stylized and orna-
mented, this mythical lion offers a challenge in relief carving.
Note the careful use of texturing from veiner lines to punch-dotted
background. Fig. 763 (top right). The turtle, also from Sri Lanka,
offers a sharp contrast in detail. Note the two head shapes.

Figs. 764 (above right), 766 (below). Made in a range of sizes, these
elephants are an interesting project. They are in soft wood and
painted in bright colors. The tusks can be white plastic inserts, or
ivory, of course.

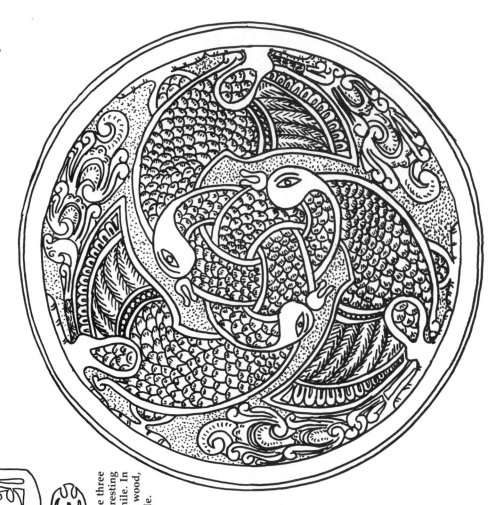

Fig. 773. Buddhists use the sacred goose of hansa in many designs. This one is more elaborate than most, a triple hansa in a light, hard wood. The original is 10 in (254 mm) in diameter, and it makes an excellent hot plate.

Figs. 767–772 (above). These are designs for scraps. The cat is ebony, 2 in (51 mm) tall, with moonstone eyes; the flower, buckles and buttons are whittled coconut shell.

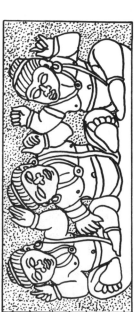

Figs. 774, 775 (below). The three demons make an interesting panel with an inherent smile. In the original walnutlike wood, the growth wood is visible.

42

Toraja Reliefs

The Celebes are now a part of Indonesia and called Sulawesi. However, this big multi-lobed island was once the haunt of pirates as well as the source of most of the sea transport of that part of the world. A land of swamps and mountains with many little harbors, it was already a hangout for pirates when the Dutch discovered it in the sixteenth century. It is a multi-racial island, as so many in that area are, with about 9 million population, including a major seafaring group, the Bujis, who designed and built a characteristic big cargo sailing ship, and a woodcarving group called the Torajas. These two were constantly at war. The Torajas, in fact, developed their unique method of burying their dead in crypts in a cliff (accessible only by special ladders) to prevent their being despoiled by raiding Bujis. This also led to the building of galleries along the cliff face, bearing effigies with hand-carved faces and limbs. These were usually life-size and dressed in clothes suitable to their rank, although

Fig. 776. These two low-relief panels, about 10 in (254 mm) tall, depict a Toraja dwelling (left) and a rice house. Both are entered through frontal trap doors via ladders. The first floors of the dwelling are for storage and animals; the rice house first floors are working and dining areas.

they never were real portraits—that was considered to be bad luck.

There are about 300,000 Torajans now, descended from Indo-Chinese ancestry. The Dutch never subdued them until 1905, then found them a fierce and suspicious race. With their spears, they can bring down a bird or animal at 15 metres and a man at twice that distance, so it's best to be friendly in their neighborhood.

However, it is their relief carving, done as panels decorating their unusual buildings, that is really outstanding. Their traditional buildings, like those of the Bataks of North Sumatra, are shaped like a Chinese junk (or, some say, water-buffalo horns) set high above the ground on piles. Viewed from the side, the center of the roof sags and the ends project at the top, often so far that they must be supported by sticks as the buildings age. The surfaces under the roof, particularly the front and rear, are elaborately decorated with relief panels in color. Like the Batak buildings, the space between the piles, which may or may not

Fig. 777 (left). A rare Toraja in-the-round carving depicts a woman with a bowl. The 6 in (152 mm) figure is of wood, with arms hinged at the shoulder. She is dressed in textiles, like the life-sized ones in grave galleries.

Figs. 778 (right), 779–786 (below). Nine typical Toraja panel designs are largely black and white, with occasional red highlights. The carving is low relief and very precise.

be enclosed, is used for storage; the family lives on the second floor in a practically windowless area. Similar but separate buildings are used for the storage of rice, the staple food.

Although their house designs can be traced to Indo-Chinese ancestry, the decorative motifs cannot. The designs are very geometric and laid out with precision, and painted largely in black and white. There is some added decoration on house fronts such as racks of water-buffalo horn pairs, but it is the painted panels and borders that dominate.

Figs. 787, 788. A decorative bird in soft wood has a 10½ in (267 mm) body with inserted wings. Colors are shown in the sketch. Although the motifs are traditional after a fashion, the design is quite modern and probably for tourists.

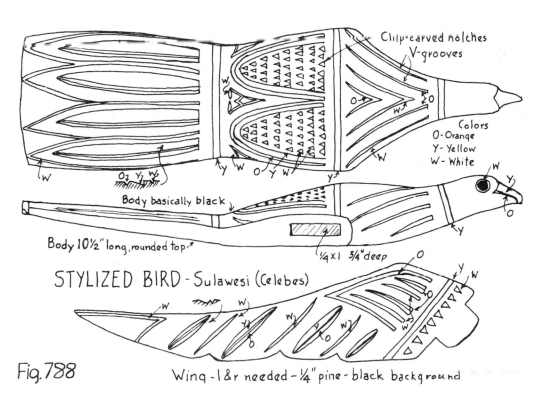

Clip-carved notches
V-grooves

Colors
O - Orange
Y - Yellow
W - White

Body basically black

Body 10½" long, rounded top

¼ x 1 ¾" deep

STYLIZED BIRD - Sulawesi (Celebes)

Fig. 788

Wing - l & r needed - ¼" pine - black background

43

The Sepik Is Prolific in Patterns

New Guinea is the world's second-largest island (Greenland is bigger) and one of its most beautiful, but we knew very little about it until this century. The Dutch had claimed the western half, the English had settled a few people in the southeast, with the Germans in the center area and later also at Rabaul on nearby New Britain, but the interior was believed to be not only inaccessible but uninhabited. The Germans were eliminated in World War I and Australia given the mandate over the entire southeastern half, and it was Australians who in the early thirties, seeking gold, found the interior inhabited by perhaps a million people in hundreds of isolated villages, many believing they were the only

Figs. 789–791. Large masks (and mask shields on next page) of the Sepik area show the variety. Each can be traced to a particular village based on design. Small cowrie shells, hair, fibre and other materials may be used for decoration, and some masks may be 4–5 ft (1.2–1.5 m) tall.

people on earth. There were some 750 different dialects; villages three miles apart could not communicate and were in a constant state of minor war. There was, however, a highly developed civilization in some areas, a great deal of craft skill—and tremendous resources in ore and timber.

The result has been development and some exploitation. The Dutch area became part of Indonesia after World War II and is now known as Irian Jaya. The Australian area was granted freedom in 1975 and is now the Republic of Papua New Guinea. The latter area has been a gold mine for anthropologists for some years, and is gradually being opened up to tourists. There are still many areas where government officials enter only at risk, and headhunting continues to break out. Local wars are frequent, although banned. But the nation is becoming stronger and recently completed a parliament building that should be the envy of Western nations, most of whom have slavishly copied traditional classic architecture. This building is strictly national in its architecture and is finished with many crafts, including woodcarving, bark painting, and woven textiles.

Best known and most accessible of inland New Guinean areas is the Sepik River, which can be explored by boat. (There are still almost no roads.) In two visits there (1982 and 1985), I have collected a number of pieces.

The middle and lower Sepik area is relatively flat country, and although the Sepik winds, it carries a tremendous volume of water at relatively high speed, five or six knots. The natives have used it as a highway—there are few others in the country—plying it in dugout canoes that can be surprisingly long. A common figurehead is the crocodile, carved integral, but this may be replaced on the upper Sepik by a praying mantis or a prawn, because many natives up there cling to their animist religion. Almost all Sepik carving is finished

Fig. 792. Sepik mask.

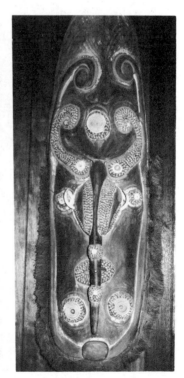
Figs. 793, 794. Sepik mask shields.

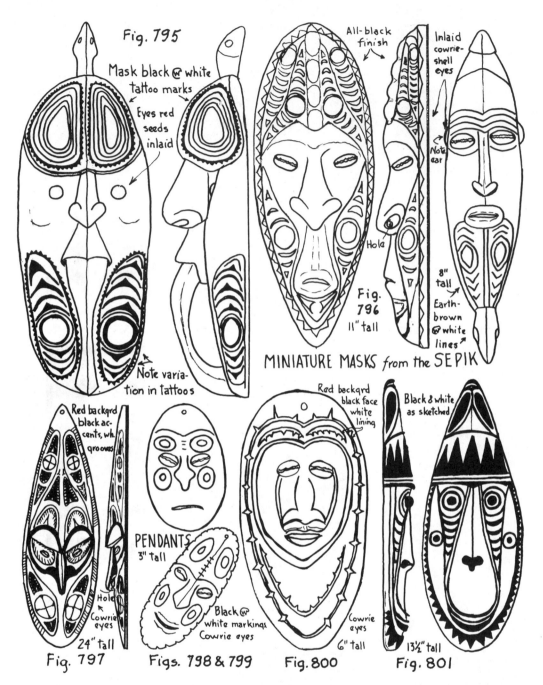

Fig. 795

Mask black & white tattoo marks

Eyes red seeds inlaid

Note variation in tattoos

All-black finish

Inlaid cowrie-shell eyes

Note ear

Hole

Fig. 796
11" tall

8" tall

Earth-brown & white lines

MINIATURE MASKS from the SEPIK

Red backgrd black accents, wh. grooves

Hole

Cowrie eyes

24" tall

Fig. 797

PENDANTS
3" tall

Black & white markings
Cowrie eyes

Figs. 798 & 799

Red backgrd black face white lining

Cowrie eyes

6" tall

Fig. 800

Black & white as sketched

13½" tall

Fig. 801

by coloring, the older colors being white from lime, black from coconut-shell charcoal, and ocher from soil. There are also occasional reds obtained from berries on the lower parts of the river. While slit drums, shields, and similar elements are decorated with carving, the major product of the river is masks, and some of these can be as tall as a man. No two are alike either in design or coloring, and the larger ones are embellished with feathers, shells, grasses, and nowadays with bits of plastic or aluminum foil, if the natives can lay hands on some. While these pieces are strong, they also tend to be crude and garish, particularly when compared with

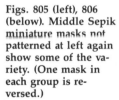

Figs. 802, 803 (above), 804 (right). These masks are miniatures from the middle Sepik. There are also two mask pendants and a food hook incorporating a mask (upper Sepik).

Figs. 805 (left), 806 (below). Middle Sepik miniature masks not patterned at left again show some of the variety. (One mask in each group is reversed.)

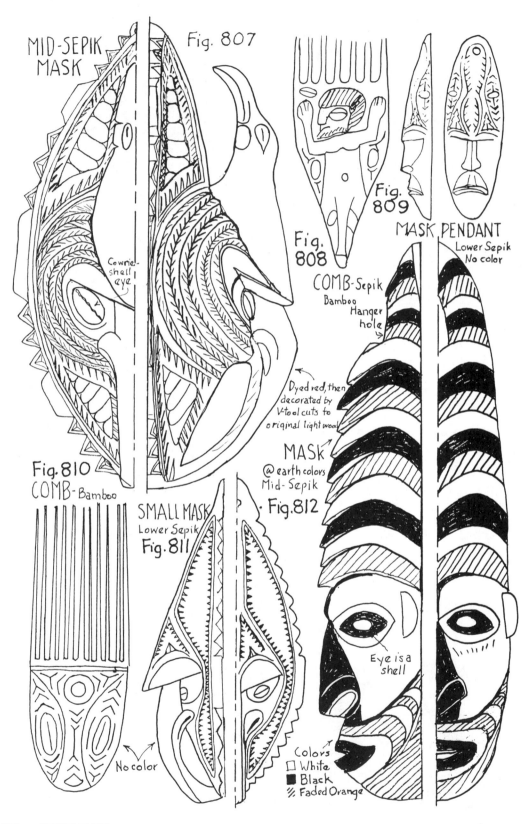

MID-SEPIK
MASK

Fig. 807

Cowrie-
shell
eye

Fig.
809

Fig.
808

COMB-Sepik
Bamboo
Hanger
hole

MASK PENDANT
Lower Sepik
No color

Dyed red, then
decorated by
V-tool cuts to
original light wood

MASK
@ earth colors
Mid-Sepik
Fig. 812

Fig. 810
COMB-Bamboo

SMALL MASK
Lower Sepik
Fig. 811

Eye is a
shell

No color

Colors
☐ White
■ Black
⧄ Faded Orange

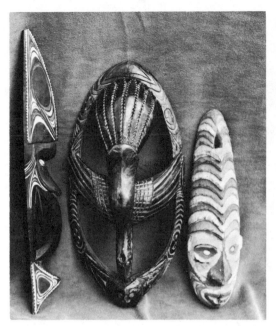

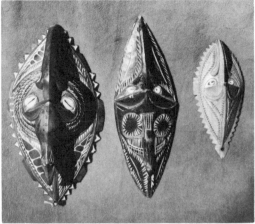

Fig. 814. Three miniature lower-Sepik masks show family resemblance. Each has the nose extending to the chin and free of the face and two have a bird neck and head over the forehead, but two have human-style eyes and one those of a reptile, although eye-balls are shells on all three.

Fig. 813. Three elaborations of the mask include that at left, a silhouette from Korego, an unusual cut-out bird mask, and a so-called spirit mask. The two at left are colored with synthetic paints, but the one at right has the traditional colors. Fig. 816 (below). These mid-Sepik masks are about 2 ft (610 mm) tall and have traditional colors. Compare the faces.

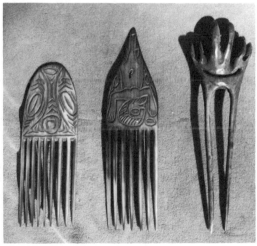

Fig. 815. Melanesians have stiff black hair, which they often decorate by sticking in feathers or flowers, or even leaves or combs such as these. The two at left are bamboo, that at right is from a cassowary bone, and is antique.

the uncolored and delicately detailed Trobriand work. Also, the river carvers use native woods like mangrove because it is easier to carve. Such pieces, in areas where tourists come, may be tinted with black shoe polish to suggest ebony, a dodge that is also familiar in African carvings of today in inferior woods.

Rather surprisingly, there is a great deal of carving done along the Sepik but relatively little in the Highlands, which are only an hour away by air. Here again, a major factor is probably the differences in way of life from village to village. In the Asmat area, along the south-coast rivers, carving is also a major craft.

SEPIK MASKS   229

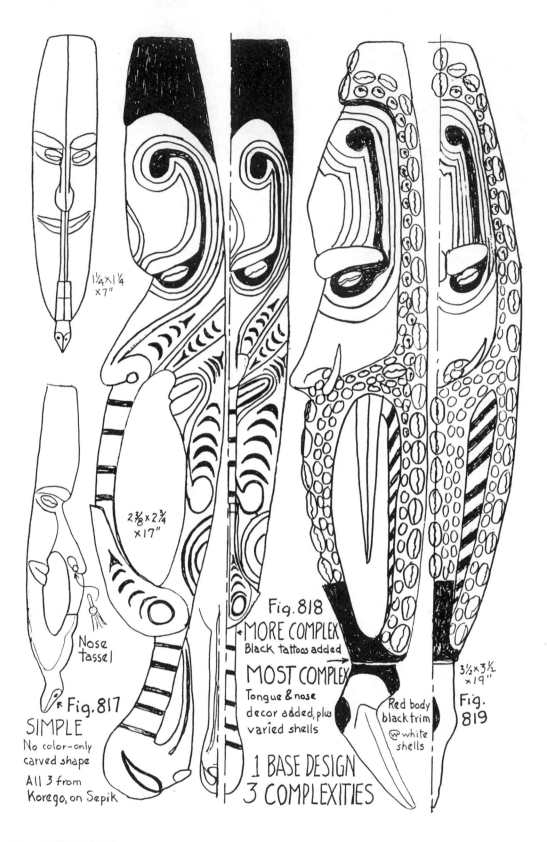

$1\frac{1}{4} \times 1\frac{1}{4}$
$\times 7''$

$2\frac{7}{8} \times 2\frac{3}{4}$
$\times 17''$

Nose
Tassel

Fig. 817
SIMPLE
No color—only
carved shape
All 3 from
Korego, on Sepik

Fig. 818
MORE COMPLEX
Black tattoos added

MOST COMPLEX
Tongue & nose
decor added, plus
varied shells

Red body
black trim
w white
shells

$3\frac{1}{2} \times 3\frac{1}{2}$
$\times 19''$

**Fig.
819**

1 BASE DESIGN
3 COMPLEXITIES

Fig. 820 (above). Three masks from Korego on the middle Sepik show stages of elaborateness in the same design. The smallest is very plain (Fig. 817) decorated only with a tassel at the nose. The second (Fig. 818) has painted tattoo marks and greater development of the bird at bottom, while the third (Fig. 819) has a tongue and elaborate cowrie-shell inlays. The pendant tongue identifies large masks from Korego.

Figs. 821, 822 (above). This Sepik "Mickey Mouse" comes from Palemboi and is unlike anything in the literature. It is about 10 in (254 mm) square and is a double face obviously carved from a tree root, with shell eyes and crocodile-teeth nose decor. Colors are traditional red, black and white. The "ears" come forward on the "Mickey Mouse" side, so are distorted by the camera to greater width.

Figs. 823 (left), 824 (below). Stools on the Sepik are carved from solid logs with integral legs, and top designs similar to those on shields. Note that the shapes are not uniform. Each village usually has an orator's chair—again one piece but with a high back and not sat in but stood next to.

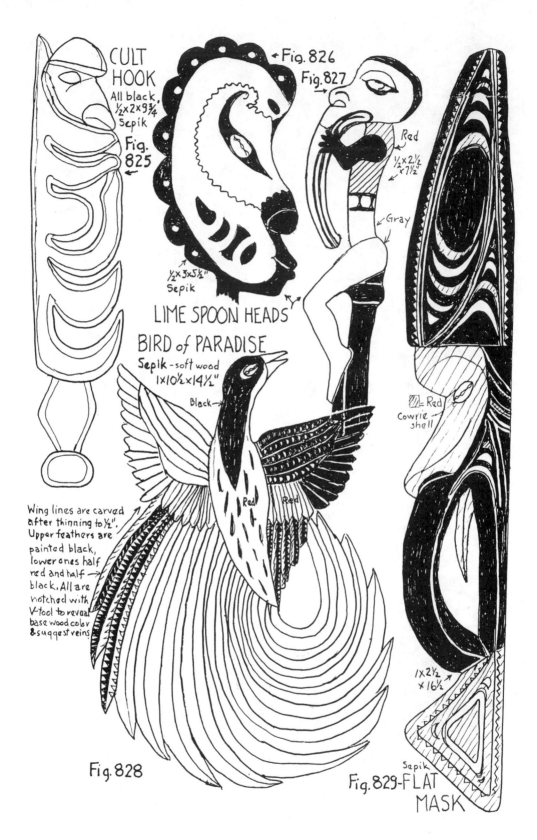

CULT HOOK
All black
½ x 2 x 9¾
Sepik
Fig. 825

← Fig. 826

Fig. 827

Red
½ x 2½ x 7½

Gray

½ x 3 x 5½"
Sepik

LIME SPOON HEADS

BIRD of PARADISE
Sepik - soft wood
1 x 10½ x 14½"

Black →

Red   Red

Wing lines are carved
after thinning to ½".
Upper feathers are
painted black,
lower ones half
red and half →
black. All are
notched with
V-tool to reveal
base wood color
& suggest veins

= Red
Cowrie
shell

Fig. 828

1 x 2½ x 16½

Sepik

Fig. 829 - FLAT
MASK

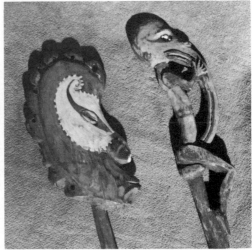

Fig. 830 (above). Among small artifacts from the Sepik are pieces such as these. The central unit is a pendant laboriously made from shell and decorated with beads and plastic bands (or woven pendants if no plastic is available). A miniature mask as a pendant is top left (pattern in Fig. 809). The darker objects are all galip nuts carved into masks, the bottom ones slit and emptied to become clickers or "crickets" (see Figs. 917, 918). At top right is a larger nut with three masks carved on its circumference, a more traditional decoration (see Fig. 919).

Fig. 831 (top right). Much imagination goes into decorating lime sticks at Palemboi. These two are carved integral with the stem and are over a foot (305 mm) tall, with heads 5½ in (140 mm) and 7½ in (190 mm) long, painted red, black, and white. The lower ends are not spatulate, but cylindrical, like a dowel.

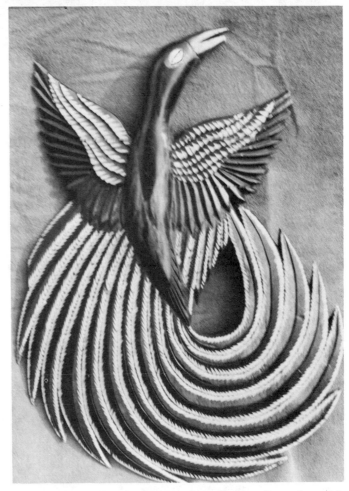

Fig. 832. This stylization of a bird of paradise is quite modern. It is 14½ in (348 mm) tall, in soft wood painted red and black. Feathered areas are ridged, and veins in the feathering are created by many parallel crosscuts with a V-tool.

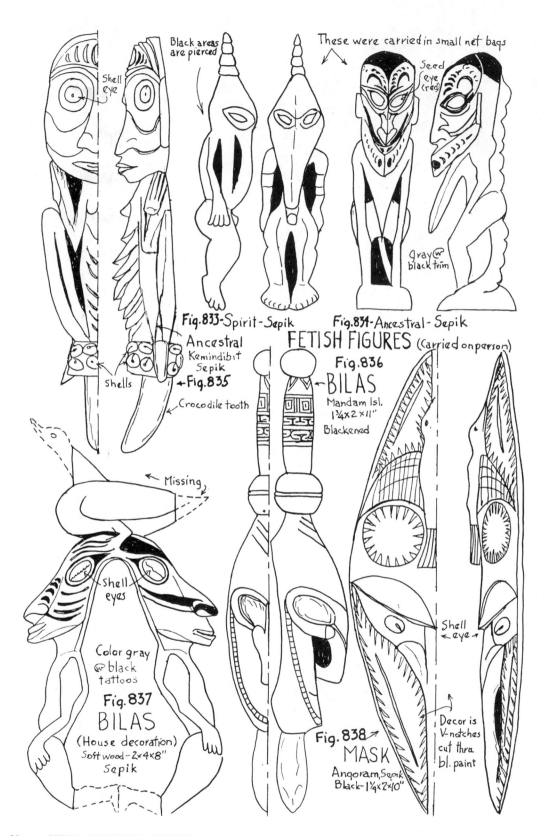

Shell eye

Black areas are pierced

These were carried in small net bags

Seed eye (red)

gray (w) black trim

Fig.833-Spirit-Sepik

Fig.834-Ancestral-Sepik

Ancestral Kemindibit Sepik

←**Fig.835**

shells

Crocodile tooth

FETISH FIGURES (carried on person)

Fig.836

BILAS

Mandam Isl.
1¾×2×11"
Blackened

← Missing

Shell eyes

Color gray (w) black tattoos

Fig. 837

BILAS

(House decoration)
Soft wood – 2×4×8"
Sepik

Shell eye

Decor is V-notches cut thru bl. paint

Fig. 838

MASK

Angoram, Sepik
Black – 1¼×7×10"

Fig. 839 (left). The spirit or cult hook is a common decoration, particularly in men's houses, called "haus tamburans." It is a very stylized flat spirit figure, usually hung to flank and protect a doorway (see Fig. 825).

Fig. 840. The size of these miniature pieces is shown by the penknife. At left is a spirit figure and at right an ancestral figure, both worn in net bags around a warrior's neck for protection. The double figure at left is a bilas or house decoration. (Head and tail of top bird and legs of the ancestor figures are missing.) The figure at right center from Tamandibit is also an ancestor statue for protection (see Fig. 841 below).

Fig. 842 (below). These three small figures would also hang in a house as protection. At left is a bilas with miniature mask. At center is a spirit hook and at right an ancestor figure decorated with shells and a crocodile tooth. All are mid-Sepik.

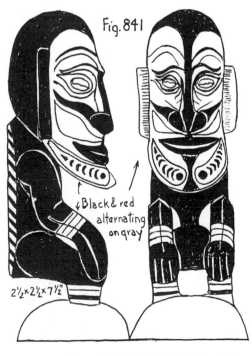

Fig. 841

← Black & red alternating on gray

2½ × 2½ × 7½"

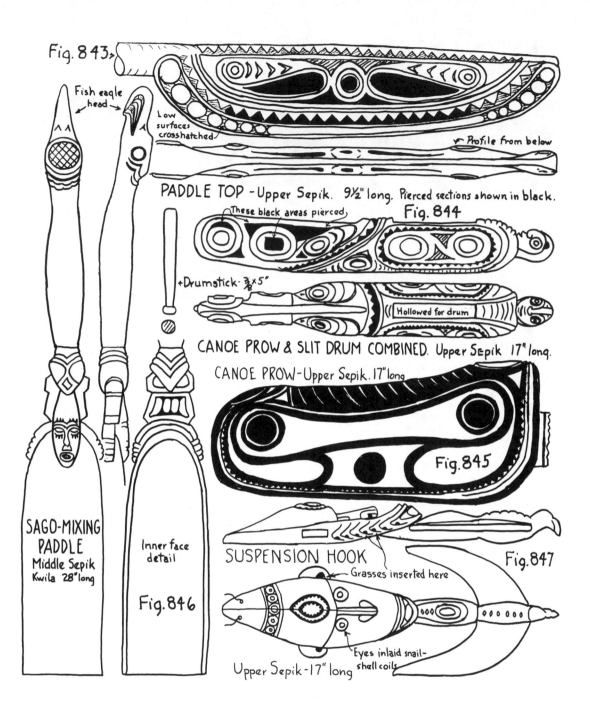

Fig. 843

Fish eagle head →

Low surfaces crosshatched

← Profile from below

PADDLE TOP - Upper Sepik. 9½" long. Pierced sections shown in black.

Fig. 844

These black areas pierced

+Drumstick· ⅜×5"

Hollowed for drum

CANOE PROW & SLIT DRUM COMBINED. Upper Sepik. 17" long.

CANOE PROW-Upper Sepik. 17" long

Fig. 845

SAGO-MIXING PADDLE
Middle Sepik
Kwila 28"long

Inner face detail

Fig. 846

SUSPENSION HOOK

Grasses inserted here

Fig. 847

Eyes inlaid snail-shell coils

Upper Sepik - 17" long

Figs. 848, 849. Upper Sepik villages are animist, so the ceremonial-paddle top (dark) at right is two prawns flanking a butterfly, as mentioned in the text. With it is an unusual piece, a miniature of a big slit drum [They can be 2 ft (210 mm) in diameter by 6 ft (1.83 m) long!] combined with an ornate canoe prow. The symbolism is a cult secret. I added color later, as shown.

Fig. 850 (right). I bought this canoe prow on the upper Sepik because it suggested a stylized crocodile to me. My guide said it represented a praying mantis. But the chief's son explained that it depicts two prawns and a butterfly. Take your pick.

Figs. 851, 852 (right). This fairly elaborate little lime holder of mangrove wood is in effect a bowl on a stand. Two men with stylized long-nose faces support the top, but are integral, of course. Of soft wood, it is finished in red and comes from the lower Sepik.

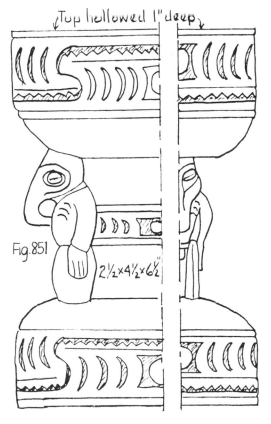

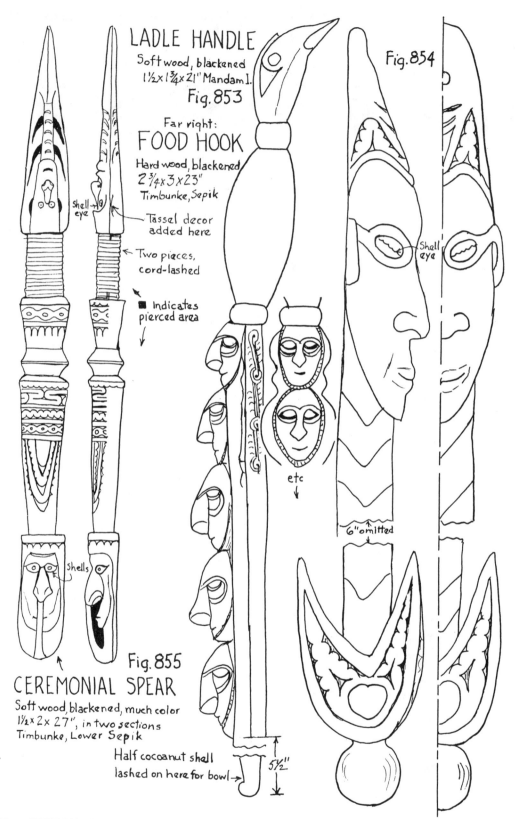

LADLE HANDLE
Soft wood, blackened
1½ x 1¾ x 21" Mandam I.
Fig. 853

Far right:
FOOD HOOK
Hard wood, blackened
2¾ x 3 x 23"
Timbunke, Sepik

Shell eye

— Tassel decor added here

— Two pieces, cord-lashed

■ Indicates pierced area

Fig. 854

Shell eye

etc

6" omitted

Shells

Fig. 855
CEREMONIAL SPEAR
Soft wood, blackened, much color
1½ x 2 x 27", in two sections
Timbunke, Lower Sepik

Half cocoanut shell
lashed on here for bowl →

5½"

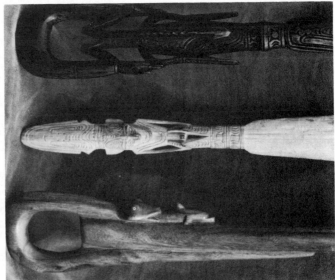

Fig. 857 (above). These three pieces are made for tourists. At bottom is a walking stick of hard cedar, with an integral snake catching a fish to form the handle (see Fig. 863). It is from Rabaul. At top is a walking stick from Mandam Island, lower Sepik, of mangrove wood stained black. It carries three series of double masks, is elaborately carved (see Fig. 861). At center is a stirring paddle for sago, with a traditional figure carved as a handle. It is from the mid-Sepik, Fig. 860.

Fig. 856 (left). Supplies are suspended in Sepik houses from food hooks that look like anchors. This one has three hooks instead of two, which identifies it as from Timbunke. Next to it is the handle for a ladle, carved with a bird and four graduated masks. At right is a ceremonial spear, with two miniature masks, one at top, one at bottom. It is painted in bright colors. (See Figs. 853–855).

Figs. 858, 859. Called story boards, medium-relief pieces like these are actually the Sepik equivalent of a photograph. In the larger of the two (9 × 23 in [229 × 584 mm]), six men paddle a dugout canoe with crocodile head, past a marsh with crocodiles (above them) and a spirit figure (a bird with bird of paradise at left). Under the crocodile is a fish. The other (6 × 17 in [152 × 432 mm]), depicts a family in a dugout, with child and dog. The sun and a monkey climbing a palm for coconuts are at left, and fish beneath the canoe. Some story boards are much larger than these, perhaps up to 3.3 × 6.6 ft (1 × 2 m).

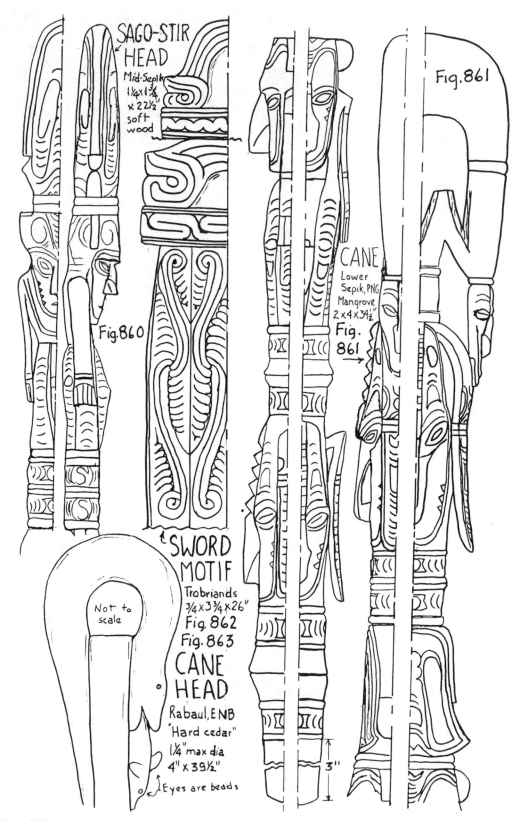

SAGO-STIR
HEAD

Mid-Sepik
1¼ x 1¾
x 22½"
soft
wood

Fig.860

SWORD
MOTIF

Trobriands
¾ x 3¾ x 26"
Fig. 862
Fig. 863

CANE
HEAD

Rabaul, ENB
"Hard cedar"
1¼" max dia
4" x 39½"

Not to
scale

Eyes are beads

CANE

Lower
Sepik, PNG
Mangrove
2 x 4 x 34½"
Fig.
861

Fig.861

3"

44

An Update on Trobriand Patterns

Some years back, I bought a small tray carved in the shape of a fish. It came from the Trobriand Islands, of which I'd never heard, and was such a good job of design and carving that it piqued my curiosity. So I looked up the islands and found that they lie about 100 miles (161 km) northeast of the southern tip of Papua New Guinea, of which new republic they are a part. The result was that I visited the Trobriands in 1982 and found them fascinating. Some of the carvings I found there are sketched and pictured in Chapter XX of my "Basic Whittling and Woodcarving" (Sterling, 1983). I made a second visit to these rarely visited islands in 1985, and again found that these unschooled carvers are perhaps

the most creative in the present world. Some of my findings are shown here, and offer brand-new and different ideas in carving and decoration. And some of the pieces are so intricately made that few Americans would take time to duplicate them.

Natives in the Trobriands are not Melanesian in origin, but Polynesian, like the Hawaiians, Samoans, and the Maori of New Zealand, and they show characteristics of this ancestry in the many spirals and curves of their designs, as well as their use of nacre (mother of pearl) inlays taken from shells, and of cat's eyes (opercula of the turban shell) for decoration. Also, their designs are often taken from

Fig. 864. Three of these pendants are in ebony and have nacre inlays. The one at left is in a light-colored hard wood, has an intentional distortion of the eyes and fibre and plastic tassels added. The first ebony piece repeats the face tattoos formerly common. The second has two very stylized faces joined by an attenuated nose, and the third is the Papua New Guinea coat of arms in miniature, showing a sea eagle atop a native drum.

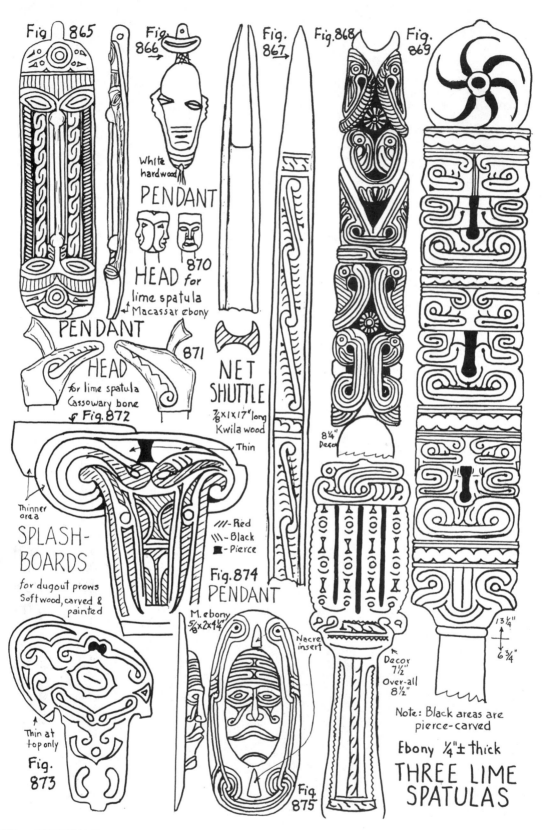

Fig. 865

Fig. 866

Fig. 867

Fig. 868

Fig. 869

White hardwood

PENDANT

HEAD for lime spatula Macassar ebony
870

PENDANT

HEAD for lime spatula Cassowary bone
871

NET SHUTTLE
⅞"×1"×17" long
Kwila wood

Fig. 872

Thin

Thinner area

SPLASH- BOARDS
for dugout prows Soft wood, carved & painted

/// - Red
/// - Black
■ - Pierce

Fig. 874
PENDANT

M. ebony
⅝"×2×4¼"

Nacre insert

8¼" Decor

Thin at top only

Fig. 873

Fig. 875

Decor 7½"
Over-all 8½"

13¼"

6¾"

Note: Black areas are pierce-carved

Ebony ¼"± thick

THREE LIME SPATULAS

the tattoo patterns they wear, because these people are still relatively unaffected by our civilization despite a century or more of missionary influence. They still live in thatched huts, wear few clothes, and exist on a healthful subsistence diet. Although their carving is now done with steel tools, these are all of the hand variety—there are no power tools because there is no electricity. What's more, much of the wood with which they work must now be imported from the Woodlark Islands, more than 100 miles away (161 km), because they prefer ebony (macassar, black or striped), kwila (light tan and very hard) or garamut (medium brown and used for

cylindrical bored-out drums to such a degree that the drums carry the same name). Their tools are adzes and chisels rather than knives, and even round objects such as deep bowls are turned out by rotating the blank with one hand while the other wields an adz.

The deep boring of a drum is a lengthy process involving the use of fire and hot rods when available, rather than conventional boring tools. A great deal of the design on flat objects and surfaces is incised, formerly done with parallel cuts, but now done with a V-tool or graver. These designs are very unfamiliar to us, being stylized versions of prawns, fish, and the like, many of them ancestral. They are quite intricate and require careful carving and a great deal of time, but this does not seem to trouble the carvers, who have no real concept of time anyway. They are un-

Figs. 876, 877 (below). Trobriand dugouts are outriggers and travel mainly at sea—islands are too small to have rivers. Long journeys are undertaken for trading and a ceremonial exchange of bracelets and necklaces with other island groups, so canoes are usually big and often elaborately decorated. Here are a typical prow and two miniatures of the odd-shaped splashboard that goes behind it. Some canoes are double-ended, so have prows and splashboards at each end, plus extensive shell decorations.

Fig. 878 (below). Swirling patterns characterize the ceremonial lime spatulas at left and right and the net shuttle at right center. All of these pieces are in ebony.

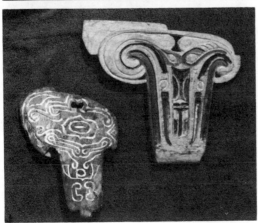

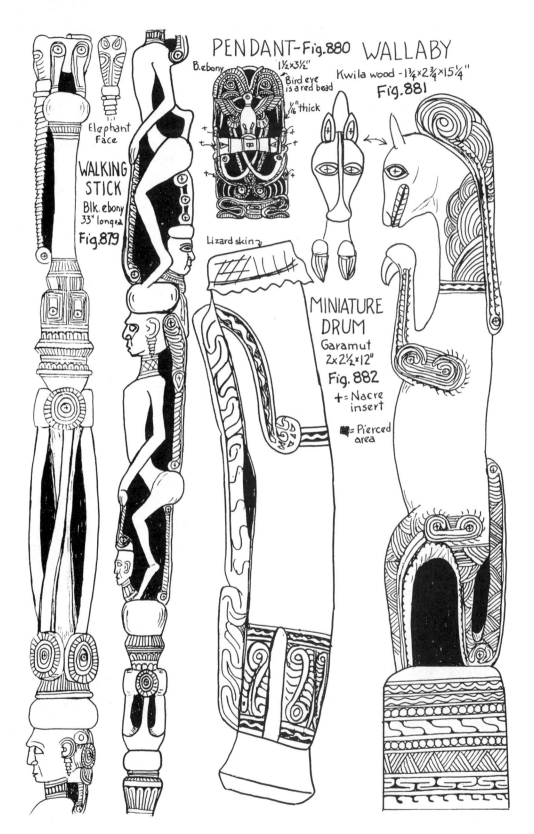

PENDANT-Fig.880 WALLABY

B. ebony
1½x3½"
Bird eye
is a red bead

Kwila wood - 1¾x2¾x15¼"
Fig.881

1/16" thick

Elephant Face

WALKING
STICK

Blk. ebony
33" long ea
Fig.879

Lizard skin

MINIATURE
DRUM

Garamut
2x2½x12"

Fig. 882

+ = Nacre
insert

= Pierced
area

troubled by our clock worship so they take whatever time is necessary to complete the job. Most of the work around home is done by wives and daughters, so the men divide their time between fishing, carving, and canoeing to adjacent islands. The islands are quite small and contain no animal life except imported dogs, snakes, and occasional pigs, only the latter of which are fed regularly, and are customarily a design subject. Much of the carving might be considered ornate by our standards, but it has the virtue that it is not monotonous—no

two pieces of Trobriand carving are ever alike; indeed, the two sides of the same carving may not match in intimate carving detail although they will agree in area, style, and treatment. Also, most designs are made by eye rather than rule, so measurements may be off by our rigid patternmaker standards. But the result is refreshing and unique carving that has a freedom which ours does not.

Trobrianders apparently price their work by whim, large objects commanding a higher asking price than small ones, regardless of intricacy. And they love to bargain, so they will, on occasion, sell something they've been using.

Fig. 883 (below). Trobriand islanders are masters of the carved ebony baton and walking stick. The most elaborate forms are those shown at center, with openwork and inlays (see Fig. 879). The ceremonial sword at right shows traditional swirling design forms (see Fig. 862 for pattern), while the battle ax behind them is an antique with a barbed wooden head tipped with a pointed leg bone from a cassowary.

Fig. 884 (below). Also typical Trobriand work are the stylized kwila wallaby at left (see Fig. 881) and the miniature garamut drum at right (see Fig. 882). The drum head is lizard skin.

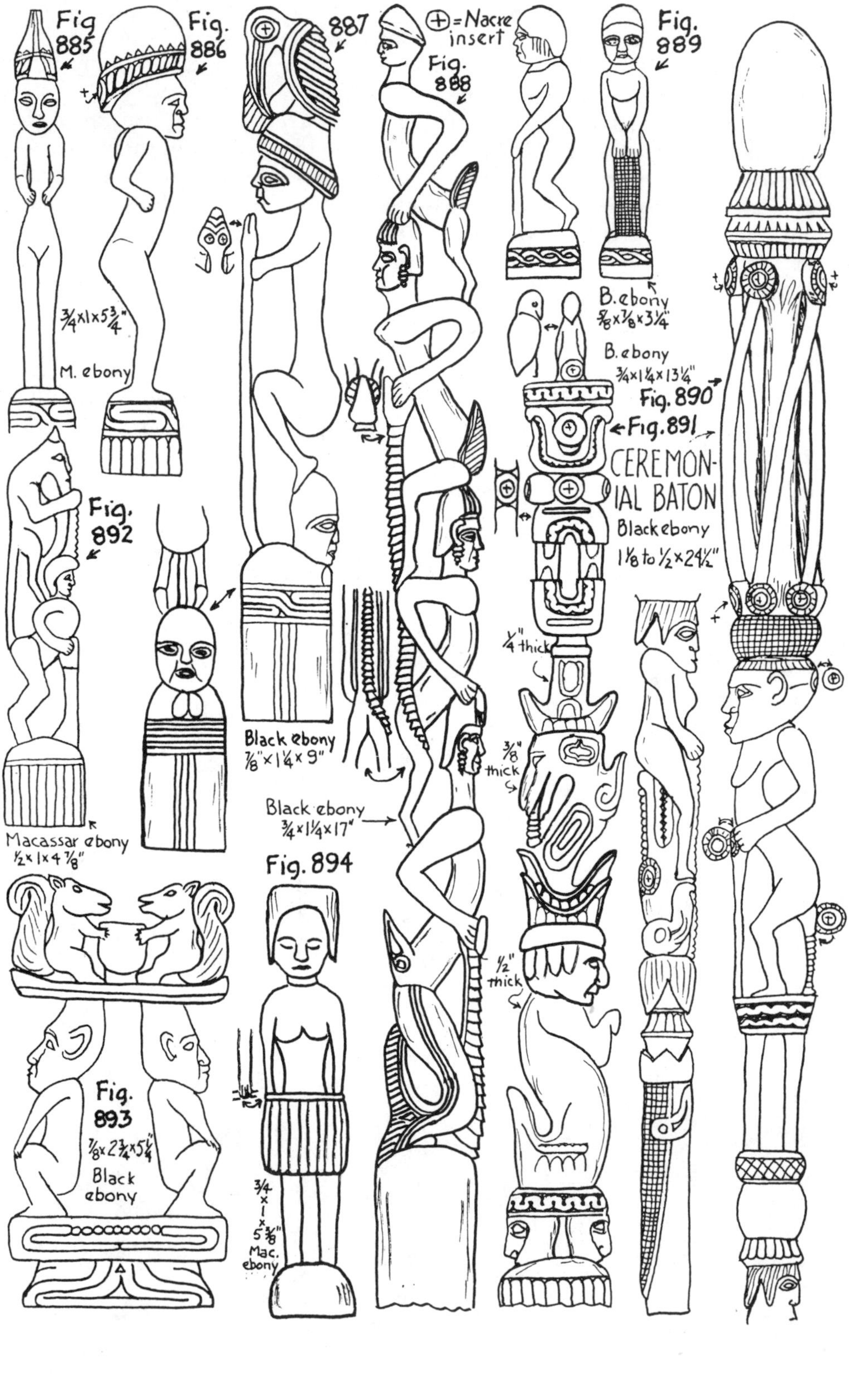
Fig 885
Fig. 886
887
⊕ = Nacre insert
Fig. 888
Fig. 889
3/4 x 1 x 5 3/4"
M. ebony
B. ebony 5/8 x 7/8 x 3 1/4"
B. ebony 3/4 x 1 1/4 x 13 1/4"
Fig. 890
Fig. 891
CEREMONIAL BATON
Black ebony 1 1/8 to 1/2 x 24 1/2"
Fig. 892
Macassar ebony 1/2 x 1 x 4 7/8"
Black ebony 7/8" x 1 1/4 x 9"
1/4" thick
3/8" thick
Black ebony 3/4 x 1 1/4 x 17"
Fig. 894
1/2" thick
Fig. 893
7/8 x 2 3/4 x 5 1/4"
Black ebony
3/4 x 1 x 5 3/8"
Mac. ebony

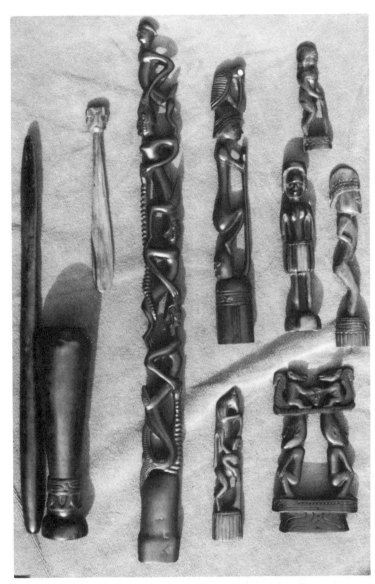

Fig. 896 (above). Bowls are usually carved of kwila, a very hard wood. Seemingly, every bowl is different, sometimes varying from end to end or side to side, as close inspection of the example above will show. Designs vary with island and individual, but the technique does not. Bowls are carved entirely by hand (there is no power available) and rough shaping is done with homemade adzes, the carver rotating the blank with one hand and swinging the adz with the other. Finishing polish is achieved by rubbing with a boar's tooth.

Fig. 895 (above). Familiar carvings from the Trobriands are these small figures, elaborately stylized and patterned at left. They range from a relatively simple figure to multiple designs with much openwork and inlays of nacre. At far left is a pestle and mortar for betel and lime. All figures are in macassar ebony.

Fig. 897. This 6-in (152-mm) bowl has integral side arms (see Fig. 908) and a base which is hollowed so a flower could be carved inside it.

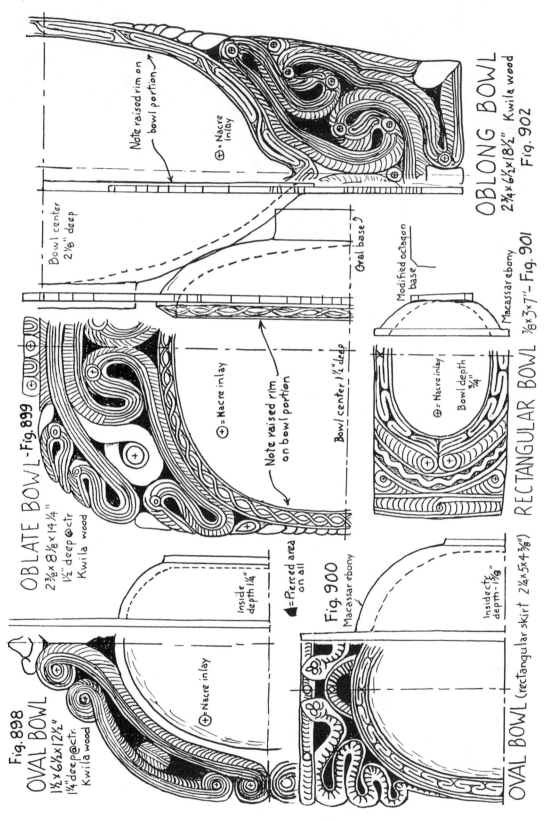

OBLONG BOWL
2¾ x 6½ x 18½" Kwila wood
Fig. 902

Note raised rim on bowl portion

⊕ = Nacre inlay

Bowl center 2⅛" deep

Oval base

Modified octagon base

Macassar ebony
⅞ x 3 x 7" – Fig. 901
RECTANGULAR BOWL

⊕ = Nacre inlay

Bowl depth ¾"

OBLATE BOWL – Fig. 899
2⅜ x 8⅛ x 14¼"
½" deep @ ctr.
Kwila wood

⊕ = Nacre inlay

Note raised rim on bowl portion

⊕ = Nacre inlay

Bowl center 1½" deep

Inside depth 1¼"

◄ = Pierced area on all

Fig. 900
Macassar ebony

Fig. 898
OVAL BOWL
1½ x 6½ x 12½"
1¼" deep @ ctr.
Kwila wood

⊕ = Nacre inlay

Inside depth 1⅜"

OVAL BOWL (rectangular skirt) 2¼ x 5 x 4⅜")

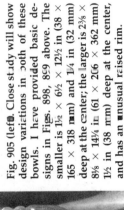

Fig. 904 (above). The upper bowl in this group is quite small, ⅞ × 3 × 7 in (22 × 76 × 178 mm) and carved in macassar ebony with nacre inlay (Fig. 901). The lower bowl is oval, with a rectangular skirt (see Fig. 900), but no inlay. Note that one end of the skirt is wider than the other. It is 2¼ × 4⅜ × 5 in (57 × 112 × 127 mm). The fish between them is in kwila, with inserted "cat's eye"—the operculum of the turban shell. The pattern for it is in the next chapter.

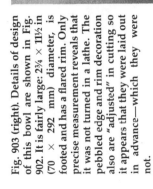

Fig. 905 (left). Close study will show design variations in both of these bowls. I have provided basic designs in Figs. 898, 899 above. The smaller is 1½ × 6½ × 12½ in (38 × 165 × 318 mm) and 1¼ in (32 mm) deep at the center; the larger is 2⅜ × 8⅜ × 14¼ in (61 × 206 × 362 mm) 1½ in (38 mm) deep at the center, and has an unusual raised rim.

Fig. 903 (right). Details of design of this bowl are shown in Fig. 902. It is fairly large: 2¾ × 11½ in (70 × 292 mm) diameter, is footed and has a flared rim. Only precise measurement reveals that it was not turned in a lathe. The pebbled edge and rim decoration also are "adjusted" in cutting so it appears that they were laid out in advance—which they were not.

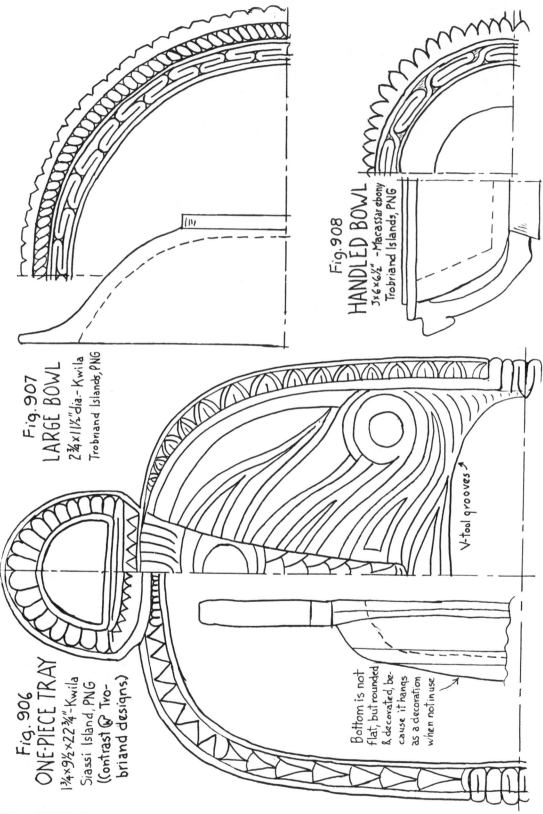

Fig. 907
LARGE BOWL
2¾ x 11½" dia. - Kwila
Trobriand Islands, PNG

Fig. 908
HANDLED BOWL
3 x 6 x 6½" - Macassar ebony
Trobriand Islands, PNG

V-tool grooves ↗

Fig. 906
ONE-PIECE TRAY
1¾ x 9½ x 22¾" - Kwila
Siassi Island, PNG
(Contrast @ Tro-
briand designs)

Bottom is not
flat, but rounded
& decorated, be-
cause it hangs
as a decoration
when not in use

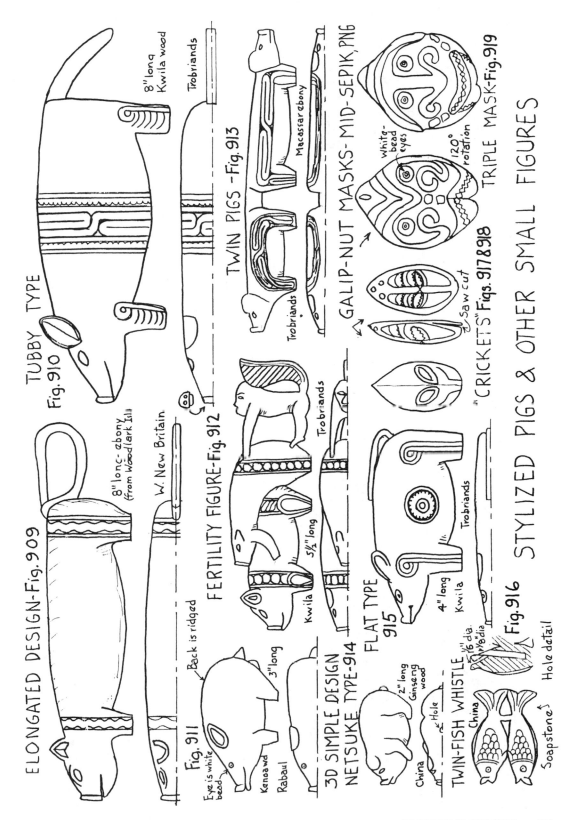

ELONGATED DESIGN-Fig.909

TUBBY TYPE Fig.910

8"long Kwila wood

Trobriands

8"long abony (from Woodlark Is.)

W. New Britain

FERTILITY FIGURE-Fig.912

Back is ridged

Fig.911

Eye is white bead

3"long

Kenoawd Rabaul

TWIN PIGS -Fig.913

Macassar abony

Trobriands

5½"long

Kwila

Trobriands

GALIP-NUT MASKS-MID-SEPIK, PNG

white bead eyes

120° rotation

TRIPLE MASK-Fig.919

Saw cut

"CRICKETS" Figs.917&918

3D SIMPLE DESIGN NETSUKE TYPE-914

FLAT TYPE 915

Trobriands

4"long Kwila

Fig.916

STYLIZED PIGS & OTHER SMALL FIGURES

2"long Ginseng wood

China

Hole

TWIN-FISH WHISTLE

1/16" dia.

3/16"dia.

China

Hole detail

Soapstone

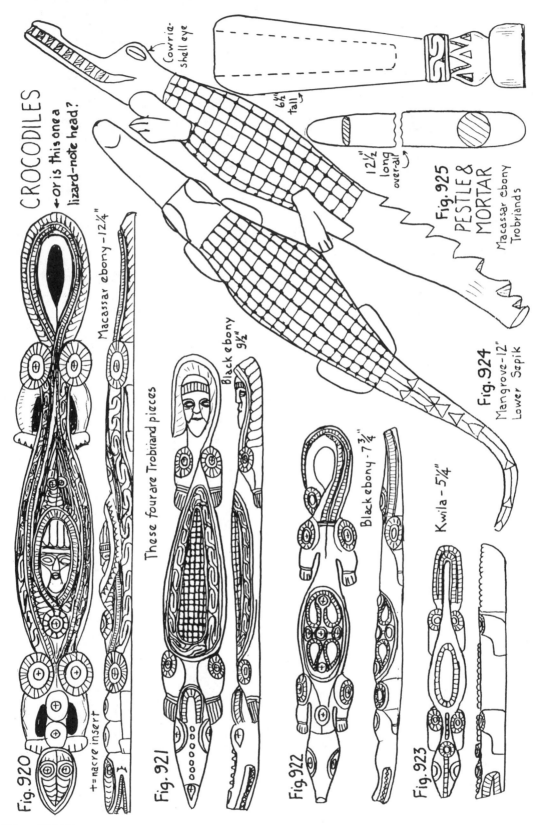

CROCODILES

→ or is this one a lizard—note head?

Cowrie-shall eye

6½" tall

12½" long overall

Fig. 925 PESTLE & MORTAR
Macassar ebony
Trobriands

Fig. 924
Mangrove—12"
Lower Sepik

Macassar ebony—12¼"

These four are Trobriand pieces

Black ebony 9½"

Black ebony – 7¾"

Kwila – 5¼"

+ = nacre insert

Fig. 920

Fig. 921

Fig. 922

Fig. 923

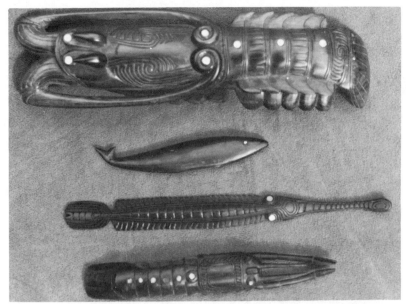

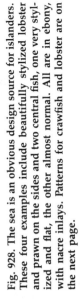

Fig. 928. The sea is an obvious design source for islanders. These four examples include beautifully stylized lobster and prawn on the sides and two central fish, one very stylized and flat, the other almost normal. All are in ebony, with nacre inlays. Patterns for crawfish and lobster are on the next page.

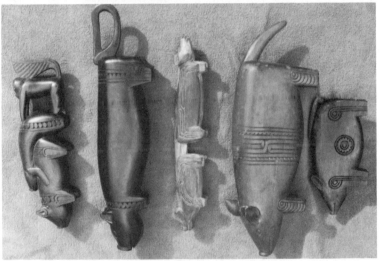

Fig. 927. Pigs are the portable wealth of most families, eaten only on very festive occasions. They are also an obvious design source, as these examples prove. No two are ever alike, as far as I've seen; they may be in various woods and varied in size. Perhaps whatever scraps are available is the determining factor. See Figs. 909–915 on preceding page.

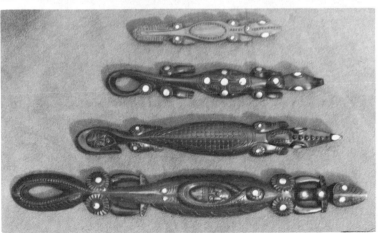

Fig. 926. The crocodile is a favorite subject for stylizing, and no two depictions are the same. Here are four examples, one in kwila and three in ebony. All are decorated with nacre inlays and have intricate surface carving, while the two at right have human masks embodied in the decoration. Or is the right-hand one a lizard?

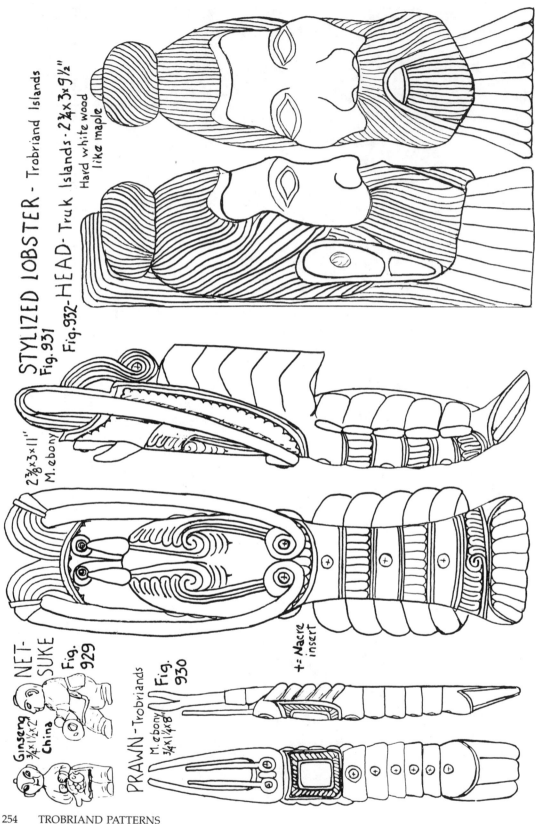

STYLIZED LOBSTER - Trobriand Islands
Fig. 931

Fig.932-HEAD- Truk Islands - 2¼ x 3 x 9½"
Hard white wood
like maple

2⅞ x 3 x 11"
M. ebony

+= Nacre
insert

NET-
SUKE
Fig.
929

Ginseng
¾ x 1½ x 2"
China

PRAWN - Trobriands
M. ebony
¾ x 1¼ x 8"
Fig.
930

45

Carvings As You Go By

SERENDIPITY—just being there—has played a large part in my finding of unusual and interesting carved pieces. I learned about Cherokee stone carvings because I taught in Brasstown, NC, and went to Cherokee over a weekend. I found out first about the Campbell Folk School at Brasstown because my business took me to Chicago in the Thirties—and there were Brasstown folk carvings in the gift shop at the Palmer House. (Liberace, then an unknown young piano player from Milwaukee, was playing in the Empire Room upstairs at dinnertime.) Because I went to Brasstown via Atlanta, I taught a couple of seminars there and learned of the beautiful carvings in the boardroom at the Emory University Hospital there.

International travel is even more rewarding, because one will inevitably find carvings from third-world countries being sold wherever tourists gather. Most are typical souvenirs, but there are always odd items among them, sometimes from unknown

Fig. 933 (below). The Chinese are the masters of small carving. Here are two Chinese (!) netsukes in ginseng: a boy, a fish, and a pig. Also a double-fish whistle in soapstone. Each is about 2 in (51 mm) long. Patterns are in Figs. 914, 916, 919.

Fig. 934 (right). From the Truk Islands comes this strong head. It is 9 in (229 mm) tall. Pattern in Fig. 932.

Fig. 935 Thin lines show painting- largely green & brown

BULLFROG Caricature
Indonesia- 6"

White

Red

Green

2-tone pale purple

Orange

Dark 2-tone tan

Dark over light tan

Pink

Fig. 936- SLEEPING BIRD China- 4"
Entire surface is glued-on multi-color shavings

China

Basic bead

Fig. 937-Larger bead or pendant
2" (51mm) tall

China

Alternate hand poses

Fig. 938- Necklace unit
1⅛"(28mm) tall

sources. And even here at home nowadays, imported carvings appear in very unlikely shops—as I found carvings from Korea and China in Mystic, Conn. My point is, I guess, to keep your eyes open; you can find ideas for your own carving almost anywhere. They're not always in wood, but they can be converted to patterns for woodcarvings or suggest a hunt for a piece of similar material. I bought a number of crocodile teeth in New Guinea to carve after I got home. I bought sea-

urchin spines and latan nuts in Hawaii, tree seeds that can be made into beads in Mexico, red pipestone in the U.S., and bits of wood all over the place. This was not all curiosity—some was economical as well—a good carved crocodile tooth may cost $100 in New Guinea; an uncarved one is about a dollar.

Some of the pieces I've collected recently are shown here, to expand on the idea. Those from more remote places were made by hand, often with very primitive tools, some (like the Hawaiian pieces) were made with rotary power tools. (As a matter of fact, the easy way to carve crocodile teeth is with a hand grinder, but the upriver natives on the Sepik have no power.) Some of the pieces are surprising in design, like the fish from Woodlark Island, which are very simple and modern in styling, al-

Fig. 939. From China, this 3 in (76 mm) bird has its head tucked back. Every feather is a separate dyed shaving glued in place (see Fig. 936), and the entire bird is almost iridescent. I found it in a Mystic, CT, gift shop!

Figs. 940 (below, left), 941 (below). Absurd sprawling frog comes from Indonesia, although I never saw him there; I found him in Mystic, CT. He is about 6 in (152 mm) wide, of soft wood painted in brilliant greens and yellows. See Fig. 935 for pattern.

Fig. 942 (left). Ginseng-wood necklace from China has priests for beads—but they differ in hand pose (see Fig. 938)! The larger priest bead or pendant (drilled top to bottom) is detailed in Fig. 937. (The third piece is an ancient jade.)

CHINA, INDONESIA   257

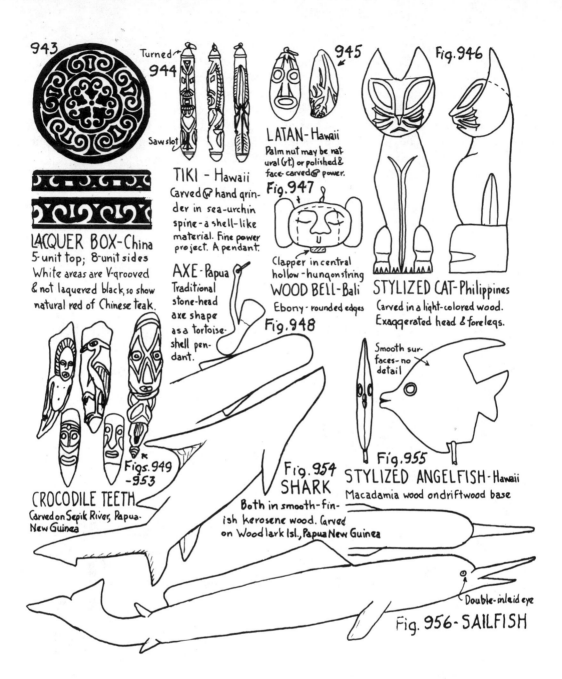

943

Turned →
944

Saw slot

LACQUER BOX - China
5-unit top; 8-unit sides
White areas are V-grooved
& not laquered black, so show
natural red of Chinese teak.

TIKI - Hawaii
Carved ⓦ hand grin-
der in sea-urchin
spine - a shell-like
material. Fine power
project. A pendant.

AXE - Papua
Traditional
stone-head
axe shape
as a tortoise-
shell pen-
dant.

945

LATAN - Hawaii
Palm nut may be nat-
ural (rt.) or polished &
face-carved ⓦ power.

Fig. 947
Clapper in central
hollow - hung on string
WOOD BELL - Bali
Ebony - rounded edges
Fig. 948

Fig. 946

STYLIZED CAT - Philippines
Carved in a light-colored wood.
Exaggerated head & forelegs.

Smooth sur-
faces - no
detail

**Figs. 949
-953**

CROCODILE TEETH
Carved on Sepik River, Papua.
New Guinea

**Fig. 954
SHARK**
Both in smooth-fin-
ish kerosene wood. Carved
on Woodlark Isl., Papua New Guinea

**Fig. 955
STYLIZED ANGELFISH - Hawaii**
Macadamia wood on driftwood base

Double-inlaid eye
Fig. 956 - SAILFISH

though they come from a remote island rarely visited, a couple of hundred miles off the New Guinea coast. They are reminiscent of the unadorned and powerful carvings of the Seri Indians in Mexico. Woodlark carvings are made from a wood called ghiti, or kerosene wood, because it will burn readily even when soaking wet. I also found that macadamia wood has as flavorful a figure in it as the nuts have

taste. Another point: In most cases, the finishes are natural—local oils, earth colors, berry or bark stains (when colors are used; they're not all that common).

There is one disadvantage when a carving is discovered at other than the place where it was made. There is no opportunity in many cases to get a true provenance; the seller can only tell what he or she has heard about the piece, which may

Fig. 957 (right). "Loot" from scouring shops in Honolulu include a stylized Philippine cat (left) two ebony grinning-face bells from Bali and a macadamia-wood angelfish from Hawaii itself. The cat is about 5 in (127 mm) tall. See Figs. 946, 947, 955. The axe of Fig. 948 was a find in a Madang, Papua New Guinea, boutique.

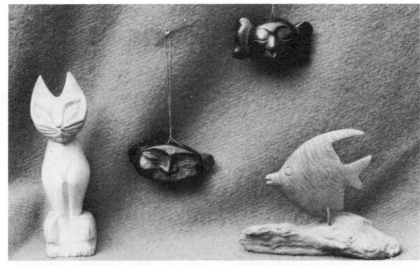

Fig. 958 (right). Natural materials are adapted by carvers everywhere. At left is a carved crocodile tooth I bought from a village chief up the Sepik in Papua New Guinea. Next to it are a latan nut and a sea-urchin spine (see Figs. 944, 945), both carved with rotary tools in Hawaii. The boar's tusk and large crocodile tooth at right are also from Papua New Guinea. I have since carved those into a bracelet and pendant.

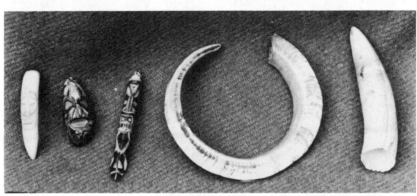

Fig. 959 (right). Six carved crocodile teeth, only the third from right carved by a Sepik native. The others are mine.

Figs. 960, 961 (left, below). Two stylized fish in ghiti or kerosene wood from Woodlark, 200 miles at sea. See Figs. 954–956.

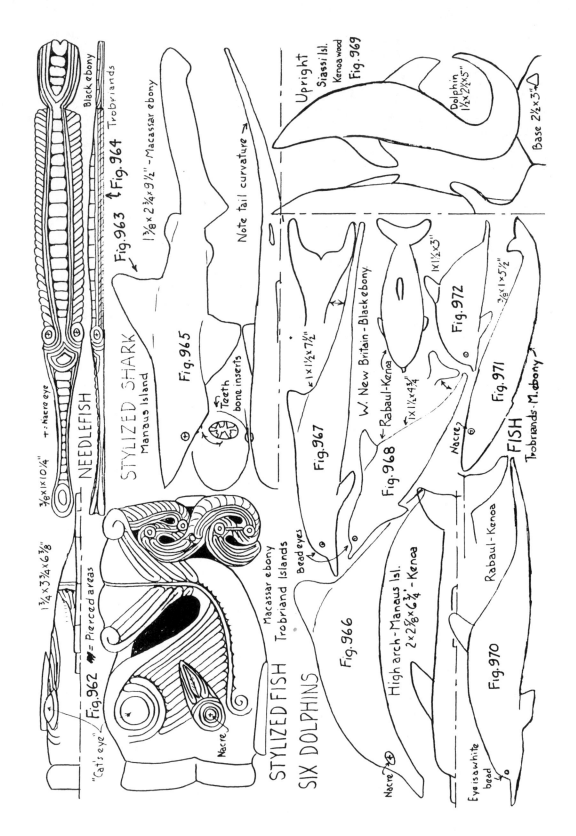

Black ebony

Fig.963 ↑Fig.964 Trobriands

1⅜ x 2¾ x 9½" - Macassar ebony

Note tail curvature →

+ : Nacre eye

⅜"x1"x10¼"

NEEDLEFISH

STYLIZED SHARK
Manaus Island

Fig.965

Teeth
bone inserts

Upright
Siassi Isl.
Kanoa wood
Fig.969

Dolphin
1½ x 2½ x 5"

Base 2½ x 3"

←1"x1½"x7½"

W. New Britain - Black ebony

Fig.967

Fig.968 ←Rabaul-Kanoa

1"x1½"x4¾"

Nacre

1x1½x3"

Fig.972

Fig.971

3/8 x 1 x 5½"

FISH
Trobriands - M. ebony →

1¾ x 3¾ x 6⅜"

Fig.962 ❀ = Pierced areas

"Cat's eye"

Nacre

STYLIZED FISH
Trobriand Islands

Macassar ebony

SIX DOLPHINS

Bead eyes

Fig.966

High arch-Manaus Isl.
2 x 2⅝ x 6¾ - Kanoa

Nacre

Fig.970

Rabaul-Kanoa

Eye is a white
bead

Nacre

Fig. 973 (right). Dolphins are a favorite subject on Papua New Guinea islands. These that I collected for a mobile include examples from Siassi, Rabaul, Manaus and West New Britain. Patterns are in Figs. 956–970, 972. Woods include kenoa (probably kerosene or ghiti) and ebony.

Fig. 974 (right). This mobile combines two sharks, a sailfish, two dolphins and a tunalike fish from four different islands. The suspension is monofilament nylon through dorsal fins from music-wire whiffle trees.

be inadequate or wrong. Thus, it is hard to find out what wood and what finish, but harder still to find out the significance of a design. That, however, is not solely a serendipity problem; one day I tried to find out from an Indian on the Sepik what the significance was of symbols on a miniature canoe prow. Stony silence. Not until later did the lady interpreter and I figure out a probable reason: They were clan symbols, secret except to members of the clan, and certainly not to be revealed under any circumstances to a woman, or through a woman, whatever color her skin.

One last point: Your purchases in remote places may characterize you and lead to other pieces that are rare. For example, the fact that I bought a couple of little carvings on one Trobriand island led to offers of much finer little pieces from other warriors which they would not sell to my cruise companions. Or again, my expressed interest in a carved motif on a canoe prow on the Sepik River led to the offer of a beautifully carved paddle top by the chief's son—he'd broken the paddle but kept the top. I got spirit whistles in Borneo because I'd bought a spirit board. A kiwi-shell necklace in Port Moresby came from talk about masks. It can happen—serendipity.

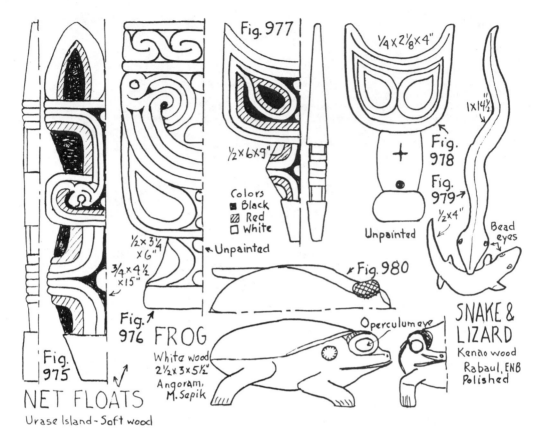

Fig. 977

$\frac{1}{2} \times 6 \times 9''$

Colors
■ Black
▨ Red
□ White

←Unpainted

$\frac{1}{2} \times 3\frac{1}{4}$
$\times 6''$

$\frac{3}{4} \times 4\frac{1}{2}$
$\times 15''$

Fig. 976↑

FROG
White wood
$2\frac{1}{2} \times 3 \times 5\frac{1}{2}''$
Angoram,
M. Sepik

Fig. 975

NET FLOATS
Urase Island - Soft wood

$\frac{1}{4} \times 2\frac{1}{8} \times 4''$

Fig. 978

Fig. 979→

$\frac{1}{2} \times 4''$

$1 \times 14\frac{1}{2}''$

Bead eyes

Unpainted

←Fig. 980

Operculum eye

SNAKE & LIZARD
Kenao wood
Rabaul, ENB
Polished

Fig. 981 (right). Fish-net floats from Urase Island, PNG, are in soft wood, some painted in red, black, and white. Size varies with that of the net. The bird could be an owl, but is a fish-eating water bird with an owl-like head. Patterns above.

Fig. 982 (below). "Carving" bargains in flea markets may be fakes. This "Chinese ivory" is neither ivory nor Chinese—it is a plastic and bonedust casting, carefully antiqued. I found similar fakes in Mexico several years ago, both as pendants and as copies of small chinese ivory statuettes.

Fig. 983 (above). Carving may be authentic but totally atypical of their source. The snake and lizard, 17 in (432 mm) long overall, is one of a kind from New Britain island; the frog, 2½ × 3 × 5½ in (64 × 76 × 140 mm) is a very sophisticated piece from the primitive Middle Sepik River.

Figs. 984–5 (right). Trays, when not in use on many islands, become house decorations, thus bottoms are often rounded. This big tray, from Siassi Island, PNG, is in kwila, a very hard wood, incised on the back and chip-carved on the face. The pattern is in Fig. 906.

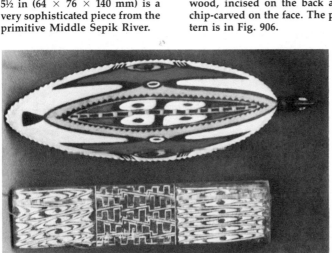

Fig. 986 (above). From near the Asmat country of Irian Jaya come these two low-relief pieces, a panel and a tray, each about 16 in (406 mm) long. Both are soft wood, the panel black with white and the tray in black, white, ecru and brown—all natural pigments. The carver explained that the panel shows fish in water at right, fish in stormy water at left, with a chief's house in between. The tray carver said his motif was fish. Note that the tray decoration is on the curved bottom.

Fig. 987 (left). Design ideas can be adapted from remote sources. This rocking horse for a dollhouse was adapted from a single-horse sketch in a British magazine. It will hold a baby doll.

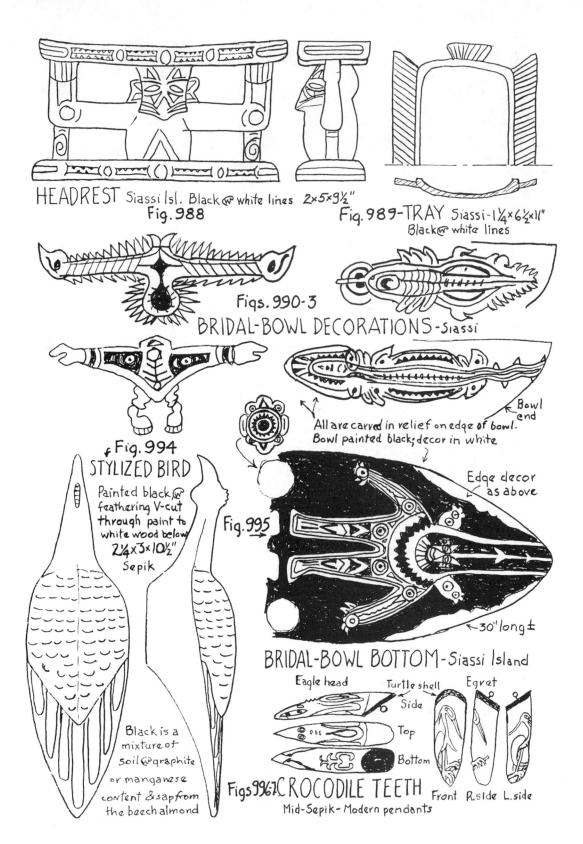

HEADREST Siassi Isl. Black & white lines 2×5×9½"
Fig. 988

Fig. 989-TRAY Siassi-1¼×6½×11"
Black & white lines

Figs. 990-3
BRIDAL-BOWL DECORATIONS -Siassi

All are carved in relief on edge of bowl.
Bowl painted black; decor in white

Bowl end

Fig. 994
STYLIZED BIRD

Painted black &
feathering V-cut
through paint to
white wood below
2¼×3×10½"
Sepik

Fig. 995

Edge decor as above

30"long ±

BRIDAL-BOWL BOTTOM-Siassi Island

Black is a
mixture of
soil & graphite
or manganese
content & sap from
the beech almond

Eagle head   Turtle shell   Egret
                Side
                Top
                Bottom

Figs 996-7 CROCODILE TEETH   Front R.side L.side
Mid-Sepik-Modern pendants

Fig. 998 (above). Siassi islanders go in for black over-all finishes with white (lime) trim. Here are a head rest and a tray (patterns in Figs. 988–993) and a bird from the Sepik River finished similarly, except that the feathering is V-cuts through to the base wood.

Figs. 999, 1000 (below). An Australian aborigine carved this 5-in (127-mm) emu egg with a small flat gouge. The egg is dark green, with a rough surface, but underneath is white. The emu is related to the ostrich and second largest of birds.

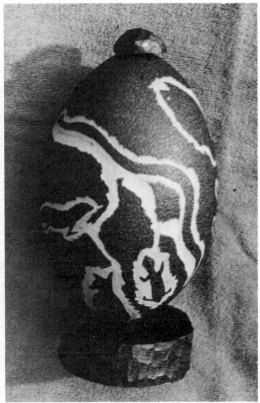

46

Carving South of the Border

IN MORE THAN A SCORE of visits to Mexico in the last thirty years, I have met and visited a great many woodcarvers and carpenters (really local cabinetmakers) there. Woodcarving tends to be concentrated in villages and is usually a supplementary occupation of farmers, adobe makers, and herders—all Indians—for added income. Further, many of the designs are traditional and differ from place to place, although all are of course governed very much by what can be sold and where. In and around Oaxaca, carvings tend to be real folk art, mostly of animals, in local woods like copal, and finished by painting. Further, the carvings are caricatures and very often assembled by tacking on tails and legs, and sticking in ears. There is very little sophistication in the pieces—they are best described as toys. In one village, however, the local farmers carve an endless number of variations of skeletons, of humans and various domestic animals. These are traditional and have to do with

Figs. 1001–1006. Many Mexican carvings are primitive, but many are not. These are by Xavier Diaz, who became fascinated by reading about the California gold rush and sculpted fourteen figures in palo santo as a result. Some are as much as 14 in (355 mm) tall. Fig. 1001, far left, is a larger figure (18 in–457 mm) done for a Houston gallery. (Palo santo is slightly harder than pine and has visible brownish grain.)

the annual Day of the Dead, November 1, which is an older, much more religious variant of our present-day Halloween, or more properly, All Hallows Eve. An occasional carving of this type is really exceptional.

In Guerrero, the carvings are in more spectacular woods and include quite sophisticated animals and birds, plus frogs, turtles and other designs with hinged tops, so they become boxes. Indians from that area carry these pieces to sell in major cities all over Mexico. In and around Pátzcuaro, the carvings are ladles, spoons, combs (of a citrus wood) and human figures, many with a Spanish heritage. Some are panels, and quite large. Some are chip-carved boxes. The Seris in Sonora, when they first discovered people would buy their unusual carvings, carried them to resort areas far from home; I bought my first ones on a beach at the lower tip of Baja California! In Mexico City, of course, the carvings are very sophisticated—and very expensive. There are several shops that sell a line of statuettes produced in "factories" and marketed in gift shops all over Mexico. From time to time also, an individual carver or a group in an area will come up with something that sells well for a time— a fad like decoys.

In the carving villages, where there are any number of carvers, there soon is one villager, or an outsider (often a mestizo), who functions as a factor or marketer for the group. As would be expected, the markup from carver to city shop is substantial, and the carvers are often pressured into making a good-selling item repeatedly. In recent years, both the state and the federal governments have set up shops to market native crafts, and these have helped the Indian sell directly, as well as locating really good pieces to be sold to galleries, museums and important foreign collectors. Several states now have large stores in their capital cities which certify quality and have fixed, not inflated, prices despite Mexico's chronic inflation.

In Mexico City, there are three or four

craft stores run by different branches of the government, as well as a network of stores set up by a semi-government company. These latter have standardized merchandise in quantity, so relatively little unique design can be found there. As always, the best and most interesting pieces are to be found in the homes or towns of the carvers or in small shops in nearby towns—which is where the pieces pictured here were acquired.

The usual carver cuts his own wood locally and suits his carving to it. The local cabinetmaker will have only three or four kinds of wood for regular use, pine, cedar, mahogany, and their equivalents as boards. But almost everyone will have a piece or two of fine hard wood put away. Carvers forego commercial woods because they are costly, and the occasional carver who has some formal background will use cocobola, mesquite, palo santo (a very soft wood, actually), ironwood and the like that he seeks out himself or buys from local

Indians. (I knew one American sculptor there who was paying Indians the equivalent of $1 American per log about 6 in (152 mm) in diameter by 6 ft (almost 2 m) long! The Indians called it "ironwood" because it was hard and sank in water. It was really cocobola—worth about $500 a log in the U.S.! Although Mexico has 2,800 varieties of trees, most of them grow on the Pacific slope near the Isthmus, so carvings from the Tehuántepec area are likely to be both sophisticated and in very good and unusual woods, in contrast to others.

I have attempted here to show some of the variety of Mexican carving, so that you can select the sort of thing that interests you. Some of the items shown are ones I collected recently and some are older—items that may have appeared in earlier books as photos without patterns or vice versa. The majority, however, are distinctive, attractive, and quite easy to carve because their original carvers were almost totally self-taught.

Figs. 1007, 1008 (left). Carved by an untaught Indian in palo santo wood, this "Misterio" (precedes the Nativity) is extremely well done and obviously inspired by church carvings. Only the hands are a bit oversize, and painting is also carefully done. Taller figures are about 12 in (305 mm). Mexicans are very religious Catholics and believe gifts are brought by the Three Kings, not by Santa. The Three Kings in Fig. 1009 (below) are turned out in some quantity. The body is standard except for differences in painting; inserted hands and gifts differ.

Figs. 1010–1016 (left). Here are three variations of the Three Kings, ranging from simple to difficult, and three variations of the Madonna, as well as a very primitive Christus, all evidences of the strong religious feeling of the Indians. Fig. 1017 (below) brings out another facet; the Indian also fears the Devil, and depicts him on occasion, sometimes as a fallen angel.

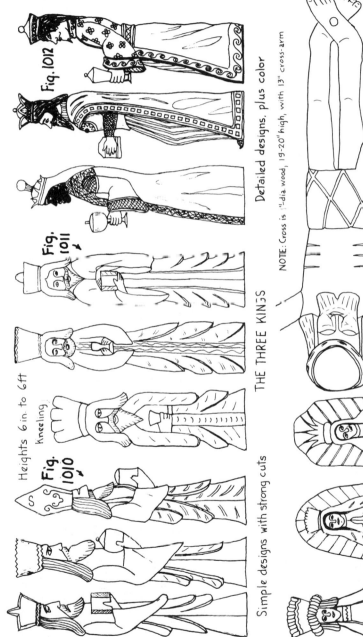

Fig. 1012

Fig. 1011

THE THREE KINGS

Fig. 1010

Heights 6 in. to 6ft

Kneeling

Simple designs with strong cuts

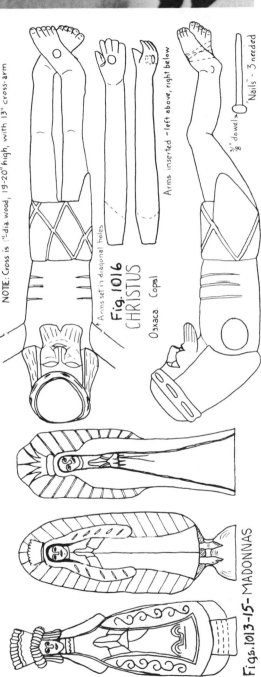

Detailed designs, plus color

NOTE: Cross is 1"-dia wood, 19-20" high, with 13" cross-arm

Arms set in diagonal holes

Fig. 1016
CHRISTUS
Oaxaca Copal

Arms inserted - left above, right below

"Nails - 3 needed

⅜" dowels

Figs. 1013-15 — MADONNAS

Fig. 1018

Fig. 1019

1020

1021

1022

1023→

1024

DANCER↑ CAMPESINO↑ QUIXOTE↑

MARDI GRAS FARMER

Fig. 1025

Fig. 1026↙

Fig. 1027

INDIANS – 2-6 feet tall

Plaques are all silhouettes with strong, deep carving and some pierced sections. Note use of Sioux head-dress

Figs. 1028-30

Fig. 1031

Fig. 1032

Fig. 1033

1034

Note: Detail varies as does design truth

Figs. 1018–1034. In the Pátzcuaro area, Indians carve silhouette plaques of themselves and their ancestors as they see them—not always authentically. Some plaques can be 6 ft (1.83 m) tall. Busts and other historical characters are carved as well, some as caricatures. Here I have provided patterns for a number of such figures. They may be finished by staining or in vivid colors, also often imaginative rather than authentic. But they decorate adobes in that area.

"Ribbons"

Heel cap ⓦ
← thongs →

Separate
rifle inserted

ZINCONTECO MAN– Chiapas, Mex.
Fig. 1035 ↑   Fig. 1036 →

REBELDO–Chiapas, Mex.

Fig. 1037 (left). Cedar is a favored carving wood in southern Mexico. The man at left and the rebel above were carved in San Cristóbal de las Casas.

Figs. 1038, 1039 (right). Pochotlé bark has long been carved by Indians into miniature towns (see Figs. 1046–1048), but José Cortez D, a jeweler in Oaxaca, carves it into patterns for lost-wax casting. This one is for a Oaxaca feather-dancer pendant and pictured at twice its actual size! The bark is dark red and tough, so it will hold detail.

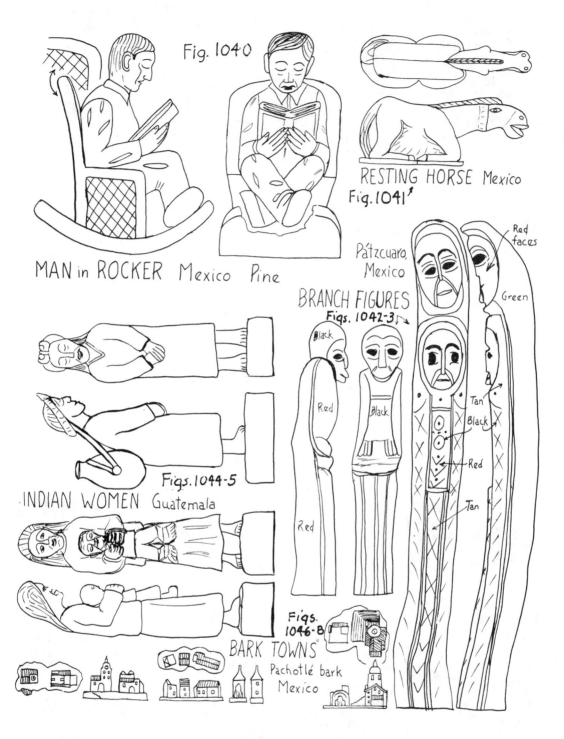

Fig. 1040

RESTING HORSE Mexico
Fig. 1041

MAN in ROCKER Mexico Pine

Pátzcuaro, Mexico

Red faces

Green

BRANCH FIGURES
Figs. 1042-3

Black

Red

Black

Tan

Black

Red

Red

Tan

INDIAN WOMEN Guatemala

Figs. 1044-5

Figs. 1046-8

BARK TOWNS
Pachotlé bark
Mexico

Figs. 1040–1048. The resting horse of Fig. 1041 and the bark houses of Figs. 1046–1048 are not shown in photographs; the drawings are sufficiently clear. Since the troubles in Guatemala began, some Indians have migrated to Mexico, and produce carvings like the two women in Figs. 1044–5 and 1054 for a livelihood. The man in the rocker (Figs. 1040, 1049) is unusual; note the solid base of the rocker—which rocks. The figures of 1042–3, pictured in Fig. 1051, are Tarascan from Pátzcuaro and carved to fit any available branch, then painted.

Fig. 1049 (above). The man reading is 5 in (127 mm) tall, in pine.

Fig. 1050 (above, right). "La Malinché" is very unusual, an imaginative portrait of the coastal Indian traitoress who helped Cortez defeat the Aztecs. It is in soft wood and painted, about 15 in (382 mm) tall.

Figs. 1052–3 (below and right). Someone gave me a piece of breal, white inside with red bark, so I carved a woman from Tehauntepac, leaving the outer bark for the skirt and tinting some areas to match. She is 10 in (254 mm) tall.

TEHUANA

EJT in Mexico - breal

Headdress back

Fig. 1052

Figs. 1051 (above), 1054 (below). See discussion on preceding page of these contrasting native figures.

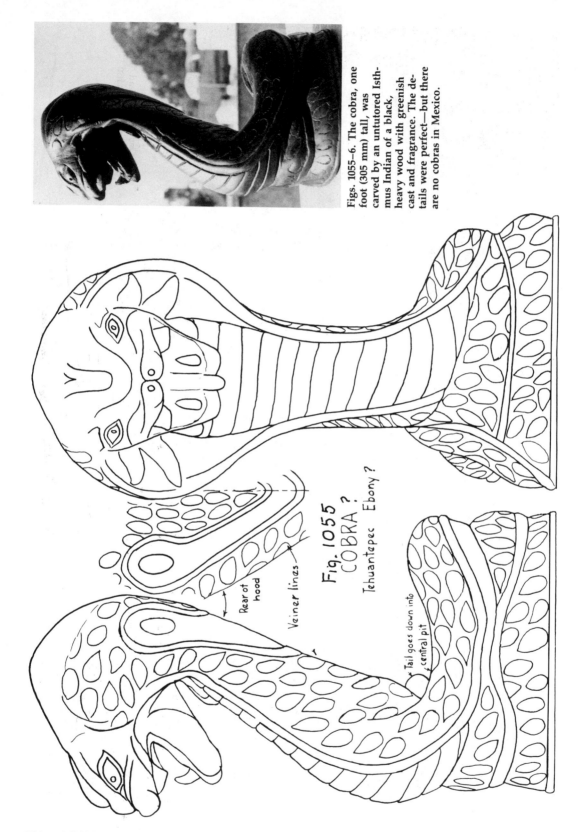

Figs. 1055–6. The cobra, one foot (305 mm) tall, was carved by an untutored Isthmus Indian of a black, heavy wood with greenish cast and fragrance. The details were perfect—but there are no cobras in Mexico.

Fig. 1055
COBRA ?
Tehuantepec   Ebony ?

Rear of hood

Vainer lines

Tail goes down into central pit

Figs. 1057–1065. Except for the road runner (see Fig. 1083), these unusual pieces come from near Oaxaca. All are in pine or copal, the mermaid a total fantasy, the skeletons to celebrate the Day of the Dead. The utensils are made by hand.

Alternate skull & arm designs

From a bent branch

SKELETON
Oaxaca. Copal
Fig. 1058
Fig. 1059-60

Gouge-cut designs thru point

Figs. 1061-3
CHALICE & CANDLESTICK
Oaxaca. Copal

Size: Approx. 2½ x 10 x 24"
Fig. 1057

ROAD RUNNER Seri Ironwood

– 8" –

Fig. 1064

MERMAID By Celestino Cruz, in pine

MEXICAN FANTASIES   275

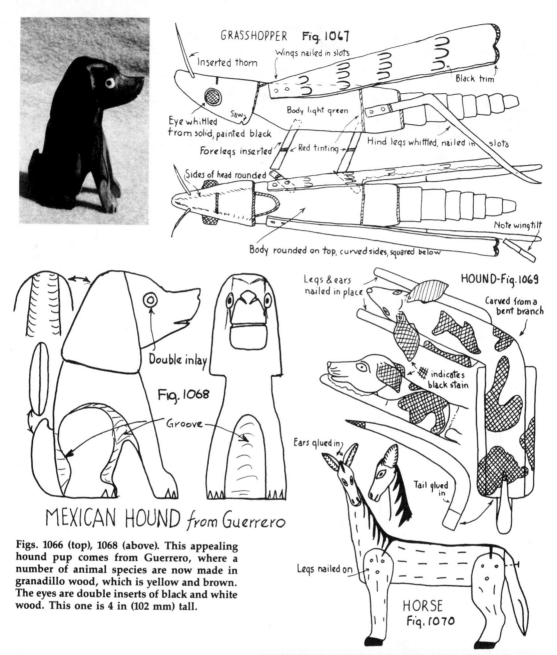

GRASSHOPPER Fig. 1067

Inserted thorn

Wings nailed in slots

Black trim

Eye whittled from solid, painted black

Saw

Body light green

Red tinting

Hind legs whittled, nailed in slots

Fore legs inserted

Sides of head rounded

Note wing tilt

Body rounded on top, curved sides, squared below

Double inlay

Fig. 1068

Groove

MEXICAN HOUND *from Guerrero*

Legs & ears nailed in place

HOUND-Fig. 1069

Carved from a bent branch

# indicates black stain

Ears glued in

Tail glued in

Legs nailed on

HORSE Fig. 1070

Figs. 1066 (top), 1068 (above). This appealing hound pup comes from Guerrero, where a number of animal species are now made in granadillo wood, which is yellow and brown. The eyes are double inserts of black and white wood. This one is 4 in (102 mm) tall.

Figs. 1067, 1069, 1070 (above, right). Many toy animals are made in the Oaxaca area, often of scraps of wood or branches and based on the wood shape, as in the hound of Fig. 1069. Others may be elaborate assemblies like the grasshopper of Figs. 1067, 1071 (right). The legs are obviously nailed in place, and the ears inserted in drilled holes, and the whole is brightly painted.

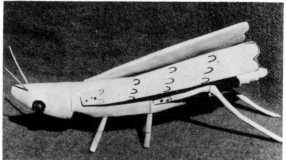

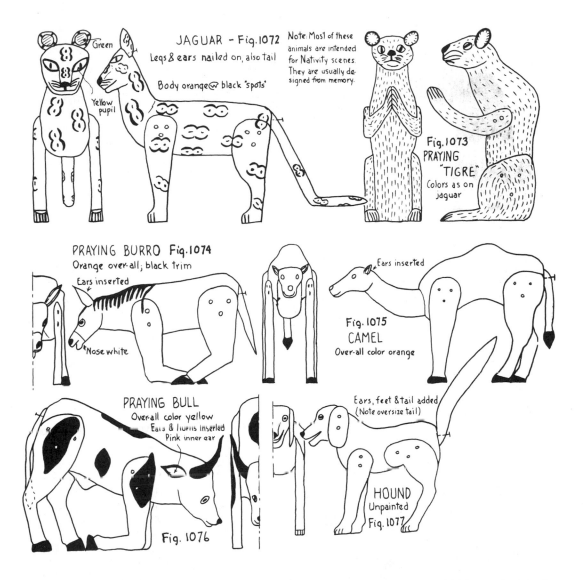

JAGUAR – Fig. 1072

Legs & ears nailed on, also tail

Body orange w/ black "spots"

Green

Yellow pupil

Note: Most of these animals are intended for Nativity scenes. They are usually designed from memory.

Fig. 1073
PRAYING "TIGRE"
Colors as on jaguar

PRAYING BURRO Fig. 1074
Orange over-all; black trim

Ears inserted

Nose white

Ears inserted

Fig. 1075
CAMEL
Over-all color orange

PRAYING BULL
Over-all color yellow
Ears & horns inserted
Pink inner ear

Fig. 1076

Ears, feet & tail added
(Note oversize tail)

HOUND
Unpainted
Fig. 1077

Figs. 1072–1079. Nativity scenes are popular in Mexico, and may include a great variety of animals, as well as entire added scenes, sometimes a hundred or more pieces. And the animals may be posed like humans, as in the case of the praying burro and bull shown here. (I have even seen large Nativity scenes including the Last Supper and Christ on the cross!). Here again, the animals are assembled from available pieces of wood and brightly painted. They may be any size, to suit the scene; I have seen them more than a foot (305 mm) tall.

Figs. 1080 (above), 1082 (far right). Masks are essential in Mexico for fiestas and playlets as well as house decoration. Here are some simple and two very complex ones. All can be worn. Some are decorated with horse hair and may have dog teeth, etc.

Fig. 1081 (right). "Gordo" (which means "fat") gave me this 13 in (330 mm) piece of copal, partly carved, then abandoned. He expected me to finish it, with skulls, rabbit skeletons, and the like to celebrate the Day of the Dead. I did.

Fig. 1083 (right). The Seri Indians of Sonora began to carve figures like these in desert ironwood about 30 years ago. Very stylized for primitive carvers, they sold well to Americans, so well that they are now being made in a "factory" in Hermosillo, and the Seris have gone back to fishing for a living.

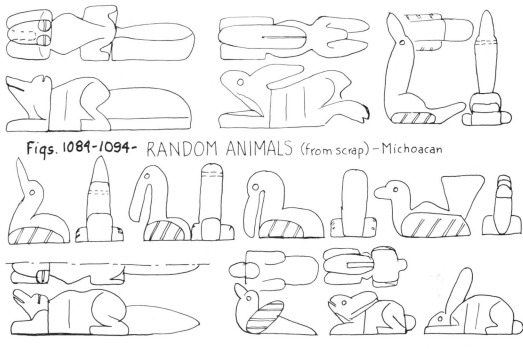

Figs. 1084-1094 - RANDOM ANIMALS (from scrap) - Michoacan

Figs. 1084–1094 (top), 1096 (above). Somebody in Michoacan had some scraps of a hard, dense red wood and a coping or band saw—plus a very vivid imagination. These little figures are typical of some 15 that I bought in San Miguel de Allende, sorting them out of several batches during a month. No two were alike, and the store that had them couldn't keep them in stock.

Fig. 1095 (above). This little peon figure is in mesquite and is 18 in (457 mm) tall. I carved him some years back as a copy of a small figure I bought in Guadalajara. A knot at his right foot became an iguana. The virtue of this carving is that there are no hands or face to worry over—only his big feet. And he requires no pedestal—he stands well on the floor.

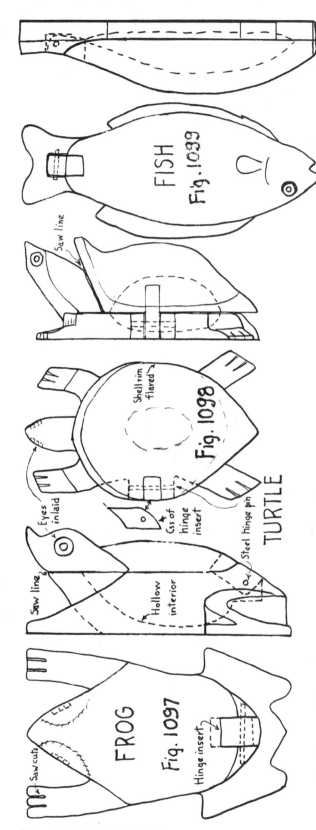

FISH
Fig. 1099

Saw line

TURTLE

Shell rim flared

Fig. 1098

Eyes inlaid

Css of hinge insert

Steel hinge pin

Saw line

Hollow interior

FROG
Fig. 1097

Saw cuts

Hinge insert

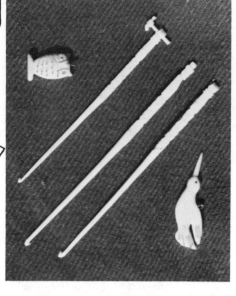

Figs. 1097–1100 (left and above). In Guerrero, they make a series of carved animals like these which are hollowed out and have hinged tops. All have the double-inserted eyes.

Fig. 1101 (right). Guanajuato specializes in carvings in bone. The crochet hooks have been made for years, with a man, a hand, or just decoration on top. The flying bird and owl are new, one a pin, the other a pendant.

47

A Dozen Designs

These pictures of carvings from my collection will, I trust, help you in making or adapting designs for your purposes. They may even be of direct use to you—they are certainly varied enough! Some of these I have had for a number of years, and some I have passed on to others where I thought they would inspire or suggest. The important thing in planning any original carving is to let your imagination work; don't be bound by ironclad "rules of art." There are no such rules. Let yourself go!

Fig. 1103. INTRIGUE. This Ecuadorean figure in walnut is 11¼ in (292 mm) tall and is one of a kind in that prolific carving country. It invites you to guess what it is—and you'll be wrong. It is a male fiesta dancer acting the part of a cowgirl. He has shoved aside his mask to take a drink from the bottle, which is his only sustenance during three days of dancing, and he has a reserve bottle on his hip. Contrast his face and that of the mask.

Fig. 1102. STRENGTH. The Bolivian Indian who carved this pair of heads made them strong and distinctive. Both faces look brutal to us, but note the subtle distinctions between female and male—the Adam's apple and neck cords on the man, the harsher lines of his face. These heads are life-sized, in an ebony-like wood. The treatment of her hair and his knitted cap is excellent.

Fig. 1104. TELL A STORY. Cordoba, Spain, is the source of this 8½ × 24 in (216 × 610 mm) oak panel which depicts Miguel Cervantes writing, while what he is writing shows above him: Don Quixote on his deathbed is talking to a grieving Sancho Panza.

Fig. 1105. INTRICACY. In contrast to the preceding simple panel, this one is an exercise in intricate design. It is very "busy," yet delicate, showing a goddess from the Ramayana. It is from Bali, in a mahogany-like wood and is 9 × 27 in (229 × 686 mm).

Fig. 1106 (above). CONTRAST. The Seri Indians, working in ironwood, understood the value of texture in achieving contrast. The seal, highly polished, stands on a rough-finished rock. The piece is about 7 in (178 mm) tall.

Fig. 1107 (upper right). COLOR. Excellent use of color increases the "eye-grasping" ability of this Sri Lankan mask. The large mask is flanked by 18 smaller ones, to protect wearer or patient against all sorts of evils, real and imagined. The color helps make it dramatic and effective for its purpose.

Fig. 1108 (right). UNITY. This little Japanese pill-box shows a delicate pattern of Oriental maple leaves in detailed low relief. The box itself is of maple, and other boxes, in other woods, bear similarly suitable leaves. The appropriateness adds to its effectiveness.

Fig. 1109 (left). MINIATURIZATION. Little carvings always attract. These two, one depicting the Nativity, the other the Nativity and Crucifixion (in a walnut shell), were made in Oberammergau, West Germany. The figures are actually carved slivers of wood glued in place, but very dramatic.

A DOZEN DESIGNS   283

Fig. 1111 (above). PA-
TRIOTISM. The figa, or
thumb in fist, is a Brazilian
symbol. Here the carver has
combined it with the head
of a planter to make a pleasing vertical combination.

Fig. 1110 (top). BALANCE. A Haitian carved
this Obeah panel some years ago. In it, he
combined a series of symbols in a well-spaced
and balanced composition. It is simple, but
makes its point.

Fig. 1112 (above). TRADITION. A Viking
carved these wedding spoons for his intended
and draped her with them when he went
avoyaging. Such spoons are still carved in
Sweden, and still out of one piece of soft pine.

Fig. 1113 (right). BUT NOT TOO MUCH TRA-
DITION. Avoid slavish copying. Here are two
carvings from remote Easter Island, one a
miniature of a kneeling Moai of international
fame, the other an effort in a new direction, a
sort of stylized flower growing out of the head
of an islander. The leaves carry appropriate
symbols—and it is not a copy of anything.
There is a place in our world for both. Try
your own thing—it may be better than tradition.